Standard & Poor's Guide to Sector Investing

Standard & Poor's Guide to Sector Investing

1995 Edition

Sam Stovall

McGraw-Hill, Inc.
New York   San Francisco   Washington, D.C.   Auckland   Bogotá
Caracas   Lisbon   London   Madrid   Mexico City   Milan
Montreal   New Delhi   San Juan   Singapore
Sydney   Tokyo   Toronto

International Standard Serial Number:
Standard & Poor's Guide to Sector Investing
ISSN 1081-051X

1 2 3 4 5 6 7 8 9 0   AGM/AGM   9 0 0 9 8 7 6 5

ISBN 0-07-061717-1

*The sponsoring editor for this book was David Conti, the editing supervisor was
Paul R. Sobel, and the production supervisor was Suzanne W. B. Rapcavage. It
was set in Palatino by Dina E. John of McGraw-Hill's Professional Book Group
composition unit.*

Printed and bound by Quebecor.

McGraw-Hill books are available at special quantity discounts to use as
premiums and sales promotions, or for use in corporate training programs.
For more information, please write to the Director of Special Sales,
McGraw-Hill, Inc., 11 West 19th Street, New York, NY 10011. Or contact
your local bookstore.

This publication is designed to provide accurate and authoritative information in regard to the subject matter covered. It is sold with the understanding that the publisher is not engaged in rendering legal, accounting,
or other professional service. If legal advice or other expert assistance is
required, the services of a competent professional person should be
sought.

*— from a delaration of principles jointly adapted by a committee
of the American Bar Association and a committee of publishers*

 This book is printed on recycled, acid-free paper containing
a minimum of 50% recycled de-inked fiber.

Contents

Introduction

The $63,000 Question

If you were to ask a group of average investors to name the optimal way to make a killing in the stock market, they would probably shout—market timing! (Market timing is the technique of successfully "buying low and selling high" by pinpointing the peak and trough in stock prices.) And although they might be enthusiastic, they would be wrong. For not only is market timing that classic technique that few have mastered, but it is also less successful than an alternative technique by more than 4 to 1. That technique? Sector investing.

A study performed by CDA/Weisenberger, an investment research firm out of Rockville, Maryland, compared the performances of three investment strategies—market timing, sector investing, and "buy and hold"—over a 10-year period. The market timing technique was defined by correctly predicting price changes in the overall stock market of 10% or more in either direction, buying when prices were about to rise and selling when prices were about to decline. The sector selector strategy invested the entire portfolio in one of six sectors— energy, financial services, gold, health care, technology, or utilities—at the beginning of each year. The "buy-and-hold" strategy bought and held the S&P 500.

Each investment technique started with $1,000. At the end of the 10-year period, the "buy-and-hold" investor walked away with a little more than $6,000, while the market timer netted almost

$15,000. Yet the sector selector amassed nearly $63,000! Not bad for an overlooked investment technique.

An Alternative Investment Approach

A conservative investor will typically take the oft-advised "diversified" approach to investing by putting his money to work in either an index or broadly based equity mutual fund, which owns hundreds of stocks in dozens of industries. This investor is willing to bypass the big killings (thus lowering their return) in order to reduce the volatility, or risk, of their portfolio.

A more aggressive investor, on the other hand, may place bets on only a few stocks in a limited number of industries, accepting the increased risk in the hope of enhancing the return on their investment.

But for some investors, the above strategies may be too hot or cold. For them, some other discipline may be just right.

Enter Sector Investing, a technique that is more aggressive than investing in broadly based mutual funds, yet less risky than investing in only a handful of stocks. And, it can be accomplished either with stocks or mutual funds.

Advice on market timing and individual stock picking abound; investors have a plethora of guides to timing the market, allocating assets and selecting stocks. Yet the evaluation and selection of the right sector has been ignored. Almost nowhere can one find a comprehensive guide to understanding sector investing.

Enter *The Standard & Poor's Guide to Sector Investing*. This book—updated on an annual basis—will introduce the reader to an old saying on Wall Street: "A rising tide lifts all boats." That is, if a particular industry is "hot," all stocks within that particular industry will likely benefit. And this adage is based on fact. Studies have indicated that as much as 60% of a stock's price move can be attributed to the direction of the overall market and whether the company's industry group is in or out of favor with investors. The remaining influence pertains to the underlying company-specific factors.

The book will walk you through the "top-down" approach to investing. It will:

- Analyze the typical economic cycle of recovery and recession, dividing it into five phases and identifying the sectors and industries that perform best during each phase.

- Describe the tools of measurement used to evaluate growth trends in the overall economy and each of the industries that comprise the S&P 500 Composite Index.

- Evaluate performances (investment returns, standard deviation and beta) and valuations (price-to-earnings ratios, relative P/Es, and yields) for all industries.

- Review the definitions, characteristics and investment outlooks for these industries, as well as display peer comparisons on more than 1000 component stocks.

- Provide S&P's economic and investment outlook for 1995.

- Identify mutual funds by their sector/industry focus.

This book is geared toward the individual investor, to whom Standard & Poor's has been providing information and advice for more than 100 years. And while the book will assume the reader is aware of such terms as P/E, yield, and total return, not much more will be expected. This book will be used to expand upon the reader's basic understanding of investment concepts and techniques.

Sector Investing Is Not For Everyone

It may sound as if everyone could benefit from participating in sector investing. This is not entirely true.

Investors with little time to devote to the successful management of a portfolio, who take the "diversified" approach to investing and typically have a lower risk tolerance, should not engage in sector investing.

More active investors, however, may be willing to expose a portion of their portfolio to a limited number of industries that they think will outperform the general market in the months ahead. These investors have evaluated their tolerance for handling investment risk and are able to accept the increased risk in the hope of enhancing the overall return on their investment. They may engage their entire portfolio in this investment technique, but typically they should use only that portion that has been allocated to aggressive investments.

A Dose of Reality

The reason why sector funds may be inappropriate for passive/conservative investors yet appropriate for active/aggressive investors can be summed up in one word: volatility—the variability of investment returns. The quantitative measurement of this risk is known as standard deviation, or the amount by which an annual return may differ (or deviate) from the average (or standard) return over a specific period of time. The larger the standard deviation, the greater the risk. And it is this standard deviation that allows investors to compare the risks and rewards associated with the price performance of specific industries, sectors or the overall market. For example, the S&P 500 Composite Index (a broadly diversified assortment of 500 companies in 88 industries) sported a standard deviation of 14.7 over the 1970–1994 period, whereas the Gold, Machine Tools and Entertainment industries posted standard deviations of 42.3, 33.8 and 35.9, respectively, for the same period. (A complete listing of the S&P industries and their standard deviations can be found in Chap. 3.)

Therefore, it is important to realize that even though a one-year advance of 50% by the S&P Health Care Index in 1991 would have been welcomed by both the passive and active investor alike, it's the active investor who more likely would have had the investment temperament or mindset to weather the near-20% drop recorded for this index in 1992. Indeed, it is prudent for all investors to understand that a buy-and-hold approach is typically not recommended when dealing in sector funds. These funds should be looked upon as short-to-intermediate-term trading vehicles and not long-term total return instruments. Remember, a 50% loss in one year requires a 100% gain in the next year just to break even!

Acknowledgments

This successful completion of this book would not have been possible without the help of: Jim Dunn, who helped me stay on track; David Blitzer, who made sure my claims could be substantiated; the S&P equity analysts, who did the work so that I could take the credit: Stephen R. Biggar, Thomas M. Canning, CFA, John D. Coyle, CFA, William H. Donald, Christopher J. Grant, Edward G. Graves, Tom Graves, CFA, Joshua M. Harari, CFA, Paul L. Huberman, CFA, Stephen R. Klein, Leo Larkin, Mark Mattke, Richard O'Reilly, CFA, Michael V. Pizzi, Karen J. Sack, CFA, Herman B. Saftlas, Catherine A. Seifert, Kenneth A. Shea, Anthony M. Sorrentino, CFA, Richard Spiegel, Susan Stahl-Gibney, Paul H. Valentine, CFA, Elizabeth A. Vandeventer, and Peter C. Wood, CFA. And finally, David Conti, my editor, without whom the idea would not have become a reality.

Sam Stovall

1
The Basics Behind Sector Investing

What's a Sector?

Before we can begin to discuss how you can improve your investment awareness and results using sector investing, it's necessary to understand two key components: *sectors* and *industries*. Many use these terms interchangeably. But they are not the same. A sector is a group of industries that have similar fundamental characteristics, whereas an industry is a collection of companies with similar primary lines of business.

Although the definition is easy, the arrangement of sectors and industries isn't, for there is no uniformly agreed-upon arrangement of sectors and industries that comprise the universe of companies in which you can invest. The U.S. Government's Standard Industry Classification (SIC) system offers hundreds of different SIC codes that provide for a defined breakdown of a company's primary and secondary lines of business. But many regard this system as too large and unwieldy, as well as out of date. Other industry breakdowns also have been established by investment publications and brokerage firms.

But one industry grouping has been embraced by individual and institutional investors alike as a realistic proxy for the universe of stocks found in the New York, American, and National exchanges. That universe? The S&P 500 Composite Price index.

Why the S&P 500?

No other benchmark of stock market performance is more widely followed or more closely analyzed than the S&P 500. It is a market-value-weighted index (shares outstanding times stock price) in which each company's influence on the index's performance is directly proportional to its market value. It is this characteristic that makes the S&P 500 such a valuable tool for measuring the performance of actual portfolios. Although the 500 companies chosen for the S&P 500 are not the largest companies in terms of market value, they are chosen for inclusion because they tend to be leaders in important industries within the U.S. economy. The market value of companies in the S&P 500 represents about 75% of the aggregate market value of common stocks traded on the NYSE, and a little less than 70% of all U.S. equities.

The origins of the S&P 500 go back to 1923 when S&P introduced a series of indices that included 233 companies in 26 industries. Since then, the S&P 500 has grown to encompass 500 companies representing 88 industries, 10 sectors, and four overall segments. These segments are familiar to many: the Industrials, Financials, Utilities, and Transportation issues. The diagram below illustrates this hierarchy.

Throughout this book, it will be the industries and sectors found in the S&P 500 index that will be referred to in the text, tables, and graphs. As of December 30, 1994, this index consisted of the following sector/industry breakdown (see top of page 3).

See Appendix A for a comprehensive listing of sectors, industries, and companies in the S&P 500 Composite Index.

```
               — S & P  5 0 0  —

                       |

        ———— 4  S e g m e n t s  ————

                       |

      —————— 1 0  S e c t o r s  ——————

                       |

   ———————— 8 8  I n d u s t r i e s  ————————

                       |

————————— 5 0 0  C o m p a n i e s  —————————
```

The S&P 500 Composite Index
IT's Sectors and Industries

Basic Materials
Aluminum
Chemicals
Chemicals (Diversified)
Chemicals (Specialty)
Containers (Metal & Glass)
Containers (Paper)
Gold Mining
Metals (Miscellaneous)
Paper & Forest Products
Steel

Capital Goods
Aerospace/Defense
Conglomerates
Electrical Equipment
Engineering & Construction
Heavy Duty Trucks & Parts
Machine Tools
Machinery (Diversified)
Manufacturing (Div. Inds.)
Pollution Control

Consumer Cyclical
Auto Parts After Market
Automobiles
Broadcast Media
Building Materials
Entertainment
Hardware & Tools
Homebuilding
Hotel-Motel
Household Furn. & Appl.
Leisure Time
Manufactured Housing
Publishing
Publishing (Newspapers)
Restaurants
Retail (Department Stores)
Retail (General Merchandise)
Retail (Specialty)
Retail (Specialty-Apparel)
Shoes
Textiles
Toys

Consumer Staples
Beverages (Alcoholic)
Beverages (Soft Drinks)
Cosmetics
Distributors (Cons. Products)
Foods
Health Care (Diversified)
Health Care (Drugs)
Health Care (Miscellaneous)
Hospital Management
Household Products
Housewares
Medical Products & Supplies
Retail (Drug Stores)
Retail (Food Chains)
Tobacco

Energy
Oil & Gas Drilling
Oil (Domestic Integrated)
Oil (Exploration & Prod.)
Oil (International Integrated)
Oil Well Equip. & Serv.

Financials
Life Insurance
Major Regional Banks
Money Center Banks
Multi-Line Insurance
Personal Loans
Property-Casualty Insurance
Savings & Loan Companies
Financial (Miscellaneous)

Services
Insurance Brokers
Specialized Services
Specialty Printing

Technology
Communication Equip./Mfrs.
Computer Software & Svcs
Computer Systems
Electronics (Defense)
Electronics (Instrumentation)
Electronics (Semiconductors)
Office Equipment & Supplies
Photography/Imaging
Telecom. (Long Dist.)

Transportation
Airlines
Railroads
Truckers
Transportation (Misc.)

Utilities
Electric Companies
Natural Gas
Telephone

Other
Miscellaneous

What Then Is Sector Investing?

Now that we know what a sector is, we are ready to understand sector investing, which is as simple a concept as it sounds. Like an inverted pyramid (see top of page 4), sector investing starts with an analysis of the big picture (the outlook for the overall U.S. economy) and ends with the identification of stocks worth buying. At the "big picture" level, projections are established to answer such questions as, "Where are we in the economic cycle?"; "Have

The Economy

———

Sectors/Industries

———

Stocks

———

interest rates peaked?"; and "Is inflation accelerating?". Once these assumptions have been established, the next questions to be answered are "Which industries will benefit from the coming economic developments through an acceleration in earnings growth?" (these are the industries in which to invest, since the outlook for a company's earnings is the key determinant to the movement of its stock price); and "Which industries will experience growth, but at a decelerating rate of speed?" (these should be avoided). Finally, the investor decides "Which companies in those favored industries are projected to perform best?"

And while individual stock selection may be the goal for some, one benefit to sector investing is that significant gains can be obtained without having to select the winners from the losers. Indeed, as mentioned in the introduction, studies have shown that as much as 60% of the price fluctuation of an individual stock can be identified by economic, market, and industry influences, with the remaining 40% dependent on company-specific factors. So whether you prefer to trade in mutual funds or individual stocks, a keen awareness of sector dynamics can help improve your investment results.

Because sector investing is associated with this macro-to-micro, or economy/sector/stock, approach, it also has become known as "top-down" investing. This is in contrast to "bottom-up" investing, where stock selection is based primarily on the interpretation of company-specific fundamental (supply and demand) and technical (charting and quantitative) factors. Both types of investors can benefit from the guidelines presented in this book.

So where do we start? At the top, with the economy and its influence on the price performances of the underlying industries.

2

How the Economy Affects Industries, Companies, and Their Stock Prices

The first step that you must take to perform sector investing successfully is to be keenly aware of the present and make an educated guess about the future. In order to identify which sectors and industries are expected to outperform the overall market in the coming months, you must ascertain where we are now in the economic cycle and try to get a feel for where we are headed.

Tying Sectors to Cycles

Investment advisors frequently describe stocks as being early-, mid-, and late-cycle performers, or being defensive or interest-sensitive in nature. While this "invest-o-speak" might sound confusing at first, it's really quite straightforward. The economy is cyclical in nature: It continuously meanders through periods of expansion and contraction. What's more, stock prices usually follow a similar, though anticipating, pattern by rising about 4.5 months prior to when the economy expands and falling about 6 months before the economy begins to contract. Indeed, some industries have demonstrated a pattern of outperforming the overall stock market during certain phases of the economic cycle while underperforming during others. To help pinpoint when industries may perform best or worst, many analysts have broken the complete economic expansion/contraction cycle into five phases: three representing the expansion (early, middle, and late) and two representing the contraction (early and late). And based on this association of industry outperformance and a particular phase within the economic cycle, analysts attempt to get an edge on other investors by anticipating these changes in the economy: They time the purchase of shares that are projected to perform well and avoid those that typically get hammered during a particular phase in the economic cycle. This rolling in-favor/out-of-favor phenomena is also called "sector rotation" since investors rotate the holdings in their portfolios by buying only those stocks or sector funds that are projected to outperform the overall market during the short-to-intermediate term and selling those that have already run their course. For instance, during the early phase of an economic expansion, those stocks that are called "early-cycle" stocks frequently will soar while the overall market posts a healthy gain. And during the beginning of an economic contraction, while the overall market might suffer a double-digit decline, some industries will retreat by a significantly narrower margin. (It is because these industries suffer less, or defend a portfolio from devastating losses, that they are called "defensive" in nature.)

Until now, however, empirical evidence linking this sector rotation to the five phases of the economic cycle has been elusive. The National Bureau of Economic Research (NBER), the official keeper of information on economic cycles, indicates that there are two official phases to a complete economic cycle: *expansion* (also known as an economic recovery), and *contraction* (also called recession). An economic expansion is when most major sectors of the economy are advancing; a recession is when most are declining. The NBER's Business Cycle Dating Committee identifies turning points; usually the committee reports within a few months. For most people, this definition is a bit nebulous and open to speculation. To satisfy impatient politicians, the economist Arthur Okun (an advisor to Presidents Kennedy and Johnson) suggested that two consecutive quarters of shrinking gross domestic product (GDP) be used to signal a recession. In 1980, however, the United States entered into a recession with only one quarter of declining GDP. In addition, should one use two quarters of advancing or declining GDP as a sole guide, 6 months could go by before an investor becomes aware of (and the NBER confirms) the existence of an expansion or contraction. Thus, analysts rely on additional characteristics to identify the coming peaks and troughs in the economic cycle. In general, these additional characteristics include monthly figures on employment levels, interest rates, and the rate of inflation. Analysts have also come to learn the fairly regular pattern the economy takes when traversing the expansion and contraction phases of an economic cycle.

Characteristics of the Economic Cycle

At the beginning of an economic expansion, the picture is one of general despair: Unemployment is high; consumer and industrial demand is at a low ebb; and consumer confidence is hitting successive new monthly lows. In an effort to pull the economy out of recession, raise consumer confidence, and increase consumption (since consumers account for two-thirds of all GDP expenditures), the Federal Reserve Board has been lowering interest rates since the middle of the previous economic contraction by cutting the federal funds and discount rates. (There are 12 Federal Reserve Banks, but none set policy; the Board of Governors of the Federal Reserve System does this.) The only positive aspect of this period in the economic cycle is that since there is a lack of significant demand for goods and services, the inflation rate is either flat or declining.

Soon, these lower interest rates begin to have an effect on the economy by making it easier and cheaper to purchase the goods and services that consumers have deprived themselves of for so long. The confidence that consumers hold for the future improves and they start to spend again. This pickup in spending requires an increase in industrial output and the need for more employees, who in turn join in the demand for goods and services, which requires a further increase in industrial output and the need for more employees, and so on.

You can imagine, then, that as this pent-up demand is released there is a greater number of consumers (demand) chasing a more limited number of goods (supply), thereby putting ever increasing upward pressure on prices. And while two of three general economic goals are now beginning to be satisfied (full employment and economic growth), a third goal of stable prices is being undermined.

Therefore, in an effort to combat this upward spiral of inflation, the Federal Reserve bank typically "leans against the wind" to temper the business cycle and the pickup in inflation by raising interest rates. And while the Fed's goal is a soft landing—or a slowdown in economic growth to a more manageable level of expansion—what typically happens is that its rate-hiking moves, together with the effects of other business and economic factors, throw the economy into recession. And in a situation that is a reverse image of the early phase of the economic expansion, we find interest rates on the rise, consumer demand beginning to fall, industrial output starting to slacken, and employment levels declining. Only when the Fed realizes that it has gone too far with its interest rate policy does it again begin to ease interest rates to reignite the economic process.

"When to Hold and When to Fold" or Identifying an Industry's Track Record

As can be seen in Table 2-1, there have been four complete economic expansions in the past 25 years, the shortest of which lasted 12 months, and the longest 92 months; we are currently in the fifth. On average, the duration was nearly 50 months. There also have been five economic contractions, lasting anywhere from 6 to 16 months and averaging nearly 11.5 months. The table also shows that while the stock market attempts to anticipate a downturn in the economy, it is not always successful. In fact in 1980, the stock market peaked one month after the start of an economic contraction. In another case, it peaked 13 months in advance. In all, however, the market anticipates an economic contraction by an average of 6 months. The market is a bit more successful, and consistent, when it comes to anticipating the start of an economic expansion. The market bottomed as little as 3 months and as much as 6 months prior to an economic revival, or 4.5 months on average.

This difference in consistency and success of anticipating economic expansions and contractions is interesting: Why would investors anticipate an economic downturn through a peak in stock prices by 6 months (and quite inconsistently), yet lead a recovery (with more success) by only 4.5 months? Is it because of

Table 2-1. Peaks and Troughs in the Economy and Stock Market 1969–1994

Expansion/Contraction Start	Finish	Event	Duration (Months)	Date S&P 500 Peaked (P) or Troughed (T)		# Months S&P 500 Anticipated Economy
Dec-69	Nov-70	Contraction	11	P	Nov-68	13
Nov-70	Nov-73	Expansion	36	T	May-70	6
Nov-73	Mar-75	Contraction	16	P	Jan-73	10
Mar-75	Jan-80	Expansion	58	T	Oct-74	5
Jan-80	Jul-80	Contraction	6	P	Feb-80	-1
Jul-80	Jul-81	Expansion	12	T	Mar-80	4
Jul-81	Nov-82	Contraction	16	P	Nov-80	8
Nov-82	Jul-90	Expansion	92	T	Aug-82	3
Jul-90	Mar-91	Contraction	8	P	Jul-90	0
Mar-91	???	Expansion	45	T	Oct-90	5
Averages:	**Contraction**		**11.4**			**6.0**
	Expansion (w/o current)		**49.5**			**4.5**

SOURCES: National Bureau of Economic Research; Standard & Poor's.

the two emotions that drive the stock market—fear and greed— most investors are more motivated by fear than greed? (This implies that the risk tolerance of most investors is conservative and they are more willing to bypass an opportunity than give back a gain.) Or is it merely that more analysis on spotting tops in the market than bottoms needs to be done?

In an attempt to establish empirical evidence uncovering a pattern of market outperformance and underperformance by industries in the S&P 500, each economic expansion was separated into three equal time periods. For instance, the expansion of November 1970 to November 1973 lasted 36 months. The early, middle, and late phases were then defined as lasting 12 months each. The economic contractions, on the other hand, were divided in half. The percentage of gain or loss for each of the industries during these phases for the four expansions and five contractions were calculated and compared with the results for the S&P 500. Table 2-2 shows the number of times that an industry outperformed the S&P 500 in

Table 2-2. Sector Scorecard: Industry Outperformance by Phase of the Economy

Industry	Number of times this industry has outperformed the S&P 500 in the past Four Economic Expansions				Number of times this industry has outperformed the S&P 500 in the past Five Economic Contractions			
	# Periods Indexes Avail.	Early 1/3 (EE)	Middle 1/3 (ME)	Late 1/3 (LE)	# Periods Indexes Avail.	Early 1/2 (EC)	Late 1/2 (LC)	Batting Avg.
Aerospace/Defense	4	4	2	2	5	1	2	1
Airlines	4	2	2	1	5	2	3	1
Aluminum	4	3	3	2	5	1	1	2
Auto Parts After Market	4	1	3	1	5	1	4	2
Automobiles	4	2	2	1	5	2	2	0
Beverages (Alcoholic)	4	2	3	2	5	4	3	3
Beverages (Soft Drinks)	4	2	4	2	5	3	3	3
Broadcast Media	4	3	4	3	5	2	3	4
Building Materials	4	2	3	2	5	2	4	2
Chemicals	4	1	3	2	5	2	0	1
Chemicals (Diversified)	2	2	2	0	3	0	2	NA
Chemicals (Specialty)	1	0	1	0	1	0	1	NA
Communication Equip./Mfrs.	2	1	1	2	3	1	3	NA
Computer Software & Services	2	2	2	1	3	0	3	NA
Computer Systems	4	1	2	1	5	1	2	0
Conglomerates	4	4	1	1	5	0	2	1
Containers (Metal & Glass)	4	1	3	2	5	1	1	1
Containers (Paper)	4	2	3	1	5	2	3	2
Cosmetics	4	1	4	2	5	3	2	2
Distributors (Consumer Products)	1	0	0	1	2	1	1	NA
Electric Companies	4	0	2	1	5	3	1	1
Electrical Equipment	4	2	3	1	5	2	4	2
Electronics (Defense)	1	0	0	0	1	1	1	NA
Electronics (Instrumentation)	4	2	3	3	5	2	4	3
Electronics (Semiconductors)	4	2	2	2	5	1	4	1
Engineering & Construction	1	0	0	1	1	0	1	NA
Entertainment	4	2	4	3	5	3	2	3
Financial (Miscellaneous)	0	0	0	0	1	0	1	NA
Foods	4	2	3	2	5	4	4	3
Gold Mining	4	1	2	3	5	3	4	3
Hardware & Tools	2	0	1	0	3	0	1	NA
Health Care (Diversified)	1	0	1	1	1	1	1	NA
Health Care (Drugs)	4	1	3	2	5	4	2	2
Health Care (Miscellaneous)	1	0	0	0	1	1	1	NA
Heavy Duty Trucks & Parts	4	2	2	1	5	1	2	0
Homebuilding	4	1	2	1	5	0	4	1
Hospital Management	2	1	1	2	3	2	3	NA
Hotel-Motel	4	3	3	2	5	0	5	3
Household Furn. & Appliances	4	2	2	1	5	3	4	2
Household Products	4	1	4	3	5	4	3	4
Housewares	1	0	1	1	1	0	1	NA
Insurance Brokers	1	0	0	1	1	1	0	NA
Leisure Time	4	4	2	1	5	1	5	2
Life Insurance	4	2	3	1	5	1	4	2
Machine Tools	4	3	2	2	5	0	2	1
Machinery (Diversified)	4	2	2	2	5	2	2	0
Major Regional Banks	4	1	3	2	5	1	2	1
Manufactured Housing	4	1	1	1	5	1	5	1
Manufacturing (Div. Inds.)	1	0	1	0	1	0	1	NA
Medical Products & Supplies	4	2	3	1	5	3	3	3
Metals (Miscellaneous)	4	2	1	4	5	3	3	3
Miscellaneous	1	0	0	0	1	1	0	NA
Money Center Banks	4	0	2	2	5	2	3	1

Table 2-2. Sector Scorecard: Industry Outperformance by Phase of the Economy (*Continued*)

Industry	Number of times this industry has outperformed the S&P 500 in the past Four Economic Expansions				Number of times this industry has outperformed the S&P 500 in the past Five Economic Contractions			
	# Periods Indexes Avail.	Early 1/3 (EE)	Middle 1/3 (ME)	Late 1/3 (LE)	# Periods Indexes Avail.	Early 1/2 (EC)	Late 1/2 (LC)	Batting Avg.
Multi-Line Insurance	4	3	2	2	5	2	2	1
Natural Gas	4	3	2	1	5	2	2	1
Office Equipment & Supplies	1	0	1	0	2	0	0	NA
Oil & Gas Drilling	4	1	2	2	5	2	2	0
Oil (Domestic Integrated)	4	3	0	3	5	3	2	3
Oil (Exploration & Production)	0	0	0	0	1	1	0	NA
Oil (International Integrated)	4	3	3	2	5	4	2	3
Oil Well Equip. & Serv.	4	3	2	3	5	2	3	3
Paper & Forest Products	4	2	3	1	5	2	2	1
Personal Loans	4	2	2	1	5	0	5	1
Photography/Imaging	0	0	0	0	0	0	0	NA
Pollution Control	4	3	3	1	5	0	5	3
Property-Casualty Insurance	4	3	2	2	5	3	3	3
Publishing	4	4	2	2	5	2	5	2
Publishing (Newspapers)	4	3	3	3	5	1	5	4
Railroads	4	2	1	3	5	2	3	2
Restaurants	4	2	3	2	5	1	3	2
Retail (Department Stores)	4	2	1	2	5	2	4	1
Retail (Drug Stores)	4	4	3	1	5	1	5	3
Retail (Food Chains)	4	0	3	1	5	2	5	2
Retail (General Merchandise)	4	1	3	2	5	2	3	2
Retail (Specialty)	1	1	0	1	2	0	2	NA
Retail (Specialty-Apparel)	1	0	0	1	1	0	1	NA
Savings & Loan Companies	4	2	2	1	5	0	5	1
Shoes	4	2	2	2	5	3	5	2
Specialized Services	1	1	1	0	2	0	2	NA
Specialty Printing	0	0	0	0	0	0	0	NA
Steel	4	0	1	1	5	2	3	1
Telecommunications (Long Dist.)	1	0	0	1	1	0	0	NA
Telephone	1	0	1	0	1	1	0	NA
Textiles	4	3	3	2	5	1	3	3
Tobacco	4	1	4	3	5	5	5	4
Toys	4	2	1	3	5	2	4	2
Transportation (Miscellaneous)	0	0	0	0	1	0	1	NA
Truckers	4	2	3	2	5	2	4	2

each of these phases. (Appendix B shows the results on a percentage basis.) Take a look at the first line of Table 2-2: aerospace/defense. Since data for this index started to be kept before 1969 (the beginning of this study) it participated in all four of the economic expansions and all five of the economic contractions. (Chemicals-diversified, you'll notice, was started in the late 1970s, so it participated in only two expansions and three contractions.) Yet in the four economic expansions, aerospace stocks out-performed the S&P 500 during the early phase every time! They then underperformed the market in the middle and late expansion phases and in each of the two contraction phases. The stocks in the aerospace/defense industry, therefore, appear to be classic early-cycle performers. The industry also has a batting average of 1 for 5—more on this later.

Although it was not surprising that aerospace stocks were early-cycle performers, an interesting revelation occurred with the manu-factured housing industry. These issues have been characterized by some analysts as non-interest-sensitive (meaning they did well when interest rates fell and poorly when rates rose) because earn-ings were driven by housing prices and demographics. In a period of rising home prices, consumers were supposed to shy away from the more expensive site-built homes and opt for the more cost-effec-tive manufactured homes. In addition, demographics played a sig-nificant role as indicated by the old industry adage that these homes are "meant for the newly wed and the nearly dead." But this analysis shows that manufactured homes outperformed the market during the period of falling interest rates five out of five times, lead-ing one to conclude that while this industry's earnings may rise as a result of substitution and demographic trends, its share prices are interest-rate driven. Its batting average was also 1 for 5.

But just as there are some industries that are classic cyclical plays that are associated with the early expansion (like aerospace), middle expansion (entertainment), late expansion (metals misc.), early contraction (food), and late contraction (manufactured hous-ing) phases, there are some that performed well in several phases (and are indicated by a batting average of 3 or 4 out of 5), or near-ly always struck out (0 for 5). The batting average is merely a count of the number of times an industry outperformed the mar-ket three or four times out of four during each of the three eco-nomic expansion phases, or three, four, or five times out of five during each of the two contractionary phases. A batting average will always be between 0 and 5. Those industries with consistently high batting averages include household products, publishing-newspapers, and tobacco. Those that beat the overall market less than 50% of the time in all five phases include automobiles, com-puter systems, heavy duty trucks and parts, machinery—diversi-fied, and oil and gas drilling.

The knowledge that investors should gain from Table 2-2 and Appendix B is that the performance of the overall market is highly cyclical and that nearly 80% of the gains that are likely to be recorded take place during the more investor-friendly stock market environment of the late contraction to mid-expansion phases of an economic cycle versus the late expansion and early contraction phases, when the investing environment appears more hostile. In particular, the market experienced an average loss of nearly 14% during the first, or defensive, phase of an economic contraction but gained an average 14% during the second, or interest-sensitive, phase of the contraction, and 20%, 12%, and 12% for the early, mid, and late phases of an economic expansion, respectively.

Table 2-2 also suggests that less-aggressive investors who still wish to participate in sector investing should gravitate toward those industries with batting averages of 3 or 4 out of 5 (none was 5 out of 5), and that those investors who are more aggressive and willing to monitor the market's sector rotation may hope to reap greater rewards by investing in industries with batting averages of 1 or 2 out of 5. Industries with a batting average of 0 out of 5 should be avoided.

Above all, this table shows that one way to be successful with sector investing is to realize that gains and losses come from how skillfully an investor anticipates these sector/industry rotations. The trick is to be able to identify the current economic phase and anticipate the timing of the succeeding phase.

Timing Guidelines

General timing guideposts include:

1. Decide whether the economy is in recovery (expanding) or in recession (contracting).

2. Measure the duration of the current expansion or contraction and compare to the average as indicated in Table 2-1—this assumes that the NBER has identified such a date. In reality, however, the NBER will fix the date of an economic contraction after the subsequent expansion has already started. It is advised, therefore, to monitor the reports of well-respected Wall Street economists and use their prognostications, as well as your own input, to estimate the starting and ending dates of economic peaks and troughs.

3. Identify which industries are outperforming or underperforming the overall market and compare them to Table 2-2.

4. Monitor the general trend in those economic indicators that measure the growth or rise in consumer expectations, industrial output, inflation, interest rates, and the slope of the yield curve. This last concept merits further explanation. The yield curve is a pictorial representation of the yields offered on debt instruments from the 3-month Treasury bill through the 30-year Treasury bond; this curve typically demonstrates an upwardly sloping bias with the spread (or difference) between short-term bills and long-term bonds being around 2 percentage points (also referred to as 200 basis points). In the early stages of an economic recovery, however, the yield curve is sharp as the spread expands to 300 basis points or beyond because investors anticipate economic growth to accelerate in the months ahead (as well as a resulting pickup in inflation). Prior to an economic contraction, on the other hand, the yield curve has narrowed to the point where the spread is 100 basis points or less. There have even been times when the yield curve has become inverted, meaning that shorter-term bonds yielded more than longer-term bonds. This happens when investors anticipate a recession in the coming months, which will reduce the longer-term growth in the economy and inflationary expectations.

In general, the five phases of an economic cycle are characterized by:

Early Expansion

Duration:	First third of economic expansion, or about 17 months on average.
Consumer expectations:	Rising sharply.
Industrial production:	Flat to rising modestly.
Inflation:	Continuing to fall.
Interest rates:	Bottoming out (leads inflation).
Yield curve:	Steep.

Middle Expansion

Duration:	Second third of economic expansion, or about 17 months on average.
Consumer expectations:	Leveling off.
Industrial production:	Rising sharply.
Inflation:	Bottoming out.
Interest rates:	Rising modestly.
Yield curve:	Moderate.

Late Expansion

Duration:	Last third of economic expansion, or about 17 months on average.
Consumer expectations:	Declining.
Industrial production:	Flattening out.
Inflation:	Rising modestly and beginning to be of concern to investors and the Fed.
Interest rates:	Rising rapidly due to Fed policy (as well as the supply and demand of capital) to combat inflation.
Yield curve:	Flattening out (short rates rising as the Fed combats inflation, whereas long rates may be falling as they reflect future inflationary expectations).

Early Contraction

Duration:	First half of economic contraction, or about 6 months on average.
Consumer expectations:	Falling sharply.
Industrial production:	Declining.
Inflation:	Rising less strongly.
Interest rates:	Peaking.
Yield curve:	Flat (and sometimes inverted—short rates are higher than long rates).

Late Contraction

Duration:	Final half of economic contraction, or about 6 months on average.
Consumer expectations:	Reviving.
Industrial production:	Decline diminishing.
Inflation:	Flat to declining.
Interest rates:	Falling.
Yield curve:	Rising again.

Figure 2-1 is a graphic representation of the rotation of sectors favored by investors as the economy passes through a complete economic cycle of expansion and contraction. As the economy begins to expand, investors rotate through the transportation, technology and basic materials issues as demand increases, output expands, and inflation heats up. But as the expansion matures, too

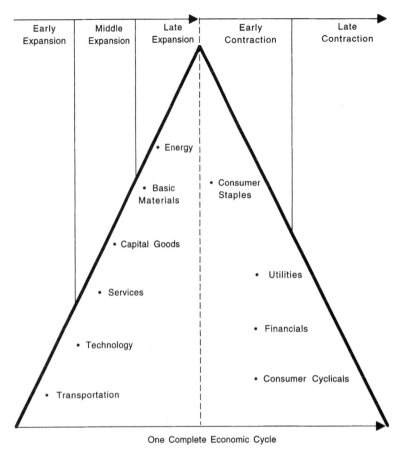

Figure 2-1. Sector rotation within the economic cycle.

much of a good thing causes interest rates to rise; investors then begin favoring the more defensive issues as the market averages start to decline. Next, as the Fed looks to pull the economy out of recession by easing its grip on interest rates, the financial issues come to life. And as lower interest rates induce increased consumption and production, the consumer cyclicals begin to take off and the sector rotation process begins again.

S&P believes that the U.S. economy is in the third phase of an economic expansion.

Caveats to Consider

There are some definitional factors that you should be aware of. First, since the S&P 500 is a market-capitalization-weighted index, extreme swings in the stock price performance of industry leaders may have skewed the industry index's return during the periods analyzed. For instance, IBM's recent price slump will make itself evident when the results for the current expansion are included. Second, the returns calculated do not include reinvested dividends, which doesn't fully portray the investment performances of such total-return industries as electric companies, baby bells, and natural gas pipelines and distributors. And finally, the method of separation of expansion and contraction phases (into thirds and halves, respectively) was chosen for simplicity. A more in-depth analysis could indeed establish a different duration for each of the five phases.

Also, although the findings of this analysis are certainly enlightening and, hopefully, profitable, investors should be aware of some additional facts.

1. The findings of a study based on 25 years of data (four-to-five economic cycles) should not be considered gospel. They should be used as a general guide and starting point.

2. The study is a measure of how these industries performed in time under economic, political, and market conditions that were particular to that point in time. And as everyone is aware, conditions constantly change. For instance, aerospace issues appear to be classic early-expansion stocks in this study. But now that the Cold War has ended, will this continue to hold true? Only time will tell. But it does serve as a perfect introduction to the next chapter. Although this study has identified general patterns, future industry-specific factors may affect future price performances for these industries. It therefore pays to be informed of the general and specific economic factors that drive certain industry groups as well as other less certain aspects, such as the acceptance of new product introductions. It is with this in mind—the need to look beneath the general trends—that we move to Chapter 3, where you will become familiar with the fundamental and investment characteristics of each of the industries in the S&P 500.

3

Industry Profiles and Projections

Standard & Poor's analysts review hundreds of reports issued by the U.S. government, industry trade organizations, and individual companies, as well as a host of investment reports from other Wall Street research firms. Although the individual investor is not expected to read this massive amount of information—let alone have access to it—there are three things the sector investor must be familiar with in order to make winning investment decisions. The first is a carry through of the top-down framework of sector investing. In order to anticipate which industries will experience an increase or decrease in orders and profits, an investor must become familiar with those economic indicators that will have an influence on an industry's earnings and share price movements. Next, an investor must have a framework from which to judge if an industry is overvalued or undervalued on a historical basis. For instance, even if the projected phase of the economic cycle might indicate that a certain industry should outperform the overall industry, if that industry already is trading at a substantial premium, an investor might just be buying these shares at the top rather than at the bottom. Finally, the investor must be familiar with the fundamental characteristics of a particular industry in order to judge whether stocks within that industry might act similarly to past performances or that dynamics within the industry will alter future price movements. This chapter is broken into two sections to help the investor accomplish the above tasks.

The first section contains three tables that show influencing indicators, performance results, and valuation measurements for the industries within the S&P 500. The tables are arranged by sector, with each member industry listed alphabetically. Table 3-1 is a quick summary of three indicators that influence earnings and share prices for those industries in the S&P 500. These indicators are usually economic reports that can be retrieved by an investor on a weekly, monthly, or quarterly basis from most financial publications. Table 3-2 is a performance measure, displaying each industry's 1-, 5-, 10-, and 25-year price performances (dividends are not included), along with its standard deviation (a measure of individual industry volatility, where the higher the number the greater the price variations), beta (that industry's volatility relative to the volatility of the S&P 500, a beta of 1.0 indicating volatility equal to that of the overall market, whereas a higher or lower beta indicates a greater or lesser magnitude of volatility, respectively), and an "Observations Since" column to tell the reader if an industry index has a shorter than 25-year average. And, finally, Table 3-3 provides the investor with an industry-by-industry comparison of valuation measurements: "The industry's 1995e price-to-earnings rato (P/E) and average P/E from 1970-1993; 1995e and average relative P/E (P/Es for the individual industries relative to the P/E of the S&P 500); and dividend yield for year-end 1994 and average yield." Investors should use these tables to gauge whether stocks within each industry are currently overvalued or undervalued on an absolute and/or relative basis as compared with its long-term average.

Table 3-1. Influencing Indicators

Sector **Industry**	Indicators		
Basic Materials			
Aluminum	Industrial Production	End Market Expectations	Product Prices
Chemicals	Industrial Production	End Market Expectations	Chem. Production Indexes
Chemicals (Diversified)	Industrial Production	End Market Expectations	Non-Chemical Factors
Chemicals (Specialty)	Industrial Production	End Market Expectations	Raw Material Costs
Containers (Metal & Glass)	Personal Income	Raw Material Costs	Agricultural Output
Containers (Paper)	GDP Growth	Industrial Production	End Market Expectations
Gold Mining	Capacity Utilization	Employment	U.S. Dollar
Metals (Miscellaneous)	World GDP Growth	Housing Starts	Auto Production
Paper & Forest Products	Interest Rates	Housing Starts	Capacity Utilization
Steel	GDP Growth	Auto Production	Construction Spending
Capital Goods			
Aerospace/Defense	GDP Growth	Defense Spending	Contract Awards
Conglomerates	Industrial Production	Consumer Confidence	Interest Rates
Electrical Equipment	GDP Growth	Capital Spending	U.S. Dollar
Engineering & Construction	Capital Spending	Order Levels	Order Backlog
Heavy Duty Trucks & Parts	GDP Growth	Industrial Production	Retail Sales
Machine Tools	GDP Growth	Capital Spending	Machine Tool Orders
Machinery (Diversified)	Interest Rates	Housing Starts	Auto Sales
Manufacturing (Div. Industries.)	Industrial Production	NAPM	Interest Rates
Pollution Control	Industrial Production	Capital Spending	Construction Spending
Consumer Cyclical			
Auto Parts After Market	Consumer Confidence	Personal Income	Interest Rates
Automobiles	Consumer Confidence	Personal Income	Interest Rates
Broadcast Media	Advertising Spending	Interest Rates	Regulatory
Building Materials	Interest Rates	Consumer Spending	Housing Starts
Entertainment	Consumer Spending	New Products	Product Quality
Hardware & Tools	Interest Rates	Housing Starts	New Products
Homebuilding	Interest Rates	Employment	Housing Starts
Hotel-Motel	Consumer Confidence	Travel Costs	Construction Levels
Household Furn. & Appliances	Interest Rates	Consumer Spending	Housing Starts
Leisure Time	Consumer Confidence	Demographics	New Products
Manufactured Housing	Interest Rates	Employment	Consumer Confidence
Publishing	GDP Growth	Consumer Confidence	Paper Costs
Publishing (Newspapers)	GDP Growth	Advertising Spending	Paper Costs
Restaurants	Consumer Confidence	Disposable Income	Cost Pressures
Retail (Department Stores)	Consumer Confidence	Disposable Income	Employment
Retail (General Merchandise)	Consumer Confidence	Disposable Income	Employment
Retail (Specialty)	Consumer Confidence	Disposable Income	Employment
Retail (Specialty-Apparel)	Consumer Confidence	Disposable Income	Employment
Shoes	Consumer Confidence	Disposable Income	Interest Rates
Textiles	Consumer Confidence	Interest Rates	Housing Starts
Toys	Consumer Confidence	Disposable Income	New Products
Consumer Staples			
Beverages (Alcoholic)	Interest Rates	Consumer Confidence	Personal Income
Beverages (Soft Drinks)	Interest Rates	Consumer Confidence	Personal Income
Cosmetics	Consumer Spending	New Products	U.S. Dollar
Distributors (Consumer Products)	Inflation	Interest Rates	Consumer Confidence
Foods	Interest Rates	Consumer Confidence	Personal Income
Health Care (Diversified)	Demographics	Gov't Policies	U.S. Dollar
Health Care (Drugs)	Demographics	Gov't Policies	U.S. Dollar
Health Care (Miscellaneous)	Demographics	Medicare Reimbursement	Employment
Hospital Management	Demographics	Medicare Reimbursement	Regulatory
Household Products	Interest Rates	Housing Starts	New Products

Table 3-1. Influencing Indicators (*Continued*)

Sector
Industry	Indicators		
Housewares	Interest Rates	Housing Starts	New Products
Medical Products & Supplies	Demographics	Medicare Reimbursement	U.S. Dollar
Retail (Drug Stores)	Inflation	Disposable Income	Demographics
Retail (Food Chains)	Inflation	Disposable Income	Consumer Confidence
Tobacco	Interest Rates	Consumer Confidence	Taxes

Energy
Oil & Gas Drilling	Commodity Prices	U.S. Dollar	Refined Product Margins
Oil (Domestic Integrated)	Commodity Prices	U.S. Dollar	Refined Product Margins
Oil (Exploration & Production)	Commodity Prices	U.S. Dollar	Refined Product Margins
Oil (International Integrated)	Commodity Prices	U.S. Dollar	Refined Product Margins
Oil Well Equip. & Services.	Commodity Prices	U.S. Dollar	Refined Product Margins

Financials
Insurance Brokers	Interest Rates	Policy Sales	Policy Pricing
Life Insurance	Interest Rates	Employment	Personal Savings
Major Regional Banks	Interest Rates	Inflation	Employment
Money Center Banks	Interest Rates	Inflation	Employment
Multi-Line Insurance	Interest Rates	GDP Growth	Pricing
Personal Loans	Interest Rates	Employment	Consumer Confidence
Property-Casualty Insurance	Interest Rates	GDP Growth	Policy Pricing
Savings & Loan Companies	Interest Rates	Employment	Housing Prices
Financial (Miscellaneous)	Interest Rates	Employment	Stock Market Outlook

Services
Specialized Services	GDP Growth	Consumer Confidence	Capacity Utilization
Specialty Printing	Interest Rates	Advertising Spending	Paper Costs

Technology
Communication Equip./Mfrs.	GDP Growth	Inflation	Regulatory
Computer Software & Services	Employment	Computer Sales	New Products
Computer Systems	Capital Spending	U.S. Dollar	New Products
Electronics (Defense)	GDP Growth	Defense Spending	Contract Awards
Electronics (Instrumentation)	Capital Spending	U.S. Dollar	R&D Spending
Electronics (Semiconductors)	Capital Spending	U.S. Dollar	Book-to-Bill Ratio
Office Equipment & Supplies	Capital Spending	Interest Rates	Employment
Photography/Imaging	Demographics	Consumer Confidence	Personal Spending
Telecommunications (Long Dist.)	GDP Growth	Inlation	Regulatory

Transportation
Airlines	GDP Growth	Consumer Confidence	Fuel Costs
Railroads	Industrial Production	Construction Spending	Weather
Truckers	Industrial Production	Interest rates	Fuel Costs
Transportation (Miscellaneous)	Industrial Production	Retail Sales	Fuel Costs

Utilities
Electric Companies	Interest Rates	Industrial Production	Regulatory
Natural Gas	Interest Rates	Industrial Production	Product Prices
Telephone	GDP Growth	Inflation	Regulatory

Table 3-2. Industry Performances and Volatility (Data Through 12/30/94)

Sector Industry	Average Annual % Change				Standard Deviation	Beta	Obs. Since
	1994	5 Yrs.	10 Yrs.	25 Yrs.			
Basic Materials							
Aluminum	20.5	1.9	8.5	5.0	24.1	1.1	1970
Chemicals	12.2	5.7	14.2	7.3	19.3	1.0	1970
Chemicals (Diversified)	4.2	10.6	13.4	NA	15.0	1.0	1978
Chemicals (Specialty)	-14.3	6.0	9.8	NA	14.7	1.2	1984
Containers (Metal & Glass)	-7.1	12.5	18.5	9.1	19.9	0.6	1970
Containers (Paper)	6.7	3.4	12.6	8.8	25.5	1.6	1970
Gold Mining	-19.9	-1.6	6.3	11.8	42.3	0.0	1970
Metals (Miscellaneous)	14.0	4.9	11.3	5.4	24.8	1.0	1970
Paper & Forest Products	1.6	5.8	10.6	6.5	18.8	1.1	1970
Steel	-3.6	10.5	8.9	2.3	24.2	1.3	1970
Capital Goods							
Aerospace/Defense	5.5	10.5	8.7	10.0	24.9	0.7	1970
Conglomerates	-7.5	3.9	9.2	5.3	26.7	1.1	1970
Electrical Equipment	-1.7	7.5	10.2	7.0	17.6	1.1	1970
Engineering & Construction	-5.6	3.8	7.9	NA	17.2	1.5	1983
Heavy Duty Trucks & Parts	-16.0	6.0	2.5	0.9	26.6	1.2	1970
Machine Tools	-19.9	-3.3	-5.7	1.9	33.8	1.7	1970
Machinery (Diversified)	-4.4	6.7	10.3	6.7	20.6	1.2	1970
Manufacturing (Div. Industries.)	1.7	9.0	12.5	NA	10.6	1.0	1983
Pollution Control	1.3	-5.7	15.1	8.3	39.7	1.4	1970
Consumer Cyclical							
Auto Parts After Market	-14.8	8.8	8.6	6.7	26.2	1.1	1970
Automobiles	-16.5	4.6	7.3	3.7	31.1	1.0	1970
Broadcast Media	-7.4	7.6	20.9	14.3	30.0	1.2	1970
Building Materials	-27.9	2.5	10.4	5.7	24.4	1.6	1970
Entertainment	-5.3	7.7	22.4	13.9	35.9	1.4	1970
Hardware & Tools	-4.8	1.3	4.8	NA	13.0	1.2	1980
Homebuilding	-42.8	7.0	4.7	1.8	37.6	1.9	1970
Hotel-Motel	-11.9	0.8	11.2	5.8	45.8	1.3	1970
Household Furn. & Appliances	-20.2	2.6	6.9	5.1	30.7	1.4	1970
Leisure Time	-4.8	-1.8	3.4	8.3	41.7	1.7	1970
Manufactured Housing	-17.9	9.0	3.9	3.4	36.1	1.2	1970
Publishing	-7.5	5.1	9.6	8.8	27.2	0.8	1970
Publishing (Newspapers)	-10.0	0.9	6.0	9.8	23.8	1.2	1970
Restaurants	-1.2	11.4	14.4	14.2	35.7	1.1	1970
Retail (Department Stores)	-11.9	5.4	14.0	8.9	29.0	1.2	1970
Retail (General Merchandise)	-15.9	8.5	12.9	5.7	28.7	1.1	1970
Retail (Specialty)	-6.3	13.0	16.0	NA	24.1	1.3	1982
Retail (Specialty-Apparel)	-16.1	6.2	NA	NA	42.3	1.4	1985
Shoes	33.6	15.2	19.2	11.8	38.0	1.7	1970
Textiles	-4.3	0.7	12.0	4.5	37.8	1.3	1970
Toys	-1.6	20.9	13.6	2.8	39.2	1.3	1970
Consumer Staples							
Beverages (Alcoholic)	7.2	5.5	15.8	6.3	28.3	1.1	1970
Beverages (Soft Drinks)	5.8	18.0	24.3	11.7	26.1	1.1	1970
Cosmetics	24.1	19.4	22.1	5.5	24.0	1.3	1970
Distributors (Consumer Products)	2.9	9.3	11.8	NA	15.2	1.0	1982
Foods	8.8	8.1	18.4	10.6	20.4	0.9	1970
Health Care (Diversified)	12.1	8.2	14.9	NA	16.7	1.0	1983
Health Care (Drugs)	12.4	7.3	17.0	8.9	18.2	1.2	1970
Health Care (Miscellaneous)	-14.3	11.0	4.6	NA	33.8	1.6	1983

Table 3-2. Industry Performances and Volatility (Data Through 12/30/94) (*Continued*)

Sector / Industry	Average Annual % Change				Standard Deviation	Beta	Obs. Since
	1994	**5 Yrs.**	**10 Yrs.**	**25 Yrs.**			
Hospital Management	6.1	0.9	4.7	NA	33.7	1.1	1978
Household Products	5.8	11.4	17.1	9.8	18.0	1.0	1970
Housewares	-4.8	13.6	20.9	NA	23.1	1.6	1984
Medical Products & Supplies	16.1	6.8	13.8	6.3	23.4	1.1	1970
Retail (Drug Stores)	13.8	9.4	10.9	11.5	34.2	1.0	1970
Retail (Food Chains)	5.0	7.1	18.3	9.5	20.8	1.0	1970
Tobacco	3.9	6.6	19.0	14.0	19.5	1.2	1970
Energy							
Oil & Gas Drilling	-20.6	-7.8	-7.3	1.5	43.3	0.8	1970
Oil (Domestic Integrated)	0.7	-3.8	4.2	7.8	23.4	0.7	1970
Oil (Exploration & Production)	-21.2	-16.9	NA	NA	11.9	0.5	1989
Oil (International Integrated)	1.5	5.2	11.9	8.2	18.1	0.6	1970
Oil Well Equip. & Services.	-10.3	-1.5	3.4	8.5	31.6	1.0	1970
Financials							
Insurance Brokers	-2.6	-1.8	8.6	NA	24.5	0.9	1984
Life Insurance	-19.7	2.8	7.7	6.8	23.0	1.2	1970
Major Regional Banks	-8.8	6.5	5.5	2.7	20.7	1.5	1970
Money Center Banks	-5.9	5.6	7.6	5.0	19.7	1.4	1970
Multi-Line Insurance	3.5	5.3	10.0	7.6	20.9	1.3	1970
Personal Loans	9.1	8.6	9.5	3.9	24.8	1.8	1970
Property-Casualty Insurance	2.3	4.9	9.4	7.1	17.9	1.1	1970
Savings & Loan Companies	-15.9	0.5	6.9	3.8	30.4	2.1	1970
Financial (Miscellaneous)	-6.1	9.0	NA	NA	20.6	1.6	1988
Services							
Specialized Services	-10.7	-6.8	3.4	NA	15.6	1.0	1982
Specialty Printing	-13.1	NA	NA	NA	NA	1.0	1993
Technology							
Communication Equip./Mfrs.	13.6	14.5	9.4	NA	22.3	1.3	1978
Computer Software & Services	17.9	16.4	16.2	NA	20.2	1.4	1978
Computer Systems	27.8	-3.3	-2.2	0.2	19.7	0.9	1970
Electronics (Defense)	-5.1	12.5	10.7	NA	13.1	0.7	1983
Electronics (Instrumentation)	22.5	16.0	9.9	9.5	28.8	0.7	1970
Electronics (Semiconductors)	16.3	29.2	16.5	11.6	30.4	1.4	1970
Office Equipment & Supplies	-0.5	7.1	10.2	NA	21.2	1.2	1982
Photography/Imaging	6.0	NA	NA	NA	NA	0.5	1993
Telecommunications (Long Dist.)	-11.0	0.7	11.0	NA	24.4	0.9	1984
Transportation							
Airlines	-30.3	-10.2	2.0	1.7	30.5	1.4	1970
Railroads	-15.7	10.8	13.1	9.4	24.7	1.2	1970
Truckers	-5.0	2.2	6.6	9.1	27.6	1.3	1970
Transportation (Miscellaneous)	-14.5	6.3	NA	NA	27.3	0.8	1988
Utilities							
Electric Companies	-18.9	0.1	4.8	1.9	16.2	0.5	1970
Natural Gas	-7.8	-4.4	4.6	6.0	22.7	0.6	1970
Telephone	-8.9	0.1	9.9	NA	16.4	0.7	1983
S&P 500 Composite	-1.5	5.7	10.8	6.7	14.7	1.0	1970

Table 3-3. Industry Valuations (Current Data as of 12/30/94)

Sector Industry	P/E (1995e)	P/E Avg. ('70-'93)	Rel. P/E (1995e)	Rel. P/E Avg. ('70-'93)	Div'd Yield (%) Current	Div'd Yield (%) Avg. ('70-'93)	Obs. Since
Basic Materials							
Aluminum	18.96	10.85	1.51	0.88	1.84	3.82	1970
Chemicals	12.71	14.56	1.01	1.08	3.32	4.60	1970
Chemicals (Diversified)	12.33	14.90	0.98	1.08	2.55	4.11	1978
Chemicals (Specialty)	13.62	15.19	1.09	0.97	2.02	3.20	1984
Containers (Metal & Glass)	16.83	11.69	1.34	0.89	0.42	3.81	1970
Containers (Paper)	40.60	12.30	3.24	1.01	1.72	3.56	1970
Gold Mining	28.41	21.18	2.27	1.78	0.95	1.48	1970
Metals (Miscellaneous)	13.89	11.27	1.11	0.95	2.47	3.38	1970
Paper & Forest Products	18.18	15.07	1.45	1.08	2.55	4.12	1970
Steel	10.66	7.95	0.85	0.70	0.96	4.34	1970
Capital Goods							
Aerospace/Defense	12.32	9.85	0.98	0.78	2.68	3.61	1970
Conglomerates	10.43	10.85	0.83	0.84	2.98	4.35	1970
Electrical Equipment	14.04	15.01	1.12	1.19	2.93	3.45	1970
Engineering & Construction	15.61	27.11	1.24	1.81	2.02	2.30	1983
Heavy Duty Trucks & Parts	9.22	19.09	0.74	1.35	2.89	4.03	1970
Machine Tools	12.95	19.37	1.03	1.58	1.26	3.81	1970
Machinery (Diversified)	10.70	16.45	0.85	1.24	2.05	3.65	1970
Manufacturing (Div. Inds.)	13.12	18.41	1.05	1.23	1.92	2.59	1983
Pollution Control	14.49	19.90	1.16	1.52	2.35	1.92	1970
Consumer Cyclical							
Auto Parts After Market	11.00	15.22	0.88	1.23	2.50	3.30	1971
Automobiles	4.62	8.71	0.37	0.71	2.74	6.14	1970
Broadcast Media	29.99	20.34	2.39	1.48	0.23	2.07	1970
Building Materials	10.77	14.06	0.86	1.06	2.18	3.79	1970
Entertainment	29.76	16.68	2.37	1.31	0.58	1.84	1970
Hardware & Tools	13.23	18.61	1.05	1.29	2.85	3.14	1980
Homebuilding	9.56	19.53	0.76	1.50	1.41	1.76	1970
Hotel-Motel	18.51	16.96	1.48	1.28	0.98	3.10	1970
Household Furn. & Appliances	9.29	14.86	0.74	1.17	2.63	4.27	1970
Leisure Time	10.85	12.98	0.86	1.05	2.41	3.15	1970
Manufactured Housing	9.23	18.87	0.74	1.62	2.81	2.50	1970
Publishing	13.85	14.39	1.10	1.19	4.35	3.28	1970
Publishing (Newspapers)	16.12	16.46	1.28	1.28	2.83	2.55	1970
Restaurants	14.89	17.69	1.19	1.38	0.92	1.02	1970
Retail (Department Stores)	10.33	12.40	0.82	0.97	2.59	3.29	1970
Retail (General Merchandise)	12.10	14.95	0.96	1.20	1.83	3.24	1970
Retail (Specialty)	16.91	20.34	1.35	1.40	0.75	1.01	1982
Retail (Specialty-Apparel)	11.36	18.98	0.91	1.18	1.80	1.21	1985
Shoes	13.04	10.91	1.04	0.85	1.61	3.69	1970
Textiles	10.93	12.76	0.87	1.00	2.35	3.57	1970
Toys	12.52	12.45	1.00	1.03	0.91	1.77	1970
Consumer Staples							
Beverages (Alcoholic)	11.91	15.87	0.95	1.24	2.77	2.35	1970
Beverages (Soft Drinks)	19.70	18.44	1.57	1.44	1.68	3.13	1970
Cosmetics	18.97	19.24	1.51	1.48	1.87	3.64	1970
Distributors (Consumer Products)	13.98	16.34	1.11	1.14	2.43	1.85	1982
Foods	16.09	13.11	1.28	1.00	2.59	3.75	1970
Health Care (Diversified)	14.30	17.25	1.14	1.16	3.35	3.15	1983
Health Care (Drugs)	14.57	18.30	1.16	1.46	3.18	2.88	1970

Table 3-3. Industry Valuations (Current Data as of 12/30/94) (*Continued*)

Sector Industry	P/E		Rel. P/E		Div'd Yield (%)		Obs.
	(1995e)	**Avg. ('70-'93)**	**(1995e)**	**Avg. ('70-'93)**	**Current**	**Avg. ('70-'93)**	**Since**
Health Care (Miscellaneous)	16.51	38.84	1.32	2.99	0.52	0.24	1983
Hospital Management	12.74	15.73	1.02	1.29	0.27	2.10	1978
Household Products	15.06	14.39	1.20	1.14	2.40	3.66	1970
Housewares	15.21	17.68	1.21	1.13	1.83	1.70	1984
Medical Products & Supplies	14.93	24.14	1.19	1.82	2.01	1.68	1970
Retail (Drug Stores)	15.12	16.92	1.21	1.32	2.22	1.99	1970
Retail (Food Chains)	13.21	13.61	1.05	1.09	1.90	3.81	1970
Tobacco	9.75	10.30	0.78	0.82	5.41	4.41	1970
Energy							
Oil & Gas Drilling	−467.30	15.49	NM	1.35	0.98	1.24	1970
Oil (Domestic Integrated)	22.25	15.79	1.77	1.10	4.18	4.50	1970
Oil (Exploration & Production)	−29.58	34.03	NM	1.82	1.01	3.12	1989
Oil (International Integrated)	15.08	9.36	1.20	0.71	4.31	6.38	1970
Oil Well Equip. & Serv.	22.56	21.87	1.80	1.73	2.44	2.36	1970
Financials							
Insurance Brokers	14.22	18.13	1.13	1.21	3.56	3.81	1984
Life Insurance	8.51	8.68	0.68	0.74	3.39	3.98	1974
Major Regional Banks	7.45	14.21	0.59	1.13	4.47	4.78	1970
Money Center Banks	6.40	9.41	0.51	0.72	3.83	5.23	1970
Multi-Line Insurance	11.43	10.90	0.91	0.92	1.75	3.53	1974
Personal Loans	8.81	9.45	0.70	0.75	3.77	5.60	1970
Property-Casualty Insurance	10.91	11.16	0.87	0.95	1.76	5.19	1974
Savings & Loan Companies	7.50	12.20	0.60	0.85	3.86	3.44	1970
Financial (Miscellaneous)	8.39	10.56	0.67	0.54	2.76	3.11	1990
Services							
Specialized Services	15.57	17.44	1.24	1.22	2.91	3.17	1982
Specialty Printing	13.16	18.37	1.05	0.92	3.43	2.77	1990
Technology							
Communication Equip./Mfrs.	21.18	19.38	1.69	1.71	0.42	1.13	1978
Computer Software & Services	22.78	20.06	1.82	1.61	0.19	0.93	1978
Computer Systems	12.77	17.93	1.02	1.49	0.92	3.00	1970
Electronics (Defense)	10.48	13.31	0.84	0.93	2.27	2.13	1983
Electronics (Instrumentation)	13.57	21.87	1.08	1.77	1.30	0.87	1970
Electronics (Semiconductors)	12.38	22.13	0.99	1.80	0.59	1.13	1970
Office Equipment & Supplies	11.98	19.03	0.96	1.22	3.10	4.67	1982
Photography/Imaging	14.54	22.23	1.16	1.12	3.37	4.34	1990
Telecommunications (Long Dist.)	13.25	19.34	1.06	1.18	2.45	3.93	1984
Transportation							
Airlines	14.21	21.96	1.13	2.02	0.16	1.17	1970
Railroads	10.42	10.69	0.83	0.86	2.85	4.35	1970
Truckers	14.12	16.37	1.13	1.30	2.52	2.75	1973
Transportation (Miscellaneous)	11.30	25.98	0.90	1.68	0.94	1.30	1988
Utilities							
Electric Companies	10.54	9.57	0.84	0.76	7.04	8.35	1970
Natural Gas	11.90	12.32	0.95	0.97	3.73	5.32	1970
Telephone	12.30	13.71	0.98	0.85	5.53	6.01	1984
S&P 500 Composite	**12.54**	**13.06**	**NA**	**NA**	**2.90**	**4.14**	**1970**

The second section is a snapshot of each industry in the S&P 500, providing a three-part review of the industry: a *description* of the products and/or services provided; a discussion of the *characteristics* of the industry, including the influencing indicators listed in Table 3-1, and other industry-specific factors that could affect share prices for companies within this industry, such as seasonal price variations and the effect of government regulations. And, finally, there is an investment *outlook* for each industry, highlighting what the S&P analyst believes lies ahead for the companies within each industry over the coming year and beyond. (These outlooks were updated as of December 30, 1994, so all referenced statistics and reports were the most current available.) Those industries found in S&P's monthly *Industry Reports* publication are accompanied by a 5-year industry price chart. Investors will come to rely on this section to learn to judge whether stocks within each industry may act similarly to past performances or if dynamics within the industry might alter future price movements.

Completing the picture is Chapter 4 (p. 205). It is a financial digest for more than 1000 companies followed on an analytical basis by S&P analysts. Earnings, P/Es, dividend yields, as well as STARS (S&P's unique Stock Appreciation Ranking System that offers a buy, hold, or sell recommendation) are listed for each company. These peer company listings are arranged alphabetically within industry. More about that later.

AEROSPACE/
DEFENSE

Description. The aerospace segment, quite simply, produces flying vehicles: aircraft, for both commercial and military marketplaces, as well as manned and unmanned spacecraft, helicopters, and missiles. It also produces the component parts. The defense segment produces such military items as ships, submarines, tanks, and armored personnel carriers.

Characteristics. The primary, and highly cyclical, factors affecting the performance of aerospace stocks are defense spending and the ordering of aircraft by the commercial transport companies. Each cycle can extend over several years and may not necessarily coincide with one another or with conditions in the general economy. Defense spending trends are primarily a product of the state of international relations, while commercial transport ordering reflects the equipment needs of the airline industry. Profits of military contractors can be affected by policy changes of the Defense Department, such as new contracting regulations that result in cuts in profitability for many companies. Share prices of individual companies also are influenced greatly by contract awards.

Outlook. During 1995, the investment outlook for the aerospace/defense industry will continue to be affected by the squeeze on defense budgets in effect for the past few years. However, during 1994 the group moderately outperformed the market as defense contractors responded with profitable consolidation actions. Meanwhile, the price performance of some issues in the commercial aerospace sector has improved as investors look for a bottoming in

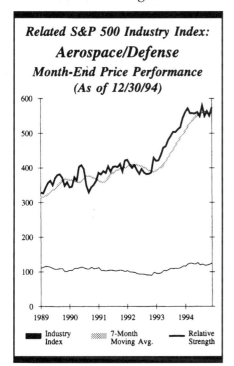

Related S&P 500 Industry Index:
Aerospace/Defense
Month-End Price Performance
(As of 12/30/94)

| Industry Index | 7-Month Moving Avg. | Relative Strength |

the long downtrend of orders for new aircraft as airline industry finances begin to recover.

We are recommending accumulation of selected military contractors that are restructuring in an effort to cope with the defense budget squeeze, particularly those whose defense operations are supplemented by strong commercial activities. The shares of the group should continue to react positively to consolidation activities, including acquisitions of assets and mergers, as contractors move to gain dominant positions in sectors of the market. The recent merger agreement involving Martin Marietta and Lockheed is the most far-reaching example, and is likely to be followed by further consolidation moves in the industry.

The disastrous financial performance of the airline industry produced a drop in new commercial aircraft orders, and the major aircraft manufacturers cut production rates in the past 3 years. Although further cuts are scheduled for early 1995, the bottom of the market's decline could be developing as deliveries of Boeing's new 777 begin in the second half. A number of airlines are expected to be profitable in 1995. This turnaround eventually should prompt a pickup in orders for new planes by the world's airlines. And while those manufacturers that are heavily dependent on the commercial market could feel further downward pressure on earnings in 1995, the beginnings of an overall comeback should develop. Share prices are normally driven more by order recovery than by the ensuing earnings pickup. In addition, there is a possibility of a bottoming-out in the decline in defense spending in the next few years, with a modest improvement in weapons procurement during the second half of the 1990s.

AIRLINES

Description. The airline industry provides transportation services to individuals over scheduled routes, and to a lesser extent through chartered flights. Freight is also carried. The individual airlines are classified according to their routes as international, domestic, or regional.

Characteristics. The airline stocks are influenced by factors affecting the trend in passenger travel, the most influential of which is the change in the economy. As corporate profits are reduced, so too is the amount of business travel—business people are the primary users of full-fare tickets. Other important factors include trends in disposable income and their effect on leisure travel as well as the result of across-the-board fare increases and fare wars. The cost factor that influences profit trends the most is that of fuel; as oil prices rise, profits decline. Historically, fuel expenses have made up about 15% of total operating costs. The third quarter (summer season) generally provides the bulk of airline earnings as passenger traffic is highest. Stock prices have shown a tendency to rise late in the year, particularly if there is general optimism toward the overall economy in the coming year. A downtrend sometimes develops in the following spring-to-summer months if the economy does not perform to expectations.

Outlook. Airline stock prices could recover in 1995 as the industry makes further progress in its move toward profitability. During 1994, airlines badly underperformed the S&P 500 as investors continued to be wary of such developments as safety concerns and the spread of fare cutting in short-haul markets, attempts to reduce labor costs by large carriers, and cuts in capacity, as well as the possibility of slowing economic growth.

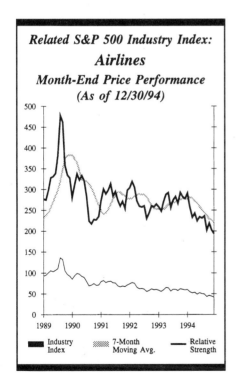

Related S&P 500 Industry Index:
Airlines
Month-End Price Performance
(As of 12/30/94)

Industry Index · 7-Month Moving Avg. · Relative Strength

33

We project higher profit totals in 1995, as the economy should support a modest level of traffic growth. The emergence of new low-fare operations resulted in a decline in average fare yields in 1994, but the effects could be more moderate in 1995. The impressive long-term performance of low-cost, low-fare Southwest Airlines and the emergence of several new low-fare competitors have caused some of the larger full-service carriers to form similar types of operations. In 1995, both Continental Airlines and United Airlines will pursue further development of their new special groups concentrating on short hauls with low-fare, no-frills service.

A key element in the emerging profits of the industry is an intensified focus on the control of operating costs. Most of the major carriers have initiated cost-cutting programs that include reductions in the work force, elimination of unprofitable routes, retirement of older planes, and general economies. As a result, unit cost of capacity (available seat-miles) generally ran below year-earlier numbers in 1994. Cost control is continuing as a major focus of activity through such tactics as the exchange of equity positions for wage and benefit cuts at UAL and other carriers, cuts in employment, and the elimination of money-losing routes. For 1995, domestic capacity will continue to be restrained, which should result in higher load factors. Moreover, significant reductions in new aircraft on order will mean large savings in capital expenditures and improvements in cash positions in the next few years.

ALUMINUM

Description.   Aluminum ingot is a metal that is not found in a natural state. It is derived from alumina through the smelter reduction process. Alumina, in turn, is refined from Bauxite, the raw material that is mined. The ingot can be upgraded to make fabricated aluminum products, such as the lightweight aluminum needed in beverage cans and the aluminum made to fine tolerances for airplanes.

Characteristics.   Aluminum ingot prices are sensitive to the balance between supply and demand, and influence the prices of fabricated aluminum products. Fabricated aluminum product prices are more stable than commodity-like ingot quotes, and profit margins of the former are generally higher than margins of the latter. Factors that influence the share prices for these firms include the outlook for industrial activity; the prospects for aluminum's most important markets, such as containers/packaging, transportation, and building/construction; and finally, since most major aluminum companies' product mix is more heavily weighted toward fabricated products, their share prices tend to correlate more closely with fabricated product quotes than ingot prices. Earnings for most aluminum companies are usually strongest in the second quarter as beverage container manufacturers order sheet to meet the high summer demand.

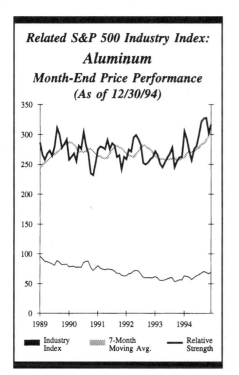

Related S&P 500 Industry Index:

Aluminum

Month-End Price Performance
(As of 12/30/94)

Outlook.   Aluminum stocks will, at best, match the market in the short term, after outpacing it for most of 1994. Domestic aluminum ingot prices have now reached high enough levels to encourage some producers to restart idled smelters and plan new greenfield capacity. Announcements to such an effect would temporarily hurt prices of aluminum and aluminum shares.

Since November 1, 1993, producers in the United States, Canada, Australia, and Europe have cut production by about 650,000 tons. While the Russian part of the former Soviet Union agreed to curtail output by up to 500,000 tons, reduced internal demand could allow aluminum exports to stay at a high level. We would not be surprised if shipments from the Commonwealth of Independent States in 1994 and 1995 approximate 1993's record 2.1 million. With very strong U.S. aluminum consumption and a pickup in European aluminum use, however, advancing world aluminum demand has crossed above declining supply. In fact, aluminum in London Metal Exchange (LME) warehouses has finally begun to decrease.

Given maintenance of cuts, sustained U.S. and better European economic growth, and a budding Japanese recovery, aluminum demand should continue to outpace supply in 1995. This trend has firmly established the higher ingot prices of the last year. But, prices are now sufficient to provide some producers with an incentive to reopen shut down smelters and to plan new green-field capacity. Greater output would be absorbed by strong demand, and any new facilities would be unlikely to come onstream until three to five years after a go-ahead decision is reached. However, such announcements would temporarily hurt aluminum prices, which also have been inflated by speculation of hedge funds.

AUTO PARTS

Description. The auto parts industry manufactures parts and accessories for motor vehicles, including autos, trucks, and off-road vehicles. The industry is divided into two segments: original equipment (parts and accessories for new vehicles) and replacement or aftermarket parts.

Characteristics. Original equipment sales depend on the number, size, and complexity of cars and trucks produced, as well as the portion of vehicles produced captively by their manufacturers. These companies are closely tied to the cyclical auto and truck industries, the sales for which are affected by personal disposable income, consumer confidence, and interest rates. The third quarter is typically the weakest in terms of sales and earnings for these companies, as they are affected by auto plant shutdowns in the summer and model changeover periods. Aftermarket parts sales depend on the number of vehicles in their prime repair years and the number of miles driven annually by the vehicles. Replacement parts sales tend to rise during recessions due to the increased propensity of vehicle owners to repair their vehicles rather than replace them.

Related S&P 500 Industry Index:

Auto Parts: After Market
Month-End Price Performance
(As of 12/30/94)

| Industry Index | 7-Month Moving Avg. | Relative Strength |

Outlook. Despite a sharp selloff for this group in 1994, we remain positive on its investment outlook, as the pressure that both original equipment manufacturers (OEMs) and aftermarket (replacement) parts companies (APMs) had been under in recent years has abated. Strengthened by improved earnings and cash flow from U.S. operations, parts companies are seeking expansion opportunities in Europe, as the valuations of European companies have declined. Many U.S. companies are now positioned to benefit from an economic upturn in Europe, which is now underway. Industry leaders are also responding to the changing demands of European automakers that are preparing to meet the challenges of a unified and open market economy in Europe.

Auto parts continue to account for about 25% of the U.S. trade deficit with Japan. Unites States government pressure has resulted in commitments from major Japanese automakers to increase their purchases from U.S. suppliers over the next few years. Parts makers will benefit from an expected rise in demand for replacement parts and services, due to new emissions regulations that are being phased in in 1994 and 1995. The new rules require centralized dynamometer testing for 4 minutes at varying speeds, versus the 30-second idling test previously performed. Companies with superior technologies or processes stand to gain from Japan's promise to boost purchases from U.S. suppliers. In 1995, the OEMs should benefit from higher car and light truck production and vigorous demand for medium and heavy duty trucks. OEMs' profits are rising, due to the higher production of vehicles in North America and a gradual increase of orders from Japanese automakers producing vehicles in the United States.

APMs are also emerging from a prolonged slowdown in unit growth that was due to various long-term trends including: fewer trips to the repair shops by more reliable vehicles; decreased demand for domestic parts, due to the proliferation of foreign vehicles; and a decline in the number of service stations, leading to less preventive maintenance. Yet industry fundamentals are improving, because of: more stringent safety and emissions inspections which will often lead to repairs; increased complexity of new vehicles, which require more costly repairs; and growth in the number of older cars in service and the number of miles driven annually, which should stimulate demand for replacement parts and tires.

AUTOMOBILES

Definition. These companies manufacture and sell automobiles and light trucks (under 10,000 pounds). The "Big Three" is comprised of General Motors, Ford, and Chrysler.

Characteristics. The U.S. auto industry has evolved into a highly competitive struggle among some 30 manufacturers located worldwide. Although there remain but three domestically owned manufacturers, nine Japanese manufacturers (called transplants) are assembling cars and trucks in North America, either independently or jointly with other Japanese or U.S. auto makers. Worldwide capacity has expanded rapidly in the past 10 years and much of the new production is aimed at the United States, which has few trade barriers. Sales of vehicles in the United States are influenced by general economic conditions, particularly changes in disposable personal income, consumer confidence, and interest rates.

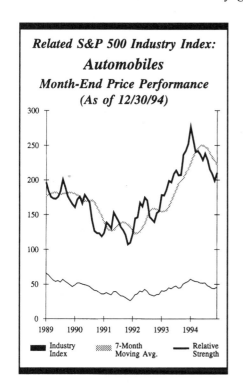

Related S&P 500 Industry Index:

Automobiles

Month-End Price Performance
(As of 12/30/94)

Industry Index
7-Month Moving Avg.
Relative Strength

Outlook. Even though the auto stocks took a beating in 1994, we remain upbeat on these stocks in the coming months. Another strong year of sales and earnings is expected in 1995 for the auto industry and we expect all three of the domestic automakers to participate in the prosperity. North American production should rise about 6% in 1995 and, with Europe exhibiting a modest economic recovery, our near-term investment outlook is positive.

Gains in earnings will continue to reflect particularly strong demand for trucks in the United States, on which the Big Three earn wider margins than on cars. This strong earnings trend should continue as all of the Big Three are participating in the introduction of a wave of new vehicles that should boost market share. Earnings will benefit from lower marketing costs (as rebates and discounts are further reduced), modest cost cutting, and lower interest and pension expense.

Increased production in Europe as the nascent recovery in vehicle demand picks up speed should provide a substantial earnings boost to GM and Ford. We believe that recent concerns that GM's productivity gains in North America may be slowing are very overblown. We expect further gains as models designed with manufacturing simplification in mind enter production. GM is also making rapid progress in solidifying its balance sheet. We upgraded GM to "buy" following the October 1994 selloff. Our "accumulate" ranking on Ford reflects concern that profit margins remain weaker than Chrysler's, despite market share gains achieved in recent years and high plant operating rates. We also rate Chrysler "buy." We expect investors to develop a more positive view of the company as it benefits from higher sales of sport utility vehicles and pickup trucks, as well as from the introduction of an extensively redesigned minivan lineup and a steady stream of new cars. Chrysler's market share should rise in North America and the company should capitalize on its recently established position as the low-cost producer in the industry. Chrysler is taking aggressive actions to boost the quality of its vehicles as measured in independent studies such as those of J. D. Power.

BEVERAGES
(ALCOHOLIC)

Description. This group includes producers of beer, distilled spirits, and wine products.

Characteristics. As defensive issues (those with earnings that are not generally tied to the overall health of the economy), any economic indicator that points to economic weakness will influence these issues favorably as it makes them more attractive to investors than the economically sensitive industries. Such indicators would include interest rates, consumer sentiment, and personal income growth. Investors should realize, however, that many of the leading U.S. alcoholic beverage companies have significantly diversified their operations over the years, both geographically and by product line, in order to help offset declining consumption patterns in the United States—for example, Seagram Co.'s 24.3% stake in duPont (EI) de Nemours (and 14.9% stake in Time Warner Inc.) and Brown-Forman Corp.'s ownership of Lenox china and Hartmann Luggage.

Outlook. The S&P Alcoholic Beverages index modestly outperformed the S&P 500 during 1994, helped by a sharp rise in Seagram shares (which were boosted by a substantial recovery in duPont earnings). However, our near-term investment outlook remains neutral, primarily due to flattish alcoholic product consumption trends in many important markets, such as the United States and Europe, and the possibility (albeit a waning one) of higher U.S. excise taxes.

The U.S. alcoholic beverages industry was given a collective reprieve from the possibility of higher federal excise taxes on its products (at

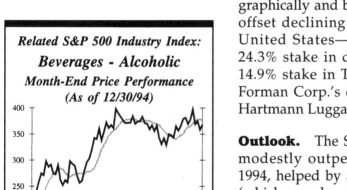

Related S&P 500 Industry Index:
Beverages - Alcoholic
Month-End Price Performance
(As of 12/30/94)

Industry Index · 7-Month Moving Avg. · Relative Strength

least for now) with the demise of the Clinton Administration's proposed health care reform plan. But industry members have not toasted yet, as the issue may be debated again in the near future. Meanwhile, U.S. alcoholic beverage consumption continues to be negatively affected by a growing consumer consumption shift toward lighter, less-alcoholic beverages. The facts continue to bear this out: In 1993, per-capita consumption of beer dipped to 22.8 gallons from 23.0; wine dipped to 1.7 gallons from 2.0; and distilled spirits remained at about 1.3 gallons.

The U.S. brewing industry extended its slow growth mode in 1993, with total domestic shipments up just 0.2% to 188.7 million 31-gallon barrels. For 1994, S&P projects U.S. brewers to eke out a 1% increase in beer shipments, helped by the receding effects from 1991's damaging excise tax increase, and from the aggressive roll-outs of new products such as ice beer and clear malt beverages. United States wine shipments declined 4% in 1993, hurt by the continuing economic malaise in California, the world's largest market. United States spirits shipments fell 2% in 1993, still hurt by lingering effects from 1991's federal excise tax increases and more moderate consumer drinking habits.

BEVERAGES
(SOFT DRINKS)

Description. The nonalcoholic beverage group includes companies that principally manufacture soft drink concentrates (Coca-Cola, Dr. Pepper/Seven-Up); those that primarily bottle the final product (Coca-Cola Enterprises); and those companies that make other nonalcoholic beverage products that may not be their sole product line (Pepsico).

Characteristics. As defensive issues (those with earnings that are not generally tied to the overall health of the economy), any economic indicator that points to economic weakness will influence these issues favorably as it makes them more attractive to investors than the economically sensitive industries. Such indicators would include interest rates, consumer sentiment, and personal income growth.

Outlook. The S&P Soft Drink index outperformed the S&P 500 during 1994, helped largely by a 15% rise in the shares of Coca-Cola (KO). KO's shares got a substantial lift following the company's strong 22% earnings per share gain in its third quarter, ended September 30, 1994, which were boosted by a sharp rebound in the important markets of Japan and Germany. Other nonalcoholic beverage stocks generally rose following KO's strong earnings. In early November 1994, The Quaker Oats Co. agreed to acquire the shares of Snapple Beverage Corp. for $14 each, in an effort to bolster its important Gatorade Beverage division.

Sales and earnings are expected to continue in a solid uptrend for U.S. soft drink concentrate manufacturers (such as Coca-Cola Co., PepsiCo Inc., and Dr. Pepper/Seven-Up Cos.) in 1995,

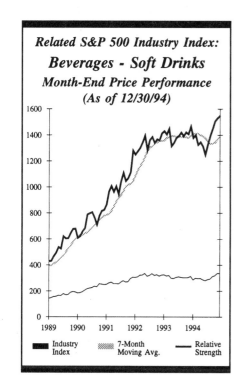

Related S&P 500 Industry Index:
Beverages - Soft Drinks
Month-End Price Performance
(As of 12/30/94)

43

driven principally by greater unit case sales volume (projected by S&P at about 3% to 5% annually) and generally stable material costs. Principal reasons for our optimistic outlook for sales volume growth include continued U.S. economic improvement, which should bolster consumer spending, and continued aggressive expansion by the industry into noncola segments (such as ready-to-drink teas, juices, bottled water, and sports drinks), which should increase overall nonalcoholic beverage consumption levels. Meanwhile, the U.S. soft drink industry should continue to reap solid profits in fast-growing international regions, where demand has risen with recent political changes and market openings. Improving economies in key overseas markets, such as Germany and Japan, should give these companies an added lift.

The outlook for U.S. bottler stocks is somewhat more subdued, despite an expected improvement in U.S. case sale volume growth. Earnings per share growth for capital-intensive Coca-Cola Enterprises should continue to be held by a high level of acquisition-related depreciation and amortization charges. Whitman Corp. is enjoying rejuvenated profit growth for its Pepsi General bottler unit, but overall company profits may be held near term by costs incurred with bottler expansion in Poland, and weakness at its Hussmann refrigeration product unit. Longer term, these companies should enjoy steady, but modest, improvement in earnings, aided by further increases in U.S. per-capita consumption of nonalcoholic beverages.

BROADCAST MEDIA

Description. This group consists of television broadcasters, radio broadcasters, and cable TV system operators.

Characteristics. Television and radio broadcasters benefit from trends in advertising spending, the health of the local economy in which they operate, changes in consumer sentiment/spending, and interest rates. Broadcasters also are driven by advertising revenues and costs of programming, with advertising largely a function of general economic activity. While cable operators are also affected by interest rates, FCC regulations that affect pricing and competition and the increase in their subscriber base are more important measures of this segment's growth opportunities. In addition, because of the capital-intensive nature of the industry, cash flow is generally a better measure of the health of a cable system operator than is net earnings, which can include sizable amounts of noncash charges. Thus, these companies are generally valued in the stock market and in private transactions based on a multiple of cash flow. There are no pure-play television broadcasters among the major media stocks, thus the outlook for entertainment, cable, and assorted publishing sectors must also be taken into consideration; it would be wise to evaluate each company on its own merits.

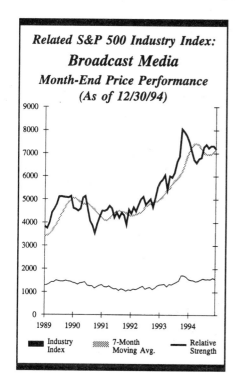

Related S&P 500 Industry Index:
Broadcast Media
Month-End Price Performance
(As of 12/30/94)

Industry Index   7-Month Moving Avg.   Relative Strength

Outlook. The outlook for cable stocks has improved following the FCC's November 10, 1994, announcement of eased restrictions on pricing. The new rules provide for positive cash flow growth over the next several years, and remove much of the cloud over the industry's future that tarnished the luster of the underlying valuation of cable properties. The relatively volatile stocks are not likely to outperform the market in the near term, however, reflecting concerns regarding the industry's competitive position vis à vis the Baby Bells. Television and radio broadcast stocks are expected to outperform the market in both the near and longer term.

The FCC's new "going forward" rules allow cablers to hike monthly rates on regulated service by a maximum of $1.50 through 1996, depending on the number of new programming channels added. Monthly rates can be raised $0.20 or more in 1997. Cablers will also be allowed inflation-indexed rate increases and other cost-of-business allowances. In addition, operators were given the go-ahead to set up new unregulated packages of cable programming. Two earlier rounds of FCC-mandated rate rollbacks (10% in September 1993 and 7% in May 1994) and a price freeze of nearly two years had hurt the industry in a number of ways, the most obvious of which was in revenues and cash flow. The restrictions also impaired the industry's attractiveness to lenders, acquirers, and investors.

We project a rise in total TV advertising of 7.1% in 1995. By category, we are looking for a 6.2% rise in network and national syndication ad spending, an 8.2% rise in local advertising, and an 8.1% gain in national spot advertising. The rise in total broadcast TV advertising for 1994 is estimated at 9.7%.

Total radio advertising could rise another 9.0% in 1995 to $11.74 billion, after an estimated 12.6% advance in 1994 to $10.77 billion. We project that local advertising will advance nearly 9% in 1995, that national spot spending will gain almost 10%, and that network spending will rise nearly 9%. The industry's stellar performance points up radio's advantages for highly targeted marketing and the relative ease and low cost to produce and air commercials. Among other factors, radio has also been doing a better job of marketing itself.

BUILDING MATERIALS

Description. Building materials are the items used to build a residential structure: lumber, structural panels, glass, insulation, doors, cement, gypsum wallboard, and plumbing.

Characteristics. Since building materials are the items used to build a home, their sales, earnings, and share-price movements are similar to those that affect homebuilding and household furnishings and appliances: interest rates, personal income/spending, and housing starts. Demand for these items typically increases as the weather warms up.

Outlook. The near-term investment outlook for building materials stocks is positive following the recent retreat in the shares of leading producers. While industry sales remain healthy, 1994's sharp rise in interest rates raised fears that construction activity will be severely curtailed and that demand for building materials will suffer. However, thus far there has been no real decline in industry shipments, as rates are still at a low enough level to support significant building activity. Business remains relatively strong compared with the early 1990s, and industry conditions have improved due to increased demand for repair-related materials in areas damaged by natural disasters. Pricing for structural panels continues to be strong enough to promise good profits for most suppliers. Obviously, the key factor in the future for the level of building materials demand is the effect of future interest rate changes on the construction markets.

Because of recent pricing weakness, most lumber types (e.g., Western spruce-pine-fir, Southern

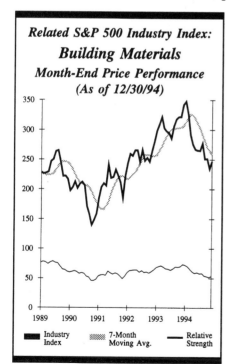

Related S&P 500 Industry Index:
Building Materials
Month-End Price Performance
(As of 12/30/94)

Industry Index | 7-Month Moving Avg. | Relative Strength

pine) are now priced somewhat lower than a year ago. If the strong economy is able to partially offset the effects of higher interest rates, allowing for continued good demand from home-builders, trends point to stronger lumber pricing over the next few years. The supply/demand picture for wood is favorable due to restrictions on logging on government-owned land resulting from environmental concerns. On the demand side, despite investors' fears, housing starts are likely to remain at healthy levels as there appears to be significant underlying pent-up demand for housing. Increased infrastructure spending and upward revisions in estimates for U.S. population growth also bode well for building material demand.

The Surface Transportation Act passed in 1991 has proven to be beneficial to cement producers, and shipments have been boosted by the need to repair earthquake damage in California. However, this industry has seen years of weak profits due to strong competitive pressures. Cement/aggregates stocks are no bargains at current valuations considering the industry's commodity nature.

The gypsum industry has benefited from improvement in pricing for wallboard, resulting in healthier profit margins. The uptrend in gypsum pricing is expected to continue.

CHEMICALS

Description. The U.S. chemicals industry produces a variety of products, including plastics, fibers, pesticides, paints, and detergents, as well as inorganic chemicals. Most products are used by other industries and, to a lesser extent, directly by consumers. Chemical products can be either high-volume, low-price commodities, or lower-volume, higher-valued specialty products. The S&P Chemicals index is comprised of traditional commodity producers.

Characteristics. The industry is generally cyclical, driven by changes in economic growth and industrial production. The industrial segment of the economy accounts for about two-thirds of demand for chemical products. The largest end users are the automotive (tires, plastics, and rubber) and housing-related markets (carpeting, furniture, paint, and vinyl siding). Longer-term growth is commonly projected at about 1.5 times real economic growth. Research and development expenditures as a percentage of sales are typically 50% more than for all manufacturing companies.

Outlook. We remain positive on commodity chemicals stocks given the industry's favorable earnings outlook for 1995. Many major chemical companies posted higher sales and double digit increases in 1994, attributing the gains to the improvement in the U.S. economy and key markets, as well as rising selling prices. We expect profits to continue to advance well into 1995. The industry has fully digested the massive production capacity added earlier in this decade and profit margins for petrochemicals and plastics are widening as operating rates climb. The industry is also benefiting from the cost reductions implemented over the past few years. Key end markets, such as housing, automotive, and

Related S&P 500 Industry Index:
Chemicals
Month-End Price Performance
(As of 12/30/94)

Legend: Industry Index | 7-Month Moving Avg. | Relative Strength

manufacturing, should remain healthy despite rising interest rates. In addition, with the European economies showing more signs of recovery, U.S. chemical companies with foreign operations should now begin to benefit. Fertilizer markets, which improved in 1994 in response to increased crop acreage, may remain strong in 1995 on good global demand.

S&P expects chemical and products production to rise more modestly in 1995 than the 4.0% increase for 1994. Output in December 1994, as measured by the Federal Reserve production index for chemicals, was at 126.3 (1987 = 100), up 4.5% from the year-earlier level. The industry's operating rates should remain at the current healthy levels which are the highest since 1988, reflecting the climb in output and the slowdown in the industry's capacity expansion of the past few years. In December 1994, the utilization rate was 81.4%, versus 80.8% for the year-earlier period. The producer price index for chemicals and products in December 1994 was 138.6 (1982 = 100), up 8.3% from the year-earlier level. Price strength is occurring in many key products including organic chemicals and plastics such as polyethylene and polyvinyl chloride resins. Chlor-alkali producers have announced further prices increases for caustic soda, which had declined sharply in the two years through 1993.

CHEMICALS (DIVERSIFIED)

Description.   These are companies whose largest individual business is chemicals related, but also have major interests in other businesses. For example, FMC Corp. produces industrial and agricultural chemicals, while also owning defense, machinery, and gold mining businesses.

Characteristics.   The factors that influence the sales, earnings and share prices of companies in this industry are similar to those in the commodity chemical industry. Depending on the nonchemical businesses, trends in these areas could dampen or magnify the cyclical chemical factors.

Outlook.   The investment outlook for this industry is similar to that of the commodity chemical industry. Investors are advised also to review the investment outlooks of the nonchemical businesses in which these companies are engaged.

CHEMICALS
(SPECIALTY)

Description. Major categories of specialty chemicals include water treatment, manufacturing, processing, additives, coatings, pesticides, catalysts, adhesives, and sealants. Specialty producers are generally smaller in terms of dollar size than traditional commodity producers; some focus on only one product line, while others boast a diverse product mix.

Characteristics. Specialty chemicals products, which are of higher value than commodity chemicals, sell on performance specifications rather than on price. Specialty chemicals also help customers meet increasingly stringent environmental regulations. Although specialties require higher R&D spending and incur a greater amount of marketing and customer service costs, their production is typically less capital intensive than for commodities. Specialty chemicals producers are generally less affected by changes in the economy and supply/demand balances than are commodity producers, and thus do not experience the same cyclical earnings surge as commodity producers.

Outlook. S&P's investment outlook for several of the companies in the S&P Specialty Chemicals index is positive, while the outlook for most of the other industry participants is generally less favorable. Specialty chemicals stocks have generally underperformed the stock market in contrast to the commodity chemicals group, reflecting market fears of the adverse impact on specialties of higher raw materials costs.

Based on S&P's forecast for real GDP to show a 3.0% growth in 1995, specialty chemicals companies' sales and earnings generally should contin-

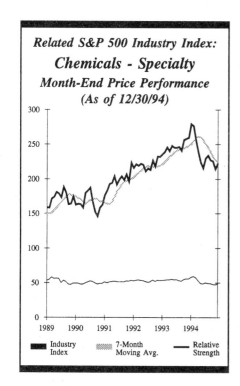

Related S&P 500 Industry Index:
Chemicals - Specialty
Month-End Price Performance
(As of 12/30/94)

Industry Index | 7-Month Moving Avg. | Relative Strength

ue to do well. Healthy conditions in the important domestic key end markets, such as manufacturing, housing, and automotive, are boosting demand for a wide variety of specialty products. As the European economy shows further signs of improvement, U.S. companies with foreign operations should begin to benefit. Rising prices for commodity chemicals are likely to hurt profit margins for specialty chemicals producers through at least early 1995, although the impact will vary by company. Although long-term prospects vary widely for different types of specialties producers, depending on their individual market conditions, overall industry sales growth is projected at about 6% a year.

COMMUNICATIONS EQUIPMENT MANUFACTURERS

Description. These companies manufacture communications equipment ranging from fiber optic cables and wireless antennas used to transmit calls, to end-user equipment such as office phone systems and consumer telephone sets.

Characteristics. Sales, earnings, and share prices are influenced by trends in the overall economy, inflationary expectations, and government regulation. Economic growth influences growth in demand for communications services, and therefore growth in demand for communications equipment. Inflation impacts the manufacturers both through the effect on the prices of their end products and through its impact on interest rates, which will increase customers' cost of capital. And, finally, regulatory policy can either encourage or discourage communications services companies' investment in infrastructure.

Outlook. The S&P Communications Equipment index put on a strong showing in the fourth quarter of 1994 reflecting, in part, the seasonality of the group. Most equipment orders are skewed to the latter half of the year. Our near-term outlook for the group is neutral to moderately positive, with companies having a strong presence in wireless and fiber optic equipment likely to outperform the group as the telcos target spending to revenue opportunities. Over the longer term, we expect the group as a whole to benefit from spending on infrastructure by developing nations and as telephone companies and cable operators upgrade their networks for the provision of new service offerings.

Related S&P 500 Industry Index:

Communications Equip.

Month-End Price Performance
(As of 12/30/94)

Industry Index | 7-Month Moving Avg. | Relative Strength

55

Visibility of earnings growth has improved as equipment orders have taken their typical seasonal track. Stronger growth in access lines and prospects of clearer regulatory policy are prompting renewed growth in spending by the major U.S. telephone companies. In particular, as regulators and lawmakers reexamine regulatory restraints on telcos and cable operators, spending on infrastructure upgrades for the provision of advanced interactive services is beginning to heat up. Sharp interest in auctions of wireless spectrum licenses portend accelerated spending by wireless service providers as cellular carriers move to upgrade their systems and companies begin building infrastructure for competing wireless technologies.

International growth opportunities are bright. Many nations are investing in their telecommunications infrastructure, replacing outdated and inadequate networks to attract foreign investment. Spending in regions such as the Far East and Latin America is likely to grow rapidly; spending in the former Soviet Union should also expand, although funding concerns may limit expenditures. Opportunities in more developed regions also exist. The unification of Western Europe creates a stunningly large market and directives from the EC Commission have opened the terminal equipment market to U.S. manufacturers.

The group is likely to exhibit extreme volatility in the foreseeable future as shares move with highly visible contract awards and regulatory actions.

COMPUTER
SOFTWARE & SERVICES

Description. Software is a series of coded computer-language instructions that direct a computer's operation. The major categories are systems software, which controls the management of a computer's resources, and applications software, which provides the computer with instructions for the performance of individual tasks. Computer service vendors help those who can't help themselves when it comes to using computers. Processing service providers generally use their own computer facilities and proprietary software to process a customer's transactions and data. Professional service vendors offer consulting, system design and development, custom software, systems integration, training, outsourcing, and disaster recovery. Information services vendors offer access to proprietary databases.

Characteristics. Sales of software are influenced by the sale of computer hardware products. However, the software industry is primarily product driven. A new software product which increases productivity or enhances quality will be in great demand. Computer services are more generally tied to the overall economy. For example, processors of weekly payroll checks will be influenced by employment rates. However, the trend is for organizations to "outsource" their computer-related resources. Service providers often offer organizations cheaper and better computer resource management by offering economies of scale through spreading the costs of hardware, software, development, and maintenance over a large base.

Outlook. We believe that the investment outlook for software stocks is positive, in general, and that the best strategy lies with investing in leaders of the various software markets. Although unit sales of mainframes and minicomputers are expected to remain sluggish, there is an expanding need for software to effectively manage and utilize the ever-

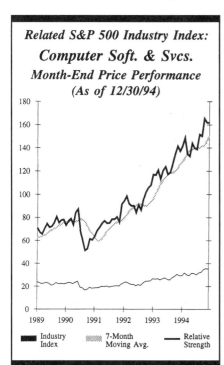

Related S&P 500 Industry Index:
Computer Soft. & Svcs.
Month-End Price Performance
(As of 12/30/94)

Industry Index · 7-Month Moving Avg. · Relative Strength

increasing power and complexity of these computers and the networks to which they are being joined. Segment revenues continue to rise because the price of software in these markets is partly related to the processing power of the computer on which it resides. The PC segment is particularly attractive; sales should be up over 20% again in 1995. Software vendors have tapped the expanded capabilities of today's newest PCs and are bringing new functionality and increased usefulness to the desktop, spurring even greater demand for the PC and its software. The number of software programs installed on each PC is rising. The PC software industry is in the final stages of a transition away from the traditional DOS environment to the easier-to-use Windows environment. The next version of Windows, recently named "Windows 95," is expected to ship by the third quarter of 1995, and should launch a major new product cycle for PC software vendors. Access to various "on-line" services, as well as gateways to the information superhighway, will provide opportunities for PC software vendors.

Our investment outlook for the computer services segment remains positive as these firms have a high level of repeat business and long contract life cycles, leading to recurring revenues, earnings stability, and predictability. In the current market environment, computer services firms that have demonstrated a consistent record of predictable earnings growth could see their P/E multiples expand further. Demand for computer services is being fueled by improvements in the price/performance of increasingly complex hardware; difficulties in integrating hardware from different vendors into a networked environment; advances in software technology; strong demand for customized software; a shortage of computer science professionals; inefficiencies associated with maintaining an in-house data processing staff; and complex and diverse information needs of the current competitive business environment.

The availability of new, less costly, and more powerful computer workstation and communications technologies has led to increasing demand for "client/server" computing systems, which are based on networks of desktop computers. Client/server networks are cheaper, more reliable, and more versatile than traditional mainframe-based systems. The growing popularity of client/server computing has led to a new industry buzzword: transformational outsourcing. This term refers to a practice whereby a computer services firm assists its customers in making the move away from its traditional mainframe computing environment to client/server systems. A continuation of the general outsourcing trend is expected in 1995.

COMPUTER SYSTEMS

Description. Computer systems, which encompass supercomputers, mainframes, minicomputers, workstations, and personal computers, are known for their ability to process huge amounts of information and to run popular software applications for home and business uses.

Characteristics. The key factors used to gauge the overall strength of an economy include capital spending trends by businesses, the general direction of interest rates, and the value of the U.S. dollar. The computer systems industry is known for short product life cycles, which can last as briefly as 6 months. Investors increasingly perceive the computer systems to be a cyclical, not growth, industry. However, not all industry segments worldwide have identical business cycles. Furthermore, most of the large computer companies have not been able to benefit from the relatively strong capital spending in the United States. The computer industry by nature is deflationary. Due to rapid price performance improvements, greater computing power is available at a lower cost each year. As a result, more units have to be shipped to reach the same dollar amount. Rather than focus on macroeconomic indicators to value these stocks, we believe that investors should focus on each company's internal product cycle.

Outlook. Our 1995 investment outlook for companies in the S&P Computer Systems Index is neutral, mainly due to the aggressive rotation into the group during the latter half of 1994 and the subsequent rise in valuations. The computer systems group was one of the best performers in

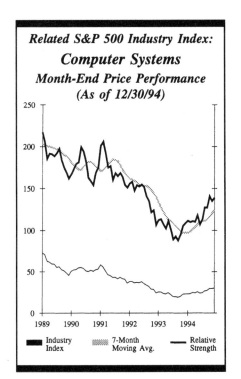

Related S&P 500 Industry Index:

Computer Systems

Month-End Price Performance
(As of 12/30/94)

Industry Index | 7-Month Moving Avg. | Relative Strength

1994. Companies not represented in this index, namely selected networking stocks and firms focusing on client-server technology, remain attractive because of more positive longer-term structural trends.

Fundamentals in the computer industry have improved versus one year ago, mainly due to a growing global appetite for technology products that increase productivity. Worldwide competition is forcing companies to become more productive, a task being accomplished largely through the employment of technology. Although this trend is favorable for computer system vendors, the industry is still dominated by intense competition that can quickly render today's leaders tomorrow's losers. Humbled heavyweights IBM and Digital Equipment are examples of companies that clung to old business practices that are no longer profitable. The new computing paradigm demands that vendors constantly introduce new, more powerful, and cheaper versions of successful products, while keeping a tight rein on operating expenses.

A profitable trend in the computer industry during 1995 is expected to be the continued evolution toward client-server computing. This model promotes the use of networks of cheap, yet powerful, PCs and PC servers versus larger, more expensive, and proprietary mainframe computers. Companies that specialize in migrating customers to this new model, like Hewlett Packard and Sequent, are expected to be strong performers, while server and workstation providers, Sun Microsystems and Silicon Graphics, are also likely to be direct beneficiaries. Computer networking stocks should again be strong in 1995, as firms seek to connect thousands of disparate systems into a seamless web of applications and information. Our favorites remain Cisco Systems, Cabletron Systems, and 3COM. The PC industry, coming off three consecutive years of strong growth, could finally slow in 1995. Major product transitions to Intel's Pentium processor and Microsoft's new Windows 95 operating system could also delay purchasing decisions. We remain mildly bullish on Compaq, owing to its dominating distribution and purchasing channels and demonstrated execution skills.

CONGLOMERATES

Description. This industry consists of a variety of companies that offer a broad array of products and services to the industrial and consumer marketplaces.

Characteristics. The companies within this industry are less likely to be affected by sector-specific events than they are by the direction of macro economic components: GDP growth, industrial production, consumer confidence, interest rates, imports and exports, and the value of the U.S. dollar.

Outlook. The unemployment rate ended 1994 at 5.4% as the economy continued to expand. And while there are a few signs that growth is beginning to level off, the overall tenor is one of strong economic activity. Recent data, including consumer confidence and the leading indicators, point to further growth.

The economy continues to grow faster than the Fed's "speed limits" of 6% unemployment, 2.5% real GDP growth, and 85% capacity utilization. Inflation rates are expected to remain under control. At present, we expect the year-to-year inflation rate to peak at less than 3.5% in mid-1995. Recently, the inflation rate has been about 3% for the CPI and less than 2% for the PPI.

Consumer-related spending sectors, which powered the economy's growth in the first and second quarters leveled off in the second half of 1994. Auto sales and production, as well as housing starts, are expected to be much smaller contributors to overall economic growth in 1995. But with confidence perking up, consumers are not expected to fold their tents.

S&P Economics projects annualized GDP growth of 3.0% for 1995 and 2.7% for 1996. Industrial production is forecast to grow 3.2% and 2.5% in 1995 and 1996, respectively, with capacity utilization expected to peak at 85.8% by the second quarter of 1995. Capital spending should surge 9.4% in 1995 and 4.4% in 1995. Finally, the yield on the 30-year Treasury bond is likely to continue its ascent, peaking at about 8.25% by mid-1995.

CONTAINERS
(METAL AND GLASS)

Description. The metal and glass containers industry supplies cans and bottles to beverage and food companies, as well as other users of such containers.

Characteristics. Virtually all of the metal and glass containers are consumer oriented (versus industrial). Most of the market segments are highly competitive with products sold primarily on a basis of price, service, quality, and performance. Manufacturers of such products tend to sell a substantial portion of their output to relatively few, but large, customers. The packaging business is capital intensive, requiring significant investments in machinery and equipment, and is sensitive to consumer income/spending, the cost of raw materials, such as aluminum and steel, the agricultural output in the case of food containers (a bad crop harvest calls for less canning), and the cost and availability of energy resources. The commodity nature of the industry has resulted in a drive to lower operating costs, maximize use of plant and equipment, and produce differentiation.

Related S&P 500 Industry Index:
Containers (Metal & Glass)
Month-End Price Performance
(As of 12/30/94)

| Industry Index | 7-Month Moving Avg. | Relative Strength |

Outlook. The investment outlook for 1995 is neutral. The overall packaging market in the United States has been characterized by slow growth, primarily due to a relatively slow-growing population. This has resulted in severe competitive pressures in the United States and steady consolidation in the industry via mergers and restructuring. In an effort to enhance operations, packaging companies have focused on faster growing regions of the world that are still developing the use of disposable containers, including Europe, Asia, and the Middle East.

63

Particularly attractive markets include Russia, Eastern Europe, and China.

A long-term trend has been to substitute aluminum or plastic containers for steel and glass, making steel and glass containers, in essence, declining market segments. The overall decline in glass had been arrested somewhat by the emergence of so-called "new age" beverages such as Snapple Iced Tea, packaged in wide-mouth glass bottles. However, increased competition among the new age beverage makers will likely result in substitution of less expensive plastic containers to maintain product margins. This will result in further erosion of the glass market, as will technological advances in plastic containers that allow applications where hot food or liquids are being packaged. The multilayered container continues to gain consumer appeal for packaging of juices and other noncarbonated beverages, but still faces environmental obstacles, namely difficulty in separating the different types of layered materials incorporated in this packaging.

CONTAINERS
(PAPER)

Description. Paper containers are corrugated boxes, as well as the linerboard used to produce them.

Characteristics. Linerboard, the heavy brown paper used to make corrugated boxes, tracks changes in industrial production very closely because corrugated containers are used mainly to ship finished goods; of course, the potential for rapid pricing changes exists on both the upside and downside. Industry earnings also are magnified by the generally high level of balance sheet leverage in the group. A large percentage of sales for both corrugated containers and specialty packaging is made to the food industry. Demand from food producers is relatively stable, compared with other industrial customers. But while stable food industry demand moderates the fluctuations in aggregate demand, changes in overall economic activity have a greater impact on pricing.

Outlook. Conditions for companies producing paper containers improved dramatically in 1994 due to the strengthening of the U.S. economy. Containerboard inventories fell with the improvement in general business conditions, and the long-awaited profit recovery for major companies in the group is underway. The surge in both domestic and overseas demand has left many mills behind on shipping orders, with customers in certain areas now being put on allocation. Containerboard prices were raised several times in 1994, and further advances are likely given the current supply/demand situation. Assuming economic growth doesn't slow significantly in the wake of interest rate hikes, paper container demand is likely to remain healthy.

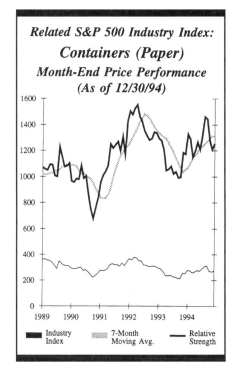

Related S&P 500 Industry Index:

Containers (Paper)

Month-End Price Performance
(As of 12/30/94)

Industry Index — 7-Month Moving Avg. — Relative Strength

65

One potential negative, however, is that pricing has soared for old corrugated containers used as recycled content in boxes, which will restrict profit gains.

Recovery potential for most container producers is impressive due to the high operating leverage in the industry. In addition, a lack of significant new production capacity coming on stream means that supplies will continue to tighten in a sustained business upturn. Due to environmental concerns, one product category experiencing steadily increasing demand is packaging made from recycled materials. Companies able to provide recycled boxes to its customers economically will continue to have an advantage over competitors, while those still needing to modernize and upgrade production equipment will be penalized by the capital expenditures involved.

COSMETICS

Description. The cosmetics industry consists of six major product categories: hair care (29% of total volume), fragrances (22%), skin care (10%), deodorants (9%), dentifrices (7%), and a miscellaneous category that includes mouthwashes, shaving preparations, and sun-care products (7%).

Characteristics. The top 10 producers control more than 60% of the market, while the rest of it is split among 500 smaller producers. Influencing factors include consumer spending patterns, new product introductions, and the value of the U.S. dollar, as most of this industry's future growth is projected to come from international marketplaces.

Outlook. Investors gobbled up cosmetic stocks in 1994 because of a rosy earnings outlook for the group. European economies are finally beginning to pick up, boosting profitability of most cosmetic companies. In addition, we believe companies that are aggressively creating a presence in China and Eastern Europe, some of the world's largest untapped markets, will see above-average growth in the longer term.

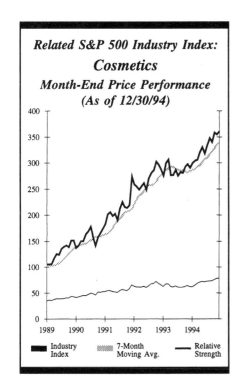

Related S&P 500 Industry Index:
Cosmetics
Month-End Price Performance
(As of 12/30/94)

Industry Index — 7-Month Moving Avg. — Relative Strength

The S&P Cosmetic index was one of the best performing indexes within the S&P 500 in 1994. And although this performance comes on the heels of a sub-par performance in 1993 (due to the decline in the dollar, European recession, and soft U.S. demand), investors should not regard 1994's result as a knee-jerk reaction, but rather a continuation of a long-term trend of superior performance. In fact, stocks of leading cosmetic companies, which include Alberto Culver, Avon, Gillette, and Tambrands among others, have outperformed the S&P 500 eight out of the last nine years.

Growth for cosmetic companies can only come from overseas in the intermediate to longer term, because the domestic cosmetic industry is mature and consolidated; longer term, domestic wholesale shipments of beauty care products are projected to grow at about 4.0% annually. Given the high usage rate and heady competition in the United States for beauty products, savvy cosmetic companies are now rapidly expanding into unsaturated and underdeveloped markets in search of growth.

DISTRIBUTORS (CONSUMER PRODUCTS)

Description. This industry is mainly made up of food and drug wholesalers. They are the "go-betweens" for the manufacturer and retailer, by distributing or buying and reselling manufacturers' products to the retailers

Characteristics. The three influencing factors of revenues, earnings, and share prices are inflation, interest rates, and consumer confidence.

Outlook. The near-term investment outlook for the distributors of consumer products is weak. The major factor hurting both food and drug wholesalers is price deflation. The longer-term outlook is more favorable, however, as company earnings should benefit from managements' focus on technological enhancements to reduce costs and increase productivity.

Strategies that worked in the past can no longer come to the rescue of distributors. With moderate-to-high levels of inflation the norm in the past decade, food and drug wholesalers turned price inflation to their advantage. In times of price inflation, increases were passed along to customers more easily as consumers grew accustomed to rising prices. Food wholesalers also would stock up on inventory that could later be sold to chains at higher prices. Price increases thereby aided sales comparisons. Since 1990, however, producer prices have been falling, reflecting ample supplies and weak demand. High drug price inflation—typically twice the CPI—has kept drug wholesalers' sales

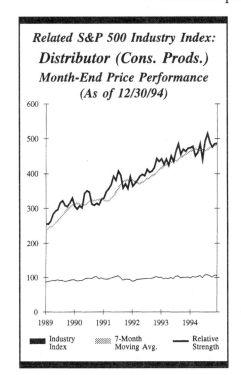

Related S&P 500 Industry Index:
Distributor (Cons. Prods.)
Month-End Price Performance
(As of 12/30/94)

Industry Index — 7-Month Moving Avg. — Relative Strength

advancing at a healthy pace in recent years. But as drug price inflation moderated, sales comparisons declined and profit margins were squeezed. Although we expect inflation to creep back into the system, competitive pressures are anticipated to force wholesalers to forgo significant price increases over the near-to-intermediate term.

To offset the absence of food-price inflation, wholesalers have focused on cost-cutting efficiencies to improve longer-term corporate profitability. Increased productivity has become the industry buzzword, and we expect companies to continue to monitor every aspect of operations and to invest in technology that will boost overall productivity. The resulting economies of scale, coupled with the deep pockets of the major players, should continue to put pressure on the smaller companies; industry consolidation will likely continue. The food wholesaling industry is a $100 billion business that has consolidated dramatically over the past decade, reducing by nearly one-half the number of food distribution companies to some 240. According to Progressive Grocer magazine, the top four companies now account for more than 40% of the industry's total sales. In drug wholesaling, three companies account for over 50% of the industry's $30 billion in sales. This consolidation trend should continue.

ELECTRIC COMPANIES

Description. Electric utilities are regulated natural monopolies that have an obligation to provide electricity to customers within their service area. The extensive state and federal regulations that govern these companies include rates charged, safety and adequacy of service, purchase and sale of assets, issuance of securities, accounting systems used, and rates of return allowed on investment.

Characteristics. Which economic factors influence this industry? Interest rates, interest rates, and interest rates. Since these stocks usually are purchased for dividend yield, they often are viewed as proxies for the 30-year Treasury bond. Indeed, the dividend yield on the S&P Electric Companies index averaged 8.4% from 1970–1993. Electric utilities, therefore, tend to perform poorly in a rising interest-rate environment. The earnings of electric companies also are affected by interest rates. Since these companies are capital intensive, and must borrow substantial amounts of money to fund their fixed investment in plant and equipment, higher interest rates result in increased interest expense, thereby reducing earnings. As a partial offset, regulators periodically examine whether equity investors are being undercompensated relative to fixed investors after adjusting for the relative level of risk. Even though earnings tend to be higher for these companies in the first and third quarters, these weather-related earnings variations have little effect on stock-price performance.

Outlook. Electric utility stocks were hurt in 1994 by both higher interest rates and concerns

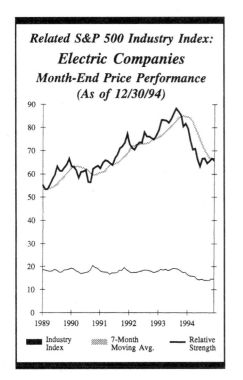

Related S&P 500 Industry Index:
Electric Companies
Month-End Price Performance
(As of 12/30/94)

Industry Index | 7-Month Moving Avg. | Relative Strength

regarding new business risks as the industry becomes more competitive. Yet we think that current electric utility stock prices discount most of the risks related to rising competition, and that interest rates should not have a significant effect on these stocks if the yield on the 30-year Treasury bond remains in a fairly narrow range through 1995. A few low-cost producers may even merit purchase at this time.

The rising competition is largely due to the October 1992 National Energy Policy Act. This law introduced electric utilities to more competition for both power generation and the sale of power at the wholesale level. Those firms with high average production costs and a large industrial customer base are likely to be hurt most by the new law. There is also a growing belief that the industry will, in the not too distant future, be subjected to "retail wheeling." Under such a scenario, large industrial customers could bypass their local utility and buy power directly from remote, low-cost utilities.

Other negatives include limited electricity demand growth prospects and a high dividend payout ratio. In May 1994, FPL Group cut its dividend 32% and announced a stock buyback program in order to, among other things, strengthen its competitive position in a rapidly changing business environment. While we see few firms following suit, we do see a continued deceleration in dividend hikes throughout the industry. In fact, we only project dividend growth of about 1.5% per year for the group in the years ahead.

An uncertainty for the industry is the long-term impact of the Clean Air Act Amendments of 1990, which set specific restrictions on, among other things, its sulfur dioxide emissions. The law calls for an initial cut in allowed emissions by 1995, with more cuts scheduled for 2000. Most of the cost of this emissions clean-up is expected to be paid ultimately by ratepayers.

ELECTRICAL EQUIPMENT

Description. Electrical equipment companies produce a wide range of electrical components used in both the industrial and consumer marketplaces.

Characteristics. These companies typically perform strongly in the later stages of an economic expansion because the capital spending that fuels their sales usually lags the economy. The major determinant of performance in the electrical equipment industry, therefore, is the projected trend for capital spending (the official name for which is nonresidential fixed investment). Since this industry is highly export-driven, fluctuations in the value of the U.S. dollar also have a significant impact on the performance of these stocks.

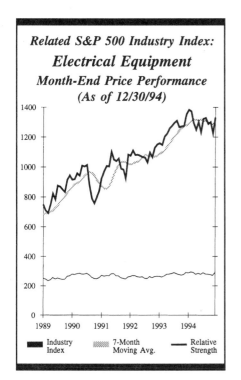

Related S&P 500 Industry Index:
Electrical Equipment
Month-End Price Performance
(As of 12/30/94)

Industry Index — 7-Month Moving Avg. — Relative Strength

Outlook. Despite underperforming the overall market in 1994, we are encouraged that continued economic growth in the United States and a recovery in Europe will result in faster earnings growth for electrical equipment companies in 1995. Margins should especially benefit from the efforts that these companies have made over the past several years to improve manufacturing efficiency and reduce costs, including restructurings.

Industry fundamentals appear positive heading into 1995. Growth in capital spending in 1995 will be complemented by increased industrial activity. Lastly, comparisons should benefit from stronger economies in Europe following an easing of recessionary conditions.

The impact of strengthening capital spending and greater industrial activity should have a magnified effect on these companies' earnings.

All of them have taken aggressive steps to reduce costs and improve productivity, which primarily has been responsible for their earnings growth in recent years.

Acquisitions and divestitures have also been making news in the industry. General Electric has announced that it will be selling the assets of its troubled Kidder Peabody subsidiary to Paine Webber. General Signal's plans to merge with Reliance Electric were derailed when Rockwell International successfully raised its bid for the company.

ELECTRONICS (DEFENSE)

Description. The defense electronics industry produces a wide variety of equipment involved in weaponry and other devices used by the military. Examples include navigational devices for aircraft and missiles, targeting equipment, surveillance and reconnaissance devices, radar, command, control and communications equipment, and electronic-based training systems.

Characteristics. The major influence on earnings and stock prices is the level and future trend of spending for electronic warfare equipment in the federal defense budgets. The overall defense budget is influenced by world affairs and threats to national security. Individual stocks are influenced by programs winning the largest appropriations.

Outlook. Despite the clouded outlook for defense spending in the intermediate term, certain defense electronic stocks could outperform the general market. Following a mid-1994 lag, the group's performance recovered in response to a pickup in merger and acquisition activity by defense companies. Some further advance could develop for companies that are expected to benefit from the industry's consolidation or that have successful commercial activities to supplement defense operations.

As defense markets have declined in the past few years, most industry members have focused on cost-cutting and debt-reduction efforts in order to improve operating margins and cash flow. An extensive consolidation movement is underway to remove excess capacity and properly size the industry to smaller demand. Some firms have bought operations in order to gain or retain a dominant position in a particular area of the industry. The most aggressive in this regard is Martin Marietta, which in mid-1994 reached an agreement to merge with Lockheed. Earlier in 1994, Northrop acquired Grumman Corporation, which has significant defense electronics operations. Also extremely active in the acquisition movement has been Loral Corporation, which made several successful purchases. These and other combinations provide opportunities for profit improvement. We expect this movement to continue.

Defense budgets are shrinking, but there is a possibility of a bottoming-out of the trend in the next few years, with a modest improvement in weapons procurement in the second half of the 1990s. The DOD budget for fiscal 1995 is approximately unchanged from that of fiscal 1994, which was about 5% below the year before. Opportunities for contractors will exist within this constricted market. With fewer new platforms (ships, planes) being developed, there will be a greater need to upgrade existing models with technologically advanced electronic systems. Other areas of concentration in the current climate are intelligence gathering equipment, command, control and communications equipment, and precision munitions. Certain types of training and electronic warfare systems should also be purchased by the government. And finally, some opportunities in international markets are likely.

ELECTRONICS
(INSTRUMENTS)

Description.   Electronic instruments are used to analyze substances in a wide range of activities from biotechnology research to criminal investigations.

Characteristics.   The major determinant in the instrument sector is technology-related capital spending, which typically lags the economy. Other factors that have an influence on instrument demand include private- and government-funded research and environmental regulation requiring analysis of air and water. The electronic instrument stocks benefit from continued emphasis on quality control, the rapidly growing biotechnology industry, efforts to clean the environment, as well as the expanding life sciences and advanced materials markets.

Related S&P 500 Industry Index:
Electronics - Instrumentation
Month-End Price Performance
(As of 12/30/94)

| Industry Index | 7-Month Moving Avg. | Relative Strength |

Outlook.   Instrument stocks have turned in an extremely strong performance this year despite generally lackluster demand throughout most of 1994 as several companies benefited from restructurings and efforts to reduce costs. We believe the current price gains will continue as demand strengthens as a result of further economic growth and a recovery in certain currently depressed markets, especially Europe.

We believe the industry's fundamentals will strengthen in 1995. The continued growth of the U.S. economy should begin to impact instrument sales, which typically lag an economic recovery. Demand from the long-depressed European market also appears to be turning around. These trends have been evident in recent orders at many firms. The failure of health care legislation to pass in 1994 means any future bill will probably be more limited than the President's original

77

plan. The biotechnology industry should also continue to fuel demand. In addition, regulatory changes should boost demand for instruments as environmental regulations are more aggressively enforced and recent changes in laws require more precise food labeling and analysis.

Longer term, a rapidly growing biotechnology industry is promising, since this is a prime market for instrument manufacturers. This was reflected in Perkin Elmer's mid-1994 agreement with ChemCore Corp. to develop microanalytical instrument systems that can rapidly amplify, detect, and quantify specific target sequences of DNA. Beckman Instruments also is placing greater emphasis on the biotechnology-based portion of its life sciences business.

ELECTRONICS (SEMICONDUCTORS)

Description. A semiconductor is a single chip of silicon that can store a million bits of information. The industry has two main product categories: discrete devices and integrated circuits. A discrete semiconductor is an individual circuit that performs a single function affecting the flow of electrical current. Integrated circuits, as the name suggests, combine two or more transistors on a base material, usually silicon. There are three types of integrated circuits: memory, logic, and those with logic and memory.

Characteristics. Companies in this industry are influenced by trends in the overall economy, nonresidential fixed investment (capital spending), and the research and development spending by such industries as biotechnology and pollution control. In addition, since much of the industry's business is international, the value of the U.S. dollar can dramatically impact a company's bottom line. The primary indicator of industry health is the book-to-bill ratio, which measures the number of orders being placed compared with the number of orders being filled. A number above 1.00 (or parity: booked orders equals fulfilled orders) indicates that there are more orders being placed today than in the past and that the industry is growing.

Outlook. A cautious approach is warranted toward the group following its extremely strong showing in the past two years. The industry's projected sales growth rate of 25% in 1994 is expected to slow to approximately 15% in 1995, while competition is increasing in key markets. We rank several stocks that have lagged the current rally as "accumulate," but many of the

Related S&P 500 Industry Index:
Electronics - Semiconductors
Month-End Price Performance
(As of 12/30/94)

Industry Index	7-Month Moving Avg.	Relative Strength

stocks in the group that participated in the recent rally are ranked "avoid" or "sell."

Following generally encouraging third-quarter earnings reports, National Semiconductor surprised Wall Street with a better-than-expected earnings for its second quarter ended November 27, 1994. Earnings reached $0.49 a share compared with the year earlier, $0.43. However, expectations had earlier been guided lower following a disappointing first quarter. This report followed generally strong third-quarter earnings for many semiconductor companies. In fact, the earnings gains in the current cycle have been nothing short of dramatic. Companies have witnessed a doubling or tripling of sales and earnings since this recovery began in earnest in mid-1992.

We believe that a slowdown in the industry's extremely rapid growth may cause margin pressures to develop at other companies over the next six to nine months. Our belief is reinforced by aggressive capital spending plans that the industry is undertaking and companies' broadening of their product lines into competitors' strongholds. Earnings disappointments have also been made easier by the high level of expectations that exist on Wall Street for earnings of semiconductor companies. In addition, it is difficult to imagine an expansion of the valuations for these stocks in such an environment.

ENGINEERING & CONSTRUCTION

Description. The S&P Engineering & Construction Index is comprised of companies that provide design, engineering, and building services to the chemical, petroleum, environmental, and electric power industries (also known as process industries). The only company in the index which is involved in civil construction, such as building dams, bridges, and major infrastructure projects, is Morrison Knudsen.

Characteristics. The principal factors affecting stock prices in the E&C industry are industry order levels, backlog growth, and capital spending by the process industries. Backlog in this industry can be erratic, which makes it difficult to identify a developing trend. Backlog and orders do not always rise in direct response to greater economic activity.

Outlook. Our investment outlook remains positive, based on strong fundamentals that include rising sales and earnings, in addition to balance sheets that contain little or no debt. Despite underperforming the S&P 500 in 1994, we believe the group should again outperform the market and rank the shares of several key players "accumulate."

The fundamental outlook for Engineering & Construction sales and profits for 1995 is positive. Oil projects in Saudi Arabia, Indonesia, and Venezuela are boosting backlogs and should aid future sales. Longer term, the ultimate reconstruction of Eastern Europe and the former Soviet republics, combined with requirements of the Clean Air Act of 1990 and worldwide growth in electrical power, are projected to enhance E&C growth during the 1990s. Projects required to

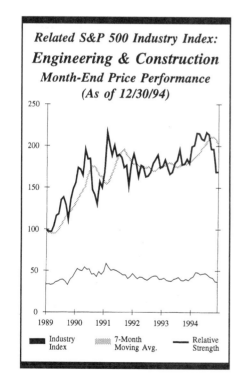

Related S&P 500 Industry Index:

Engineering & Construction

Month-End Price Performance
(As of 12/30/94)

| Industry Index | 7-Month Moving Avg. | Relative Strength |

comply with the Clear Air Act should cause an acceleration in order growth by early 1995.

Assuming a continuation of the economic recovery in the United States and an upturn in overseas economies, revenues and earnings should continue to rise in 1995. Of the five E&C companies that we cover analytically, we currently rate Fluor Corp. and Foster Wheeler "accumulate" based upon their favorable sales and earnings prospects. Fluor recently reported earnings of $0.58 for fiscal 1994's third quarter, in line with expectations. We estimate earnings of $2.70 in FY 95, from $2.32 in FY 94 (ending October). Jacobs Engineering (JEC) is ranked "accumulate" despite poor price performance resulting from flat earnings and concern over JEC's reliance on the drug industry. We believe the latter concern is overstated; the drug industry only accounts for some 15% of revenues. Nevertheless, fears over health care legislation hurt the shares. We expect a rebound in the share price on an upturn in earnings in fiscal 1995 and the failure of the health care bill to pass. We rank Granite Construction "hold" based upon its P/E ratio. We recently upgraded Morrison Knudsen to "avoid" from "sell" on price; we think that downside potential from current price levels is limited. However, we still remain concerned over losses in its rail car unit and sub-par performance in its E&C activities vis-à-vis its peer companies.

ENTERTAINMENT

Description. Companies in this industry emphasize providing enjoyment to consumers through the production of video or audio media, such as movies, TV programs, recorded music. The emphasis here is on their production; broadcast media firms provide the on-air distribution of an entertainment company's product.

Characteristics. This industry's influencing indicators include consumer confidence and consumer spending, the development of new technology, and the quality of the product, or, in other words, is the movie industry making films that people want to see? This industry is increasingly dominated by large, worldwide conglomerates. At least 80% of domestic box office dollars typically go to movies released by Time Warner, Sony (Columbia/Tri Star), Matsushita (Universal), Viacom (Paramount), and News Corp. (Fox). The worldwide recorded music industry is also dominated by Time Warner, Sony, Bertelsmann A.G., Thorn EMI, and Matsushita. These companies also have a variety of other entertainment-related interests, such as manufacturing VCRs, operating theme parks, and owning TV stations and cable networks.

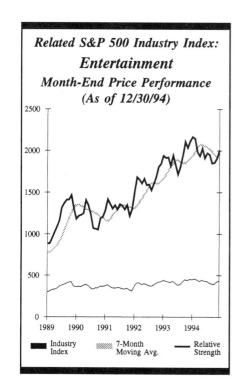

Related S&P 500 Industry Index:
Entertainment
Month-End Price Performance
(As of 12/30/94)

| Industry Index | 7-Month Moving Avg. | Relative Strength |

Outlook. Our investment outlook for the entertainment industry is positive longer term, particularly for those companies that own and create sizable amounts of filmed entertainment programming. These companies should benefit from the attempt by cable and telephone companies to deliver more programming directly to consumers' homes.

Interest in production and programming assets was indicated by the bidding to acquire Paramount Communications. After a lengthy battle with QVC Network, Inc., Viacom Inc. acquired Paramount in a transaction valued at more than $9 billion. In an increasingly interactive world, there should be growing opportunities to leverage Paramount's choice assets, which include filmed entertainment and publishing. Paramount is one of six big diversified entertainment companies, around which the supply of U.S. movies and TV shows largely revolves. Four of these (including Paramount) have been acquired within the past five years, reflecting, in part, efforts to create synergies among related businesses. Also, in mid-October 1994, three highly accomplished industry participants—executive David Geffen, former studio head Jeffrey Katzenberg, and movie director Steven Spielberg—announced plans to combine forces. We view Disney, in particular, as being vulnerable to heightened competition from the efforts of this group.

For movies, theatrical performance accounts for a much smaller portion of a film's overall revenues than it did in the past. However, TV and home video demand will be influenced by how well a film does in theaters. In home video, we expect further movement toward consumers purchasing tapes, including stimulus from lower prices. But, VCRs are now in more than 70% of U.S. households, and we do not expect domestic video demand to provide the kind of revenue growth to suppliers of movies that it had in years past. With increasingly sophisticated cable television systems, the addition of more channels and improved pay-per-view capabilities are expected to boost future revenues for program suppliers. However, current revenue from pay-per-view is still relatively small. In overseas markets, the development of home satellite and cable TV businesses should provide additional growth opportunities for U.S. suppliers of filmed entertainment.

FINANCIAL MISCELLANEOUS

Description. This group is comprised of a broad array of consumer-oriented financial service companies, offering, among other things, securities brokerage services, credit cards, and mortgages.

Characteristics. The level and direction of interest rates is a key determinant of this industry's profitability. In addition, the slope of the yield curve (gap between the typically higher yield on 30-year bonds and lower-yielding 3-month Treasury bills) is an important determinant of financing spreads (the return on assets less the related cost of funds) for many financial firms. Other influencing factors include the level of unemployment, which correlates to the number of loan defaults, and the outlook for the stock and bond markets, as two components of this index are investment firms.

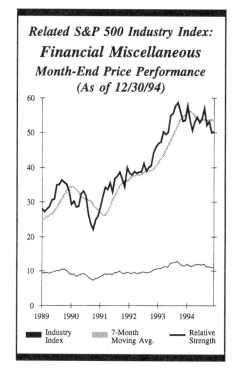

Related S&P 500 Industry Index:
Financial Miscellaneous
Month-End Price Performance
(As of 12/30/94)

Industry Index
7-Month Moving Avg.
Relative Strength

Outlook. The outlook for this interest-sensitive industry is slightly negative, because of the unfavorable impact on profit margins from projected higher interest rates. Interest rates have increased steadily since late 1993, reflecting the Fed's determination to prevent a resurgence of inflation. At the end of 1994, the yield on 3-month bills was 5.54%, up from 3.68% in October 1993. The yield on 30-year bonds was 7.87%, versus 5.87%. We anticipate that long- and short-term rates will rise further to 8.25% and 6.25%, respectively, by mid-1995, as the Fed continues its efforts to dampen inflationary forces associated with an expanding economy. After mid-1995, both long- and short-term rates are expected to decline modestly. S&P projects the yield curve to narrow slightly until mid-1995.

85

A healthy economy is generally good for financial firms, in that it stimulates borrowing and leads to reduced credit losses. In a recession, borrowing slackens and credit losses rise. GDP grew at a 4.0% rate in the third and fourth quarters of 1994. In addition, consumers remain confident and are backing up that confidence with borrowing. The Conference Board's Consumer Confidence index ended 1993 at 79.8 and finished 1994 at 102.2.

Wall Street is another story, however. After hitting an all-time high on October 12, 1993 on the tail end of a three-year bull market, share prices of securities brokers fell more than 34% in the following 14 months. The weakness reflects the widely held belief that the spectacular bull market of 1990–1993 is not likely to be repeated any time soon.

FOOD

Description. This group includes food processors at both the early stages of packaged food production (agricultural processors such as Archer-Daniels-Midland and ConAgra) as well as the later stages (cereal and general food processors and packagers such as Kellogg and General Mills).

Characteristics. As defensive issues (those with earnings that are not generally tied to the overall health of the economy), any economic indicator that points to economic weakness will influence these issues favorably as it makes them more attractive to investors than the economically sensitive industries. Such indicators would include interest rates, consumer sentiment, and personal income growth. Investors should note, however, that demand for food is generally price inelastic; these influencing indicators are not as sensitive to stock performance for this group than others.

Outlook. The S&P Food index substantially outperformed the S&P 500 in 1994. Our near-term investment outlook is positive, as this relatively defensive group is likely to stay in favor because of rising interest rates, which may negatively impact the U.S. economy. Earnings in the group are a mixed bag, however, as most U.S. food companies continue to face pricing pressures for branded food products, which may continue to dampen sales and earnings growth for the near future. S&P currently favors those food companies that are benefiting from a favorable agricultural commodity cost environment.

Record harvests of important grains (corn and soybeans) in 1994 are helping to keep raw material costs down for many U.S. food processors. Among the primary beneficiaries: raw grain processors including Archer-Daniels-Midland,

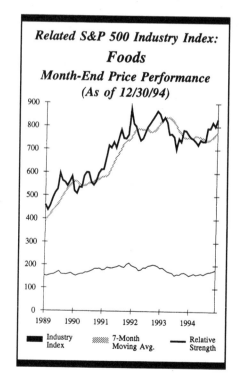

Related S&P 500 Industry Index:
Foods
Month-End Price Performance
(As of 12/30/94)

Industry Index | 7-Month Moving Avg. | Relative Strength

ConAgra, and CPC International; and chicken and livestock producers including IBP, Hormel, and Tyson Foods. These firms should benefit from low material costs well into 1995, which should allow for solid profit growth during this time frame. Most of these stocks are up significantly over the past few months, but we believe that most of these issues still offer investors above-average capital gain potential over the next 6 to 12 months. An added attraction of these companies is the defensive nature of their businesses in a rising interest rate environment.

For branded food packagers, slow U.S. population growth, combined with an increased consumer sensitivity to food price increases (despite the improving U.S. economy), is expected to further dampen demand for many of these value-added food products. The latter factor is believed to stem principally from the growing influence of warehouse stores and other discount retailers, which is in turn forcing the grocery industry to hold down prices (and force food processors to limit price increases) in order to compete.

Longer term, the packaged food industry's adept ability to meet evolving consumer life-styles and tastes should enable these companies to sustain their long, successful record of higher sales and profits. In addition, rising U.S. and world standards of living, increasing world trade liberalization, and the significant adoption of liberal economic policies throughout the world should provide U.S. food packagers adequate opportunities for long-term growth.

GOLD MINING

Description. Gold is a precious metal. Gold mining companies mine for gold, and may also mine silver and other precious metals.

Characteristics. Speculative demand is the main swing factor for gold prices. This demand is derived from gold's role as a hedge against inflation or financial crisis. Inflation does not usually accelerate until well into an economic recovery when sufficient slack has been taken up. This is usually indicated by a factory capacity utilization rate of 84–85% or higher, and an unemployment rate of 5.5–6.25% or lower. Gold tends to be inversely related to the value of the U.S. dollar. Gold mining shares move in the same direction, but fluctuate more than the price of gold. Among the most volatile of all groups, gold stocks are capable of bucking a stock market trend for sustained periods.

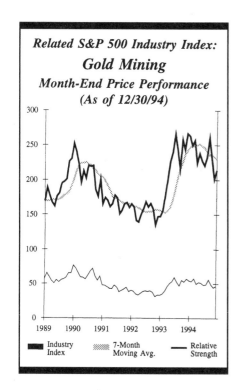

Related S&P 500 Industry Index:
Gold Mining
Month-End Price Performance
(As of 12/30/94)

Industry Index | 7-Month Moving Avg. | Relative Strength

Outlook. Gold shares will probably outperform the stock market in the next several months. That's because there is likely to be a cyclical upturn in the trend of inflation extending well into 1995, reflecting sustained U.S. economic expansion. After reaching $398 an ounce in late September 1994—the highest since August 1993—gold prices retreated to $375 in early December, and recovered to $387 presently. We believe that gold could exceed 1993's $409 high during 1995.

Capital and labor markets have tightened. In December 1994, unemployment of 5.4% was well within the 5.5–6.25% zone regarded by economists as the "natural unemployment rate," below which upward pressure is placed on wages. In addition, December's factory capacity utilization was 85.4%, at the 84–85% threshold normally associated with the start of higher inflation. These critical levels are likely to be sustained in 1995.

With the economy continuing to grow well above its long-term pace of 2.5%, the Federal Reserve has pursued a tighter monetary policy. Investors are so confident of the Fed's success in containing inflation, however, that 30-year Treasury bond yields fell sharply from a peak of 8.18%. Lower long-term rates take pressure off interest-sensitive areas such as housing. Moreover, a lapse in the vigilance of the bond market has in the past allowed raw materials inflation to become embedded in the economy. Even assuming the Fed raises interest rates faster than an acceleration of the inflation rate, such action would not slow the economy meaningfully until the second quarter of 1995 at the earliest. For now, nimble traders can speculate on a rally for which volatile gold stocks appear poised.

HARDWARE
& TOOLS

Description. These companies manufacture items for the "do-it-yourself" marketplace: hammers, screwdrivers, sanders, saws, shovels, and rakes, just to name a few.

Characteristics. This industry is influenced by factors that affect both the household product and building materials industries: interest rates, consumer confidence, housing starts, and new product introductions.

Outlook. The investment outlook for this industry is positive. The "do-it-yourself" (DIY) market is expected to hit $95.8 billion by 1997, from $73 million in 1992 and $27.5 million in 1977. This parallels the professional home-improvement market, which is expected to reach $46.2 billion in 1997, from $32.5 billion in 1992 and $10.7 billion in 1977.

The DIY market has grown rapidly for a number of reasons. The increased presence of huge home centers, such as Home Depot, has encouraged people to do some home projects on their own. The popularity of the DIY market is also bolstered by the personal satisfaction and the cost savings customers realize. We expect the leading suppliers of DIY products to benefit from increased DIY activity in the 1990s. New products, partnership relationships with customers, quick delivery, and a solid understanding of the marketplace are the keys to future success for these companies.

We believe one reason why consumers want to remodel and/or effect repairs on their homes is related to the age of the existing housing stock in the United States. Between 45–50% of the nation's dwellings were built before 1960. And even though precise statistics regarding the upkeep of these dwellings are unavailable, we believe it is likely that many of these houses need a face lift.

A subdivision of the DIY market is the "buy-it-yourself" (BIY) market. Consumers are buying more and more bathroom fixtures and kitchen cabinets themselves and either arranging for someone else to install them, or doing it themselves.

HEALTH CARE
(DIVERSIFIED)

Description.   This industry consists of leading health care product firms that have interests in not only pharmaceuticals, but also hospital management and medical products, and in some cases popular consumer products.

Characteristics.   Because of the diverse nature of this group, the factors that influence these companies are similar to those that influence the Health Care (Drugs), Hospital Management, Medical Products & Supplies, and Consumer Goods industries. In particular, such factors include demographic trends, government policies with respect to health care reform and/or legislation, as well as the value of the U.S. dollar since many of these products are sold internationally.

Outlook.   The investment outlook for this group will follow closely those of its three main components: Health Care (Drugs), Hospital Management, Medical Products & Supplies.

HEALTH CARE
(DRUGS)

Description. The companies in this group create, prepare, and distribute for sale pharmaceutical items to the consumer marketplace.

Characteristics. These issues are typically regarded as defensive plays, with their businesses unaffected by economic fluctuations. Pharmaceutical companies are affected by competitive market shares, the pace of FDA approvals, patent lives, and the strength of R&D pipelines. With most leading producers of drugs deriving substantial revenues abroad, the relative value of the dollar is another important factor. These firms are heavily dependent on R&D, which accounts for nearly 17% of industry sales.

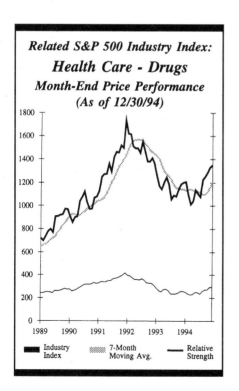

Related S&P 500 Industry Index:
Health Care - Drugs
Month-End Price Performance
(As of 12/30/94)

Industry Index | 7-Month Moving Avg. | Relative Strength

Outlook. Pharmaceutical stocks should post another good performance in 1995, extending the rally which began in the third quarter of 1994. Industry earnings should continue to grow, aided by price stabilization in certain therapeutic lines, contributions from new products, and further cost cutting measures. However, the general pharmaceutical pricing environment is expected to remain under pressure from the growing influence of HMOs and other cost-conscious managed providers. Takeover interest in the group should also continue, reflecting ongoing consolidation trends in the global drug market. We recommend investments in leading drugmakers with dominant market positions, proven R&D productivity records, and strong new drug pipelines.

The regulatory tide is also turning in favor of the pharmaceutical industry. Following the defeat of Democratic-backed health care reform initiatives in September 1994, Republican Congressional victories in November 1994 assure that the reform issue is not likely to be resurrected in 1995. Republican leaders are also pressuring the FDA for speedier and more efficient review of new drug applications and the government has also eased rules on the granting of new patents for biotechnology compounds.

Although the threat of federal legislation has diminished, pharmaceutical manufacturers are still having to live with a more difficult cost-constrained marketplace in the private sector, particularly from managed care purchasing groups. Drugmakers also face patent expirations on a large list of products and the phase down of important tax credits from manufacturing operations in Puerto Rico. These factors are expected to restrain overall industry profit to under 10%, as compared with the strong double-digit gains seen a few years ago.

Despite these negatives, companies with low cost producer status and strong research and global marketing strengths are expected to perform well in the years ahead. Positive industry fundamentals include the recession-resistant nature of drug products, the aging population, and the cost effectiveness of drugs over more expensive hospital therapies. Restructuring moves should also bolster the margins of many firms. Merger and acquisition activity in this sector is also likely to increase, as companies pool their strengths to compete more effectively in a more price-sensitive marketplace.

HEALTH CARE
(MISCELLANEOUS)

Description. This group consists of five companies in three unrelated markets: ALZA, which is a leader in the development of controlled release drug delivery systems; AMGEN, a leading biotechnology firm; Beverly Enterprises and Manor Care, leading nursing home operators; and U.S. Healthcare, an HMO.

Characteristics. Building on over 25 years of intense R&D, biotech firms have successfully commercialized over two dozen new products, with nearly 10 times that number still in clinical trials. However, most biotech firms are still in the developmental stage with their fortunes largely determined by investor perceptions of the relative merits of their R&D pipelines. With future new financings likely to be more difficult to obtain than in the past, strategic alliances between major drug companies and biotech firms are expected to increase.

Nursing home companies are influenced by demographics, specifically the elderly population, Medicaid and Medicare reimbursement, and the labor pool for staffing needs.

HMO profits and share prices are affected by demographics, government and private third-party reimbursement, and state and local regulation.

Outlook. The investment outlook is mixed, due to the diverse makeup of the group.

Biotechnology stocks are likely to remain volatile in 1995, with prices for individual companies heavily dependent on the relative success of clinical trials on their specific experimental drugs. Industry consolidation trends are also expected to accelerate, as new financing, especially for the smaller players, becomes more difficult to obtain. Merger and acquisition interest in this group has perked up in recent months, with Ciba-Geigy's planned $2.1 billion purchase of a 49.9% interest in Chiron Corp. and Amgen's proposed $262 million acquisition of Synergen. While investments in this sector carry an above-average measure of risk, positions in selected firms with promising products should be rewarded over the long term.

Catering principally to persons over 75, nursing homes are expected to experience substantial growth in their primary market over the next 10 years, reflecting increased life expectancies and greater reliance on institutional care by children unable to care for their aged parents because of the need for two incomes in the family. Based on government estimates, the numbers of people in the over-75 and over-85 segments are projected to increase 26% and 50%, respectively, during the final years of this century; by then, one out of every five people will be over 65. Total nursing home revenues are expected to rise by about 12.5% in 1995, to $96 billion, following a comparable rise indicated for 1994. Besides strong underlying demographic trends, revenue growth is being boosted by higher rates, the addition of new facilities, expanded services, and a growing number of companies offering long-term care coverage to their employees.

The outlook for HMO and other managed care stocks is also good, based on their proven ability to provide high-quality, cost-efficient medical services.

HEAVY DUTY
TRUCKS & PARTS

Description. These companies manufacture, and serve as component suppliers of, vehicles that have a gross weight of over 33,000 pounds (class 8). These are the big vehicles used for hauling 48–50-foot trailers and double trailers. They sometimes are used for off-highway construction purposes. These vehicles are called trucks by the layperson and tractors by the industry.

Characteristics. Sales, earnings, and share prices are influenced by most general economic indicators (GDP, industrial production, and retail sales). In a cascading effect, factory orders drive freight volumes, which influence order rates for trucks and finally move share prices.

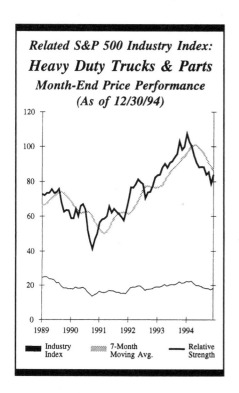

Related S&P 500 Industry Index:
Heavy Duty Trucks & Parts
Month-End Price Performance
(As of 12/30/94)

| Industry Index | 7-Month Moving Avg. | Relative Strength |

Outlook. The outlook for shares of manufacturers of heavy-duty trucks and parts has improved as we enter 1995, but may be short lived. After ignoring the consistently strong gains in unit sales during 1994, investors are starting to think that the truck cycle may remain robust for a while longer. A firmer tone to shares of heavy-duty truck manufacturers has been detected during the fourth quarter. After posting a 20% gain in 1994's first quarter, unit growth slowed to a 16% rate in 1994's second quarter but has remained at double-digit gains throughout the second half. Although we are revising upward our 1994 projection to record sales of 185,000 heavy-duty trucks (gross vehicle weights above 33,000 pounds), or a 17.7% gain, we still think volumes could slip in 1995 to 170,000 units. As this would still be an outstanding year for truck sales, and profits could improve slightly on better prices and improved productivity, we

99

think selected issues may outperform the market in the months ahead.

Demand for heavy-duty trucks during 1994 far exceeded the growth for freight volumes. The burst in truck orders was spurred by a combination of aging fleets, attractive prices for new vehicles, and low interest rates. This helped tilt the economics of ownership away from used vehicles (which require heavier maintenance and repair and get poor gas mileage) to new ones. Truck sales also were spurred by the need to curb driver turnover by providing better appointed vehicles. The slowdown seen for heavy-duty truck sales beginning in mid-1995 reflects our expectations for a weaker economy and higher interest rates. A growing glut of used vehicles by 1995 will also cause a shift in the decision process away from new trucks.

Longer-term, heavy-duty truck sales may remain sluggish for several years as the new four-year Teamsters contract includes a provision allowing truckers to use rail intermodal service for 28% of the mileage compared with about 10% currently for major players. Over time, increased use of piggyback would cut sharply into the number of tractors required by long-haul fleet operators. Another trend working against Class 8 trucks is the practice of just-in-time manufacturing. Here, too, the shorter and more frequent delivery of materials and parts which are substituted for longer haul shipments of full truckloads will shift demand to lighter classes of vehicles produced by foreign competitors.

HOMEBUILDING

Description. Companies in this industry construct new residential housing, typically called site-built homes (versus mobile homes).

Characteristics. The most important sales, earnings, and share-price influencing indicators for this industry are interest rates, employment trends, and personal spending figures, which then translate themselves into a higher monthly housing starts report; building permits are typically a leading indicator for the industry. As would be expected, sales and earnings are strongest during the prime home-sales periods of the second and third quarters when the weather is the warmest and before the kids start a new school year.

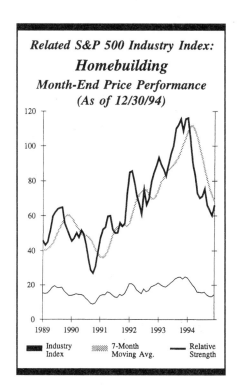

Related S&P 500 Industry Index:
Homebuilding
Month-End Price Performance
(As of 12/30/94)

Industry Index | 7-Month Moving Avg. | Relative Strength

Outlook. While low mortgage rates provided a boost to the home building industry until early 1994, six hikes to the Fed funds rate caused this industry to be the worst performer in 1994. Although single-family housing starts have held up unexpectedly well, building permits have leveled off. This may mean that builders are attempting to bring their home inventories more in line with current order rates. Despite industry caution, however, it does not appear that rates have risen enough to choke off the housing recovery entirely. An accelerating U.S. economy, although perceived as a negative for mortgage rates, has helped boost employment levels, which is a strong positive for the industry. Going forward, homebuilding stocks could rebound substantially if interest rates stabilize at a reasonable level.

After falling precipitously in 1990 and 1991, overall profits for the major builders improved strongly in 1992 and 1993, and earnings in 1994 have continued to climb despite rate fears. Individual company results are hard to predict because of wide variations among regional economies. Currently, the hottest areas include Phoenix and other Western regions where housing demand is being supported by fleeing Californians seeking better job prospects. The southern United States, particularly Florida, has also exhibited significant strength in recent periods. Over the next few years, demand for housing is likely to rise in the Rocky Mountain states.

Although the United States is likely to see fewer household formations during the remainder of this decade, it appears that housing demand is being supported by many first-time purchasers who were priced out of the market in the 1980s due to high mortgage rates. Increased utilization of adjustable-rate mortgages, which carry lower monthly payments than traditional, fixed-rate loans, has boosted home sales, as has increased activity in retirement housing. A higher level of immigration also supports improved housing demand.

Competition from less expensive alternatives to traditional homes, such as manufactured housing, may begin to exert increasing price pressures on the industry. This is especially true in the faster-growing regions of the country with relatively warm climates where there has been strong demand for manufactured homes.

HOSPITAL MANAGEMENT

Description. Principal providers of health care delivery facilities include inpatient general hospitals, independent diagnostic units, and psychiatric and rehabilitation facilities.

Characteristics. Health care delivery consists of many unrelated fields bound together by common interests in demographics and government and private third-party reimbursement. They are also affected by state and local regulation.

Outlook. Hospital management stocks should post a respectable performance in 1995, buoyed by renewed investor confidence in this sector with the demise of health care reform legislation, improving earnings, and ongoing takeover interest. Merger fever in this business intensified with Columbia/HCA's announced plans to acquire HealthTrust in a $5.4 billion transaction and National Medical Enterprises' proposed $3.3 billion merger with American Medical Holdings.

Although the specter of restrictive health care reform legislation has been removed, hospital companies must still deal with an increasingly cost constrained, managed care oriented market. Faced with much underutilized inpatient bed capacity and intensified competitive pressures, many hospitals are being forced to offer substantial discounts to health maintenance organizations, major corporations, and other large scale health insurers in order to secure their business. However, prospects for individual companies hinge importantly on their relative market position, cost structure, and physician relationships.

Although the overall U.S. hospital industry (60% of which consists of nonprofit facilities) is expected to contract under mounting pressure from managed care, leading investor owned

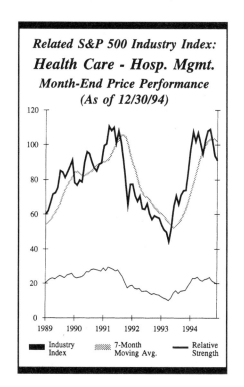

Related S&P 500 Industry Index:
Health Care - Hosp. Mgmt.
Month-End Price Performance
(As of 12/30/94)

| Industry Index | 7-Month Moving Avg. | Relative Strength |

chains such as Columbia\HCA Healthcare and National Medical Enterprises are expected to grow in the years ahead. Bolstered with the strengths of highly proficient managements, expansive geographic reach, and efficiencies derived through economies of scale, these firms should garner the lion's share of the expanding managed care market in the years ahead. They are also expected to benefit from the acquisition of many of their not-for-profit cousins unable to survive in the more cost constrained market projected for the coming years.

HOTEL-MOTEL

Description. Companies in this industry offer away-from-home lodging establishments, including casino facilities that have affiliated hotel rooms. The customer base for this industry includes both business and recreational travelers.

Characteristics. Factors influencing revenues, earnings, and share prices include consumer confidence and spending; travel costs, such as airline fares; and industry construction levels, as too much construction can create an unfavorable supply/demand situation and lead to discounting. For companies that build and own properties (such as Host Marriott), this is a capital-intensive business, and one in which cash flow may significantly exceed reported earnings, due to noncash depreciation/amortization expenses. However, some companies emphasize franchising, and largely function as service organizations. For hotel operators, this is a labor-intensive industry. Investors seeking major lodging companies without significant gaming operations will find few opportunities other than Marriott Corp. Although noncasino assets and operations are important parts of Hilton Hotels and Promus Corp., the majority of these companies' revenues now come from their gaming businesses. For investors seeking to focus primarily on gaming, the choices include Caesars World, Circus Circus Enterprises, Mirage Resorts (formerly Golden Nugget), Showboat, Aztar, and Bally Manufacturing.

Outlook. We expect the investment environment for selected casino stocks to improve in 1995, helped by improved earnings and further progress toward developing new gaming markets. In November 1994, Missouri voters approved the use of traditional slot machines.

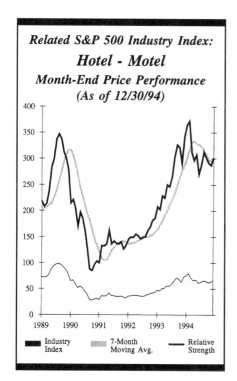

Related S&P 500 Industry Index:
Hotel - Motel
Month-End Price Performance
(As of 12/30/94)

| Industry Index | 7-Month Moving Avg. | Relative Strength |

However, a number of initiatives in other states to expand gaming activity were turned down.

Industry growth is being propelled by new casino markets. However, in some markets, competitive pressures have increased. Also, development prospects for various industry participants are quite speculative, since they are dependent on such factors as legislative approvals, court rulings, and licensing decisions.

New casino-type activity includes riverboat gambling on the Mississippi River, casinos on Indian land, and the debut of state lottery games using machines that resemble video slot machines. Such development is generally favorable for makers of coin-operated gaming machines, including industry leader International Game Technology. Water-based casinos are now open in Iowa, Illinois, Mississippi, Louisiana, and Missouri, and may debut during the year ahead in Indiana. Candidates for gaming approval in the year ahead include Pennsylvania and Alabama.

Among the major casino companies, Promus Cos. is the farthest along in developing a presence in new U.S. markets. In general, smaller companies have moved faster than the traditional industry leaders in getting new projects open. However, most, if not all, of the major gaming companies have expressed interest in geographic expansion.

In the hotel industry, operating results should improve in the year ahead, helped by a stronger economy and declines in new construction during the past several years. Industry balance sheets have been strengthened by financial restructurings and reductions in capital expenditures. For companies looking to expand, there likely will be emphasis on conversions of existing properties from other brands.

HOUSEHOLD FURNISHINGS & APPLIANCES

Description. These companies manufacture household items from the floor to the ceiling: carpeting and floor tiles, chairs, sofas, stoves, dishwashers, and lighting fixtures, just to name a few.

Characteristics. The domestic furnishings and appliances industry is influenced by general economic conditions, replacement demand, the housing cycle, and consumer buying patterns. Furnishings and appliances are characterized as being big-ticket, postponable purchases, and are usually bought on credit. The furnishings industry is fragmented, given the numerous styles and price points. An important factor driving appliance sales is the new housing market. While new housing only accounts for 20–25% of all appliance shipments, each new house has the potential to add four to six new appliances. Housing, which is driven by interest rates and consumer demand, is a critical trigger in determining both upward and downward cycles for appliance shipments. Replacements make up about 70–80% of all appliance sales. This market is largely driven by existing housing turnover and home renovations. Replacement demand is also fueled by the need to upgrade worn out appliances, which typically have a lifespan of 10–15 years. The appliance industry is more mature and is dominated by five companies—AB Electrolux, General Electric, Maytag, Whirlpool, and Raytheon.

Outlook. This industry underperformed the market in 1994 because of higher interest rates, a

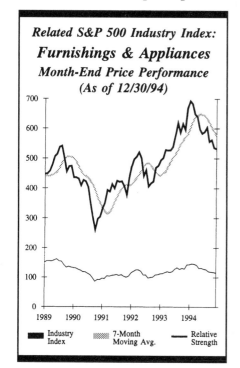

Related S&P 500 Industry Index:

Furnishings & Appliances
Month-End Price Performance
(As of 12/30/94)

Industry Index | 7-Month Moving Avg. | Relative Strength

slower housing market and satiated demand. We feel share prices of all these companies may remain under pressure through mid-1995, given the upward trend of interest rates.

According to Cahner's Economics, furniture shipments are expected to rise only marginally in 1995, as was the case in 1994. Consumers spent a considerable amount of money on furniture in 1992 and 1993, satisfying pent-up demand. Consumer demand for appliances was so strong in 1994, however, that the Association of Home Appliance Manufacturers (AHAM) raised its forecasts twice. The AHAM expects appliance shipments in North America to be increased 5.7% in 1994 to 51.3 million units. During 1995, the AHAM projects appliance shipments to reach 52.1 million, the highest ever. Yet the housing industry is not expected to help purchases of these items indefinitely. While S&P estimates that housing starts rose 10.3% in 1994, which will translate into good demand in 1995, housing starts are expected to decline 5.9% in 1995, which could mean weaker sales in 1996.

Longer term, these companies should benefit from favorable demographics. Between 1990 and 1995, the number of households run by 35–55-year-olds should grow by 18% to 42 million. This age group (1) has more discretionary income than ever before; (2) prefers high quality, brand name products; (3) tends to buy furniture that caters to leisure-time activities and "cocooning." Manufacturers of high quality, medium-to-high priced furniture are expected to benefit from these changes in demographics.

HOUSEHOLD PRODUCTS

Description. Companies in this industry manufacture soaps, detergents, and tissue and paper products for the household marketplace.

Characteristics. This industry, while valued for its defensive characteristics, is influenced by interest rates, the housing market, and new product introductions. Internationally, the household products industry is an oligopoly, with Colgate-Palmolive, Procter & Gamble, and Unilever controlling two-thirds of the worldwide market for these products.

Outlook. Household product stocks again outperformed the market. We continue to recommend the industry to risk-averse investors who are focused on a longer-term, buy-and-hold strategy and are looking for above-average price appreciation potential, along with stable yearly increases in dividends.

Expected growth for household products differs throughout the world. In the United States, for example, growth is expected to be lackluster, since Americans use more of these products on a regular basis than anyone else in the world. Overseas markets offer good growth prospects. Savvy companies are boosting their performance by expanding into huge untapped overseas markets. Countries in Eastern Europe, Latin America, and Southeast Asia—all with especially low usage rates—offer promising growth.

We expect the existing market in the United States and Europe for soaps and detergents to remain intensely competitive, particularly for brand name manufacturers which have suffered from increasing demand for cheaper private

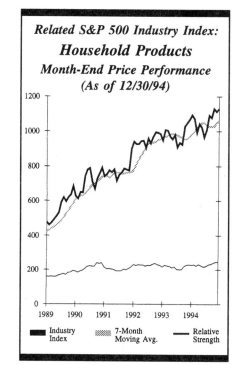

Related S&P 500 Industry Index:
Household Products
Month-End Price Performance
(As of 12/30/94)

Industry Index · 7-Month Moving Avg. · Relative Strength

label products. While branded products maintain major share, we believe consumers increasingly are turning to private label products because they are cheaper and often perform nearly as well as branded products. Brand name manufacturers of products such as bleach and ammonia have always been subject to private label competition, but manufacturers are now faced with increasing competition from private label products including detergents and other household cleaners. As a way to fight back, brand name competitors are striving to increase their presence on retailers' limited shelf space by offering a stream of new products and variations of old products.

HOUSEWARES

Description. Companies in this industry manufacture such small-ticket items as cookware, beverage glasses, flatware, and small appliances.

Characteristics. This industry is influenced by interest rates, the housing market, and new product introductions. The almost $100 billion housewares industry is very fragmented: the average company has only $15 million in annual sales. New product introductions, as well as new designs, colors, and packaging, are key to stimulating sales in this industry. Total new-product introductions normally increase about 23% a year.

Outlook. Over the near and longer term, we remain neutral on this industry, given the high saturation levels of such small-ticket items. Nevertheless, as in many other industries, there are leaders that have historically outperformed the industry and should continue to do so over the long term. Our current favorites are Rubbermaid and Premark.

The structure of the industry is changing. As mega-retailers, such as Wal-Mart, have consolidated and grown, they have become more cost-conscious and have sought partnerships with only large suppliers that can supply an enormous amount of inventory on short notice. Such suppliers as Premark, Newell Corp., and Rubbermaid offer a broad range of well-known brands, national advertising, and electronic interchange, which enable the retailers to replenish inventories quickly and reliably. We think that there will be substantial consolidation over the remainder of the decade within the housewares industry as companies try to achieve the economies of scale retailers now expect.

The majority of new products introduced at a

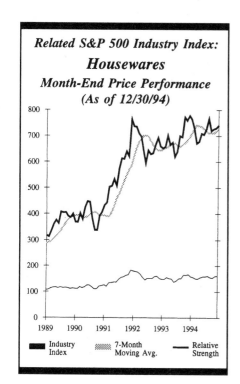

Related S&P 500 Industry Index:
Housewares
Month-End Price Performance
(As of 12/30/94)

Industry Index — 7-Month Moving Avg. — Relative Strength

recent annual International Housewares Show stressed the environment, convenience, ergonomic design, and health. In our opinion, those companies that can (1) bring out successful new products; (2) have the financial muscle to promote them among consumers; and (3) efficiently distribute them to retailers will become the market leaders. In addition, consumers have become very value conscious; this should keep competition among manufacturers heated and prices low.

INSURANCE BROKERS

Definition. These companies act as intermediaries between underwriters and purchasers of insurance. In exchange for placing insurance with a policy holder, the broker receives a commission from the underwriter that is based on the value of the insurance premium.

Characteristics. Insurance brokers derive most of their revenues from commissions earned in the placement of insurance coverage. And since commission levels are dependent on the level of insurance premiums, the brokers' business tends to track the cyclicality of the underwriters' business. As a means of partially reducing the cyclical nature of their business, many brokers have expanded their focus to include benefits and management consulting, loss-control surveys and analysis, and self-insurance consulting services. The fortunes of brokers also are closely tied to the health of the overall economy. And since investment income represents a significant earnings source, rising interest rates (and investment yields) are a positive for brokers.

Outlook. Despite seven years of weak pricing and rising loss costs, property-casualty premium pricing, in the aggregate, remains weak. After barely recovering from the $20 billion in catastrophe losses during 1992, p-c insurers are still paying claims from a catastrophe-loss-laden 1994. As a result of these losses, property insurance rates have climbed considerably. However, ongoing competitive pricing pressures in most casualty lines will restrain overall written premium growth. We anticipate that written premiums advanced about 4.5% (to about $252.6 billion) during 1994, versus written premium growth rates of 5.6% in 1993. Written premiums will likely rise 6% in 1995.

Brokers' dependence on fee-based income such as this will likely continue to expand, as they seek to compensate for slowing commercial insurance premium growth and an increasing trend of self-insurance by commercial clients. Benefits consulting is now typically the second-largest source of revenue for brokers. While increased legislative action usually forces clients to seek the specialized services of a human resources expert, for example, further growth in this area will be aided by an economic upturn.

Consolidation is another trend emerging in the insurance brokerage community. The brokerage business is a very competitive, labor-intensive business dependent on strict cost controls to ensure profit margins. As such, smaller regional brokers are consolidating in the hopes of achieving greater economies of scale and wider geographic representation. Larger, publicly held brokers are seeking acquisitions as a means of offsetting slower internal growth.

LEISURE TIME

Description. Companies in this industry manufacture products to be used during discretionary nonwork time. Such categories include boating, golfing, skiing, and theme parks. In general, this group excludes the subject areas included in the entertainment and hotel-motel industries.

Characteristics. The primary influencing factors are consumer spending and confidence; demographics, as some industries may be better suited to particular portions of the population (e.g., golfing with people ages 40 to 75); and new products, such as theme park attractions and roller blades.

Outlook. The investment prospect for leisure stocks is mixed for 1995, partly due to the diverse make-up of the group. We recommend a selective approach, based on a variety of top-down and company-specific factors. In the year ahead, we look for leisure spending to be restrained by higher interest rates. However, we expect some further benefits from relatively high levels of consumer confidence and pent-up demand. Factors influencing long-term leisure spending include demographics, income levels, and the amount of free time available. Also the presence of two wage earners in many families has boosted household incomes. However, with people often working longer hours, spending patterns are likely to include more long-weekend getaways and greater use of the home as a setting for entertainment.

Between now and the year 2000, the number of Americans between the ages of 20 and 34 is expected to decline, while the number of 35-to-54 year-olds should rise substantially. This suggests a no-better-than modest growth prospect for pursuits that require vigorous activity, such

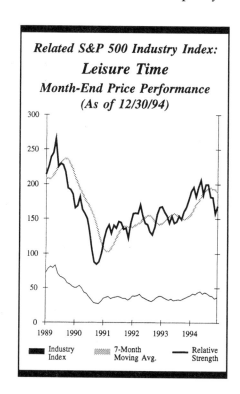

Related S&P 500 Industry Index:
Leisure Time
Month-End Price Performance
(As of 12/30/94)

| Industry Index | 7-Month Moving Avg. | Relative Strength |

as skiing and tennis, whereas it portends an improving outlook for such areas as boating and golf, which tend to be favored by middle-aged and older Americans. At least near-term, a recent baby boomlet should be favorable to the toy industry and portions of the sporting goods arena. In various consumer areas, well-known brand names can be helpful in obtaining retail shelf space and attracting customers; also, they offer potential for line extensions. However, further pricing pressure is expected for a number of products, due to competition from private labels and the value-consciousness of consumers.

LIFE INSURANCE

Definition. Life insurance is a contract between a policy-holder and an insurer whereby the payment of a stated monetary amount is guaranteed upon the death of the insured. Once merely a means of compensating for the loss of life, life insurance has evolved into an interest-sensitive, estate planning, and asset preservation tool.

Characteristics. Interest rates are perhaps the most significant economic factor affecting the results of life insurers. During periods of declining rates, life insurance profits usually rise, because the rate of interest paid on life insurance policies is adjusted downward more rapidly than the rate of interest earned on investments. Employment, savings, and tax rates also affect the purchase life insurance. Demographic shifts, such as the aging of the baby boomers, also play an important part in the growth potential for this industry.

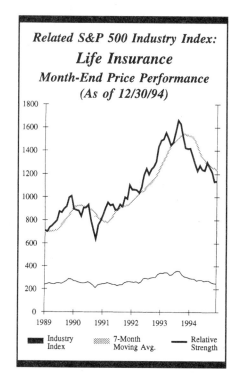

Related S&P 500 Industry Index:
Life Insurance
Month-End Price Performance
(As of 12/30/94)

| Industry Index | 7-Month Moving Avg. | Relative Strength |

Outlook. The specter of rising interest rates will likely keep the shares of most life insurers in a narrow trading range during the beginning of 1995. Life insurance stocks underperformed the overall market in both 1993 and 1994. However, as a result of this interest-rate-driven decline, many issues are trading at or near their historical lows on a valuation basis. For investors with a long-term time horizon, some compelling values currently exist within this downtrodden group. Longer term, the outlook is bright for those insurers that have tailored their product mix and pricing structure to offer a cost-effective line of savings-oriented products to an aging population.

Moreover, a sustained economic recovery, even a modest one, would help most insurers— assuming, of course, it is accompanied by a rising employment rate, which increases the

117

demand for savings and investment products. Ironically, President Clinton's failure to provide the middle class with a tax cut could prove a boon to insurers, since it widens the potential market for tax-sheltered products, like annuities. Partially offsetting these positives is the increased earnings volatility arising from a shift in the industry's product mix to more investment-oriented types of policies, like universal life. In an effort to stem the tide of policyholder defections to the money markets during the higher interest rate era of the early 1980s, some life insurers also began aggressively pricing their policies, promising unrealistically high credited rates. The decline in interest rates forced many to reprice their policies, squeezing the margins of many.

The largest participants in the life insurance industry are mutual insurance companies, which are insurers that are owned by their policyholders. During the 1980s, many pursued aggressive investment strategies that enabled them to capture market share from the stock companies through more aggressive product pricing. Forced to reprice their products when rates declined, many saw their capital bases weaken further amid a collapse of the commercial real estate market and tighter regulatory requirements aimed at increasing capital requirements. Thus, an increasing number of mutuals are likely to convert to a shareholder-owned structure to gain access to the capital markets.

MACHINE TOOLS

Definition. Machine tools are power-driven metal working machines that shape or form metal by cutting, pressure, impact, electrical techniques, or a combination of these processes. Machine tool companies also make factory automation systems.

Characteristics. The principal economic factors influencing stock prices in the machine tool industry are the strength in the overall economy, capital spending for the metalworking and automobile industries, and the monthly machine tool orders report. While there is little seasonality to sales and earnings, orders tend to slow in July and August in anticipation of the International Machine Tool Show held every September. Share prices typically are unaffected by this slowdown. The most distinguishing feature of this industry is its very small size relative to other capital goods industries. Total sales are about $5.0 billion, which is less that the annual sales of several large capitalization manufacturers. The index is comprised of just two companies, Cincinnati Milacron and Giddings & Lewis.

Outlook. After significantly underperforming the S&P 500 in 1994, the index machine tool should stage a comeback in 1995, as GIDL begins to post anticipated gains.

Based upon our 1995 projection of 3.0% growth in real GDP, a 9.1% increase in spending for producers' durable equipment, and an expansion in European economies, we expect tool orders, shipments, and profits to increase next year, albeit at a less robust rate than 1994. Longer-term industry demand will benefit from the need for manufacturers to upgrade equipment to become more competitive, as well as from the trend toward substituting capital for labor in manufacturing.

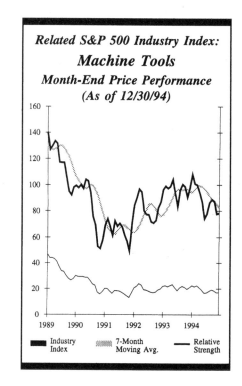

Related S&P 500 Industry Index:
Machine Tools
Month-End Price Performance
(As of 12/30/94)

Industry Index | 7-Month Moving Avg. | Relative Strength

According the Association for Manufacturing Technology, machine tool orders for 1994 are projected to have risen 35–40% on strength in the U.S. economy in general and from auto company orders in particular. The uptrend should continue in 1995, but probably at a rate of 15% to 20%.

Despite lower earnings and a battered stock price in 1994, we maintained our "accumulate" ranking for Giddings & Lewis as we entered 1995. We remain optimistic on GIDL's prospects, given its strong market position, debt-free balance sheet, and rising order trend. Moreover, the stock is only selling at a slight premium over its book value and a modest P/E based on estimated 1995 earnings. Accordingly, we believe the shares represent good value. Cincinnati Milacron (CMZ) reported progressively higher quarterly earnings in 1994 led mostly by gains in plastics machinery. Although still unprofitable, machine tool orders also improved. We are encouraged by the progress because the unit has not fully benefited from restructuring. Better market conditions and lower costs from restructuring will result in future profits for the unit.

MACHINERY (DIVERSIFIED)

Description. The S&P diversified machinery index consists mostly of companies that manufacture heavy equipment for the agriculture and construction industries.

Characteristics. The principal factors affecting stock prices in this industry group are interest rates, housing starts, and automobile sales. Sales and earnings for these companies usually decline in the third quarter due to vacation schedules and planned maintenance.

Outlook. Although we expect continued sales and profit gains in 1995, we remain neutral on the near and intermediate-term investment outlook for most of the machinery stocks. Our longer-term outlook is positive, however, based on the continuation of the current economic recovery and the competitive position these companies hold in the global marketplace. A further decline in share prices would cause us to change our near-term neutral view and recommend purchase of the stocks.

Moreover, based on the S&P forecast of real GDP growth of 3.0% for 1995, we expect to see the growth in sales and profits for companies in the diversified machinery industry slow considerably from 1994's rate of gain. Positive factors include stabilization in commercial real estate, a projected 9.8% increase in aggregate capital expenditures in 1995 (including a 9.7% rise in spending for producers durable equipment), a probable trough in aerospace, and a greater impact from the highway spending bill. Other positive factors include improving overseas business conditions and an upturn in both the

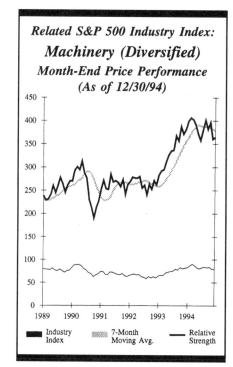

Related S&P 500 Industry Index:
Machinery (Diversified)
Month-End Price Performance
(As of 12/30/94)

Industry Index — 7-Month Moving Avg. — Relative Strength

chemical and pulp and paper industries. Negative factors for 1995 include an estimated 5.9% decline in housing starts, flat auto sales, rising interest rates, and a still anemic market for petroleum equipment spending.

At the present time, most of the companies in the index look fairly priced on a P/E basis. Deere & Co. is the only stock in the group that we rate "accumulate" based upon its modest P/E ratios relative to the other companies in the index. Currently Deere is selling at 8 times our fiscal 1995 estimate of $8.50. Recently, we downgraded Harnischfeger (HPH) to "hold" from "accumulate" based on price. Although we believe HPH's earnings will peak later than its peer companies (which implies more upside potential for the shares), we believe that near term HPH is fully valued at 19 times our fiscal 1995 estimate of $1.20. We continue to rank the shares of such companies as Briggs & Stratton, Caterpillar, Clark Equipment, and Ingersoll-Rand "hold."

MAJOR REGIONAL BANKS

Description. These banks are distributors of capital by acting as lending sources to businesses in the form of commercial loans, as well as consumer debt through credit cards. Their lending and deposit bases tend to be concentrated in regional areas.

Characteristics. Revenues, earnings, and share prices are affected by (1) interest rates, as higher rates tend to dampen loan growth whereas lower rates spur growth—higher rates also adversely affect financing spreads by narrowing the difference (profit margin) between the rate at which money is borrowed and lent; (2) inflationary expectations (CPI), since increasing prices may cause consumers to defer purchases; and (3) employment trends, for an increase in the number of people working usually causes loan demand to rise. These institutions also are affected by the health of the regional economies.

Outlook. Earnings for most regional banks remained strong in 1994, as a rising level of interest-earning assets, reflecting healthy loan demand, and reduced credit costs offset slimmer net interest margins resulting from higher interest rates. Given the rising interest rate environment, share prices for many in the group entered 1995 well below their 1993 highs. With loan growth mostly offsetting thinner net interest margins, together with improved asset quality, a focus on cost controls, and expected gains in noninterest income, we expect the group to outperform the overall market in 1995.

Most regional banks have come to accept the likely scenario of declining interest margins in the higher rate environment, deciding instead to

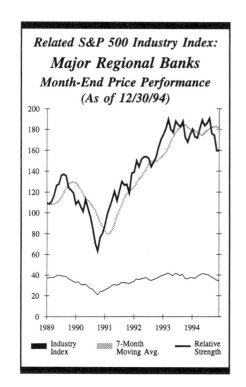

Related S&P 500 Industry Index:

Major Regional Banks

Month-End Price Performance
(As of 12/30/94)

Industry Index — 7-Month Moving Avg. — Relative Strength

focus on growth in the loan portfolio, which has been helped by a strengthening economy and, in some cases, acquisitions of smaller bank institutions. In 1995, banks will continue to place increased emphasis on growing noninterest income, such as trust fees and mortgage banking income, which also represent a more stable source of revenues.

Declining credit costs should also significantly aid profitability's going forward. With more than adequate reserves and receding problem asset levels, we expect provisions to fall further in 1995. Growth in loans has been solid throughout most categories, and we do not think that banks, despite today's competitive loan market, will begin to compromise on credit quality for the sake of loan growth.

Even though KeyCorp and Society Corp. merged in March 1994, forming the twelfth largest bank holding company in the United States, the industry needed the major BankAmerica-Continental deal to prop up merger activity. However, with the recent signing of interstate banking legislation, industry consolidation is expected to gather speed as banks attempt to increase efficiencies and grow market share, providing longer-term growth for the industry. Excess capital could also lead to continued share buybacks and dividend boosts.

MANUFACTURED HOUSING

Definition. Manufactured homes are structures built in a factory and transported to a home site. These structures are frequently referred to as mobile homes. Most producers also make recreational vehicles (trailers and motor homes).

Characteristics. There is an old saying in the industry that a manufactured home is bought by the newly wed and the nearly dead. This implies that manufactured homes are sold on a cost basis (they are typically cheaper than site-built homes and may be a cost-effective alternative to renting). Demographics also play a key role as most manufactured homes are sold to cost-conscious newlyweds and pensioners in the Sunbelt region of the United States. Also important are consumer confidence and employment trends. Interest rates are probably the dominant role in share-price performance, even though manufactured housing sales are not as sensitive to increasing rates as is the conventional housing market, due to the fact that the change in monthly payments is so much smaller for any given change in rates. Investors still regard these companies as interest-sensitive issues.

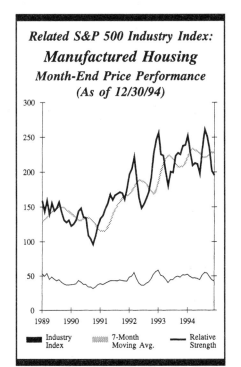

Related S&P 500 Industry Index:
Manufactured Housing
Month-End Price Performance
(As of 12/30/94)

Industry Index | 7-Month Moving Avg. | Relative Strength

Outlook. The S&P Manufactured Housing index has rebounded from weakness earlier in 1994 as industry shipments continue to climb despite fears that higher interest rates would stifle growth. The industry is likely to remain on the upswing in 1995 as pent-up demand and increased acceptance of factory-built homes boost sales. In 1992, shipments increased for the first time in eight years, and 1993 shipments climbed 21%. For 1994, the U.S. Commerce

Department projects an additional 9% advance. Earnings in 1994 were very strong, despite concerns over poor weather earlier in the year and rising interest rates.

Many of the factors that hurt site-built housing several years ago, including tight money and uncertainty on the job front, were also to blame for declining manufactured housing sales. For the moment, manufactured housing is more than holding its own vis-à-vis site-built, and manufactured housing could potentially gain market share from the site-built sector as economic uncertainty pushes more buyers into the less expensive manufactured housing market. Manufactured housing enjoys a tremendous cost advantage over site-built homes. Another advantage is quality control, which tends to be tighter and more consistent because of the factory environment in which it is produced.

While these advantages should encourage market share gains, most home buyers still prefer site-built homes, reflecting style and quality perceptions. Hurricane Andrew's impact on Florida was a two-edged sword: creating demand for affordable replacement housing, but at the same time showing the vulnerability of manufactured housing to strong winds. However, the graying of America is a positive for the industry since retirees make up a large percentage of sales.

MANUFACTURING (DIVERSIFIED)

Description. This industry consists of a variety of companies that offer a broad array of manufactured products and services to the industrial marketplace.

Characteristics. The companies within this industry are less likely to be affected by industry-specific events than they are by the direction of macro-economic components: GDP growth, industrial production, the National Association of Purchasing Manager's confidence measurement (NAPM), interest rates, imports and exports, and the value of the U.S. dollar.

Outlook. The unemployment rate ended 1994 at 5.4% as the economy continued to expand. And while there are a few signs that growth is beginning to level off, the overall tenor is one of strong economic activity. Recent data, including the NAPM Survey and the leading indicators, point to further growth.

The economy continues to grow faster than the Fed's "speed limits" of 6% unemployment, 2.5% real GDP growth, and 85% capacity utilization. Another Fed tightening is expected to continue through the second quarter of 1995. Inflation rates are expected to remain under control. At present, we expect the year-to-year inflation rate to peak at less than 3.5%. Recently, the inflation rate has been about 3% for the CPI and less than 2% for the PPI.

Business investment continues to expand, but slower growth in computer spending dampened the pace of expansion in the first half of 1994. However, upbeat business sentiment should lead to spending growth in other investment categories, including construction. Moreover, further

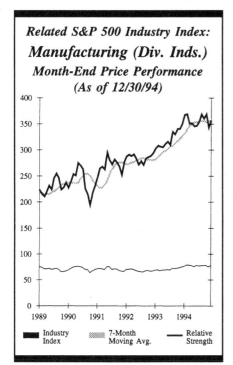

Related S&P 500 Industry Index:

Manufacturing (Div. Inds.)

Month-End Price Performance
(As of 12/30/94)

Industry Index | 7-Month Moving Avg. | Relative Strength

declines in computer prices should reignite spending in the second half of 1994 and in 1995.

S&P Economics projects annualized GDP growth of 3.0% for 1995 and 2.5% for 1996. Industrial production is forecast to grow 3.2% and 2.5% in 1995 and 1996, respectively, with capacity utilization expected to peak at 85.8% by the second quarter of 1995. Capital spending should surge 9.4% in 1995 and 4.4% in 1996. Finally, the yield on the 30-year Treasury bond is likely to continue its ascent, peaking at about 8.25% by mid-1995.

MEDICAL PRODUCTS & SUPPLIES

Description. This industry manufacturers more than 130,000 different items that range from ordinary gauze pads to sophisticated diagnostic machines. The Commerce Department divides the industry into five broad product classifications: surgical appliances and supplies, surgical and medical instruments, electromedical equipment, x-ray apparatus and tubes, and dental equipment and supplies.

Characteristics. These issues are typically regarded as defensive plays, with their businesses unaffected by economic fluctuations. Medical Products & Supplies companies are affected by competitive market shares, the pace of FDA approvals, patent lives, and the strength of R&D pipelines. With most leading companies deriving substantial revenues abroad, the relative value of the dollar is another important factor.

Outlook. Medical supply stocks should perform well in 1995, reflecting greater investor confidence in this sector because of the demise of federal health care reform and recognition of this group's defensive, noncyclical characteristics. Industry sales and earnings are also improving, reflecting increased demand from principal hospital markets, foreign expansion, and new products. However, the gains will probably be less than previous high double-digit growth rates, as pricing remains tough in the present managed-care oriented, cost-constrained health care environment. Companies with dominant positions in growing markets which are also able to successfully develop and market new cost-effective products should continue to post the best performances in this group.

Related S&P 500 Industry Index:
Health Care - Med. Supplies
Month-End Price Performance
(As of 12/30/94)

| | Industry Index | 7-Month Moving Avg. | Relative Strength |

129

The growth of managed care in the private sector, with its emphasis on cost efficiency, has engendered more conscientious buying patterns by hospitals, especially for "big ticket" items such as multimillion dollar electronic imaging systems. Tighter reimbursement and restrictions on certain surgical procedures have also had a negative impact on industry sales. Producers have also been hurt by greater regulatory scrutiny of medical devices by the FDA, which has resulted in increased regulatory-related costs and delays in new-product approvals. However, regulatory conditions in Washington may improve somewhat with the new Republican leadership in Congress.

Largely in response to a tougher and more competitive marketplace, merger and acquisition activity has increased in this sector, as producers seek business combinations to compete more effectively and reduce costs. The most recent large scale merger in this group was Boston Scientific's planned $865 million acquisition of SCIMED, a leading producer of angioplasty catheters. Further consolidations are anticipated in the coming years.

Positive longer-term fundamentals for this industry include the nation's insistence on quality health care; the swelling ranks of the elderly (principal consumers of medical products); and rising R&D outlays, which should spawn a steady flow of new diagnostic and therapeutic products in the future. Niche-oriented companies focusing on successful specialty products, particularly in the high-technology sector, should outperform the industry average.

METALS
(MISCELLANEOUS)

Description. This industry consists of companies engaged primarily in the mining and production of copper and, to a lesser extent, nickel, lead, and zinc.

Characteristics. Since copper demand is a function of business activity, one should consider the economic outlooks for the world's major copper consumers: the United States, Japan, Europe, and newly industrialized Asian countries. Another influencing factor is the demand from such end markets as autos, building/construction, computers, and telecommunications industries. Lead is used mainly in automotive batteries, comprising 63% of Western world demand.

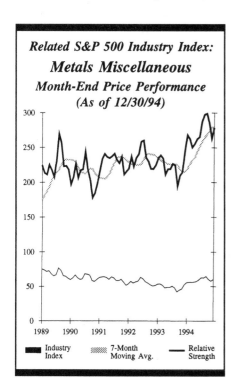

Related S&P 500 Industry Index:
Metals Miscellaneous
Month-End Price Performance
(As of 12/30/94)

Industry Index · 7-Month Moving Avg. · Relative Strength

Outlook. Stock prices of copper companies should outperform the overall market during the latter half of 1995. Copper prices, after having risen too far, too fast, may be vulnerable to a temporary decline in the early months of the year. However, world consumption is likely to exceed supply for most of 1995, as it did in 1994. With demand exceeding supply, a shortfall of copper is likely for all of 1995, comparable to 1994's shortfall in magnitude. World copper demand by market economy nations in 1995 should rise 3% to 4% from 1994's estimated record 9.6 million metric tons. Continued, but slower, growth of North American economies will result in an increase in copper use here. Continental Europe should experience a significant advance in copper consumption on stronger economic activity. A recovery from recession in Japan and renewed copper purchases by China will supplement sustained growth of copper demand among southeast Asian nations. The copper market has been bolstered by speculation of commodity funds. Thus, U.S. producer copper prices, which rose to an inflated high of $1.43 in December 1994, from October 1993's low of $0.77, may retreat for now. But, with inventories under sustained liquidation, copper is likely to resume its uptrend. For 1995, average copper quotes should far exceed 1994's $1.10 average.

We would avoid shares of companies that focus on lead, nickel, and zinc, however, as rallies in the metals are not sustainable. Global lead use should rise moderately in 1995, as further, but slower, growth of the U.S. and emerging Asian economies should combine with economic recovery in Japan and Europe. Average 1995 lead prices should modestly exceed 1994's estimated $0.25 average. The zinc market has been hurt by heavy zinc exports from Russia and reluctance of most zinc smelters to compensate by cutting their output. This has been offset by greater demand from industrialized nations. But unless more capacity is idled, zinc may retreat. Prices in 1995 could slightly better 1994's estimated $0.46 average. And finally, world nickel supply in 1995 should rise from 1994's estimated 1.62 billion pounds, on higher Western production and continued heavy Russian exports. We believe that demand in 1995 is likely to increase significantly from 1994's estimated 1.57 billion pounds, for the elimination in 1995 of 1994's surplus of 50 million pounds. But, given near-record inventories, the rally's days are numbered. In 1995, average nickel quotes are likely to modestly exceed 1994's estimated $2.85 average.

MONEY-CENTER BANKS

Description.   These banks are large distributors of capital by acting as lending sources to businesses in the form of commercial loans, as well as to consumers through credit cards, mortgages, and personal loans. These banks also engage in securities and currency trading and tend to be located in major metropolitan areas.

Characteristics.   Revenues, earnings, and share prices are affected by (1) interest rates, as higher rates tend to dampen loan growth whereas lower rates spur growth; (2) inflationary expectations (CPI), since increasing prices may cause consumers to defer purchases; and (3) employment trends, for an increase in the number of people working usually causes loan demand to rise.

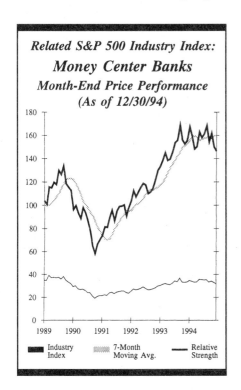

Related S&P 500 Industry Index:
Money Center Banks
Month-End Price Performance
(As of 12/30/94)

| Industry Index | 7-Month Moving Avg. | Relative Strength |

Outlook.   The expectation of continued loan growth stemming from the economic recovery, declining credit costs, and well-controlled expenses point to a favorable outlook for money center bank stocks at least through the first half of 1995. In addition, the shares for most in the group are trading at historically low P/E's and provide generous yields, leaving substantial room for price improvement. However, higher interest rates and an eventual need to boost provisions in the wake of growing loan portfolios are expected to restrain the group in the long run. The fact that the S&P Money-Center Banks index kept pace with the overall market in 1994, despite multiple interest rate hikes by the Federal Reserve, gives us cause for optimism.

Healthy loan growth and step-ups in the prime rate have led to modest growth in net interest income, despite a pinch on net interest margins from the higher rate environment. In an effort to arrest the trend of tighter yields in its basic business, banks have begun to focus on more profitable consumer businesses, such as credit cards and other variable rate lending, where the outlook for loan growth is particularly strong. With volatile trading profits continuing below record 1993 levels, banks will continue to look for more stable revenue sources in 1995. Asset quality has strengthened and, with reserves running at 200% or more of nonaccrual loans, credit costs should decline for at least the next few quarters. Stringent cost controls, including consolidations, are also expected to favorably impact earnings. In addition, merger activity could increase given the recent passing of interstate banking legislation.

Nevertheless, the long run is not without potential hazards. One primary cause for concern is that further interest rate increases by the Federal Reserve will begin to have their intended effect and slow loan growth, perhaps by the third quarter of 1995, which will have an almost immediate impact on earnings. In addition, credit costs, already at historical lows, may increase as banks start to again prop up their loan loss allowances in the wake of burgeoning loan portfolios. Pricing competition from other banks, as well as mortgage banks, credit unions, and other nonbanks, and pressure to raise deposit rates are also not expected to diminish.

MULTI-LINE INSURANCE

Description. Multi-line insurers underwrite an array of life, health, and property-casualty (p-c) insurance products for both consumers and businesses. These insurers also have a fairly large presence in the managed care arena. Still others have diversified into other financial services, such as securities brokerage and asset management.

Characteristics. The demand for insurance is a function of economic growth, inflation rates, and the need to protect assets. The supply curve for insurance is interest-sensitive. When interest rates rise, the supply of insurance also rises, as insurers are willing to provide more insurance at the same price since each premium dollar will generate a higher return. As a result, competition increases and prices decline until additional demand is reduced or until it becomes unprofitable to provide coverage and insurers withdraw from the market.

Outlook. The dynamics of this sector will be marked by a radical change in operating strategy. Realizing that the market rewards focused niche insurers with higher multiples, many multi-lines are rethinking their strategy of attempting to service all markets with all types of coverage. Hence, the pullback from selected lines already underway will likely accelerate.

Many multi-line insurers invested aggressively in commercial real estate and mortgage loans to help fund their large-case pension business. Write-offs of these investments amid a collapsed commercial real estate market plagued the multi-lines during the last several years. Now, some insurers are capitalizing on the signs of life that

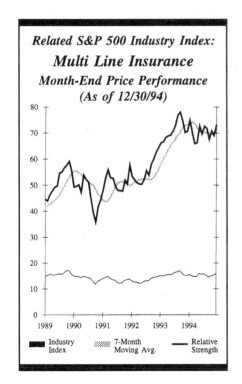

Related S&P 500 Industry Index:
Multi Line Insurance
Month-End Price Performance
(As of 12/30/94)

Industry Index · 7-Month Moving Avg. · Relative Strength

are emerging in parts of the commercial real estate market, and are selling off some of their holdings. Hence, writedowns will continue into 1995, but at a slower pace. The bulk of multi-line insurers' profits tends to come from providing some form of health insurance coverage. Against a backdrop of escalating health care costs and ever-increasing cost shifting on the part of the government, health insurance providers have turned to managed care vehicles, such as health maintenance organizations (HMOs) and preferred-provider organizations (PPOs) to help their clients manage health care expenses. However, establishing HMO/PPO networks is very capital intensive, and many multi-line insurers have yet to achieve adequate returns from their investment. A consolidation of the managed care sector is likely, as small-to-mid-size players decide they do not have the means to achieve a critical mass in managed care.

Though a Republican-controlled Congress will not likely assign a very high priority to health care reform, a growing cost consciousness on the part of the purchasers of health care will lead to a continuation of the shift to managed care from traditional indemnity (or fee for service) health care coverage. While managed care providers will see their premium volume grow, only the most cost-efficient providers will thrive under an environment that will likely be extremely price-competitive.

NATURAL GAS (DISTRIBUTORS AND PIPELINES)

Description. A distributor is a local gas utility that receives natural gas from a natural gas pipeline and in turn transports and/or sells it to the industrial or residential end user. A pipeline is a tubular structure that brings natural gas from the producing areas to the local natural gas utility or large-volume end user.

Characteristics. Prices for natural gas stocks are affected by growth in the economy, interest rates, and natural gas prices. The performance of the overall economy is a good indicator for growth in gas demand, as industrial production and housing starts will offer an idea as to the direction and magnitude of demand from the industrial and residential end users, respectively. Interest rates play a key role for these stocks as investors regard them as dividend plays. While not as generous as electric companies, the average dividend yield for these companies was 5.3% from 1970–1994. Distributors typically pay higher dividend yields than pipelines. Interest rates also affect the cost of capital for these capital-intensive companies. The price of these issues, therefore, moves inversely with the direction of interest rates. Finally, there exists a strong correlation between the price of natural gas and gas demand for utilities, and to a lesser extent pipelines. Therefore, as the price rises, demand also increases. Higher demand increases sales and earnings for the company, which should then translate into higher share prices.

Outlook. For 1995, the average utility (distributor) is projected to post small gains in operating earnings. While an improving economy should

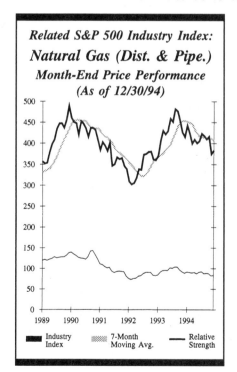

Related S&P 500 Industry Index:

Natural Gas (Dist. & Pipe.)

Month-End Price Performance
(As of 12/30/94)

Industry Index | 7-Month Moving Avg. | Relative Strength

contribute to growth in gas demand, especially in the industrial market, state regulatory commissions are likely to keep allowed rates of return at a low level and grant only small rate hikes. And while some utilities will go to great lengths to cut costs, operating expenses for the group are expected to rise, thereby limiting overall earnings gains. Therefore, these shares should only be average performers in the coming months as investors weigh pending rate cases and expectations of weather-normalized gas demand growth with the uncertainty of the peak in interest rates.

In addition, even though interest rates have been rising for over a year, and distributors are facing greater business risk stemming from FERC's Order 636, regulators are not expected to be granting meaningfully higher allowed rates of return in 1994 or 1995. Also restricting near-term price appreciation is the likelihood that dividend hikes in the next few years will be smaller than normal.

Our investment outlook for pipeline companies is neutral, as domestic expenditures to expand operations are expected to taper off after 1996 and lead to a slowing of profit growth for some pipelines. However, some companies are expected to continue to grow earnings at an attractive rate as they seize the opportunity presented by growth in gas demand worldwide and expand operations overseas where rates of return and the number of business opportunities are greater than in North America.

In 1993, pipeline companies completed a major restructuring of operations to comply with FERC Order 636. Pipeline companies were required to separate transportation services from gas sales. Order 636 established a new rate structure to make earnings and stock price behavior less sensitive to volume fluctuations and more attuned to the level of investment in pipeline assets. This new rate structure will reduce volatility in earnings during the year. Order 636 has led to the emergence of gas marketing and gas hubs whose operations add to profitability despite razor thin margins. In the long term, Order 636 should lead to increased competition, which could lead to a general decline in transportation margins. Overall, the new rate structure is viewed as a positive, since it will lessen earnings risk. Order 636 also should facilitate some expansion of the pipeline system to accommodate expected growth in demand. Gas is projected to garner a 28% share of the total energy market by 2010, up from slightly over 24% at 1994 year-end. Given its clean-burning characteristics and ample domestic supply, natural gas will be a major beneficiary of the Clean Air Act Amendment of 1990 and the National Energy Policy Act of 1992.

OFFICE EQUIPMENT & SUPPLIES

Description. Office equipment includes photocopiers, facsimile systems, mailing and shipping systems, business supplies, and business forms.

Characteristics. The key factor influencing the office equipment industry is the general strength of U.S. businesses, although foreign markets, most notably Japan and Europe, also play a role in the overall success of these firms. Some economic indicators we use to gauge the overall strength of an economy include capital spending trends by businesses, the general direction of interest rates, and employment trends.

Outlook. Our investment outlook is favorable, given the steady economic recovery. Longer-term demand should be propelled by an improvement in global economic conditions, technological advances, and increasing affordability of equipment that enhances efficiency and gives employees the flexibility to work at home.

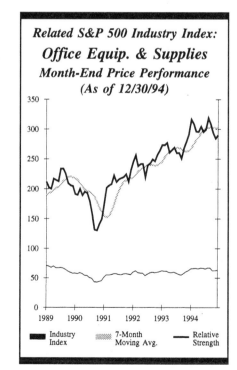

Related S&P 500 Industry Index:

Office Equip. & Supplies

Month-End Price Performance
(As of 12/30/94)

We expect Pitney Bowes and Xerox to show further operating gains, owing to recent new product introductions and restructuring moves. Pitney Bowes has taken recent steps to focus on its core strengths of preparing, delivering, tracking, and storing packages, letters, and other materials. Investment of some $500 million in research and development spending over the past six years as well as initiatives to attract more technical personnel should provide the necessary foundation for this strategy. Xerox, meanwhile, has divested operations that are not directly related to its core document-processing business and realigned its sales force. During

1994, the company reported positive operating results that are expected to carry into 1995, mainly reflecting aggressive cost-cutting efforts and further reengineering of business processes. The company also recently introduced a major industry initiative to accelerate the transformation of prime segments of traditional printing to on-demand and customized network publishing. Products related to this effort should be introduced in greater magnitude during 1995.

The outlook for the business forms segment is mixed. While the U.S. economy is improving, this segment is undergoing structural changes as companies increasingly utilize electronic data interchange and laser printer technology. Reynolds & Reynolds and Standard Register have adapted well to these changes by utilizing their proprietary forms-management systems and strengths in market niches, while focusing greater attention to customer service. These two companies should continue to do well. Smaller companies will remain under pressure to adapt to the changing technological landscape.

OIL & GAS DRILLING

Definition. Contract drilling companies rent their rigs and related crews to exploration companies. The process is initiated when exploration companies identify potential oil and natural gas reservoirs through seismic evaluations. Should the exploration company bet that the reservoir has commercial potential, they will employ drilling rigs and their crews to access the reservoir and to identify the specific volumes of oil and natural gas. Rigs are utilized in both onshore and offshore locations. Onshore, rigs can drill as deep as 30,000 feet and are used throughout the world. Offshore, there are four basic types of drilling rigs: jackups, semi-submersibles, drillships, and submersible barges. Rigs are rented or contracted out on a daily basis and the fee is referred to as the day rate.

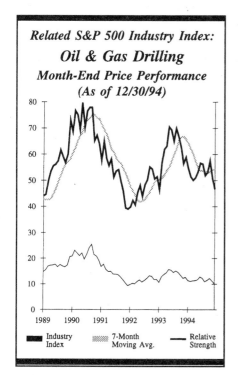

Related S&P 500 Industry Index:
Oil & Gas Drilling
Month-End Price Performance
(As of 12/30/94)

Industry Index — 7-Month Moving Avg. — Relative Strength

Characteristics. Earnings and equity prices for companies within each industry in the energy sector are affected by the same four factors: commodity prices (oil and gas); the value of the U.S. dollar, since the commodity itself is traded in U.S. dollars worldwide (a strong dollar is good for equity prices, whereas a weak dollar is not); refined product margins (e.g., the difference between crude oil and gasoline); and volumes, or the amount of product sold. Among all of the industries within the energy sector, drillers are the most sensitive to oil and natural gas prices. Higher oil and natural gas prices increase spending for oil and gas exploration. Greater exploration spending increases the demand for drilling rigs and leads to higher day rates. The principal measurement of domestic drilling activity is the Baker Hughes rig count, while the primary overseas index is the Hughes Christensen international rig count.

Outlook.   Deteriorating natural gas and crude oil fundamentals sent drilling equities reeling in 1994. Gas prices plummeted in 1994 while average oil prices were below year-earlier levels. Oil prices in 1994 averaged $17.00 a barrel, down from $18.40 a barrel in 1993. In 1995, we estimate oil prices to average $16.50 a barrel. For the balance of the decade, oil prices are foreseen to be declining.

Drilling activity in the United States had been firm during the past few years, as exploration and production companies developed natural gas reserves. With the downturn in natural gas prices in 1994, the domestic rig count fell. The December 1994 Baker Hughes domestic rig count showed 827 rigs in operation, down from 876 units in the year-earlier period. Long-term prospects for domestic natural gas drilling remain favorable, due to plentiful gas supplies and projected growth in gas consumption. Overseas, exploration projects are directed more toward oil where drilling activity has been declining. The Hughes Christensen international drilling count showed 735 units in operation, down from 788 units in the same period last year. With oil markets expected to weaken, the foreign rig count should move lower near term. Without a sustained long-term recovery in oil prices, the count should continue to decline for the foreseeable future. Despite unfavorable oil markets, drilling activity has been strong in Latin America where Argentina and Venezuela have been encouraging investment in their oil businesses. Drilling activity in Colombia has also been strong. We expect Mexico to emerge as an important drilling market because of its vast hydrocarbon potential in the Gulf of Mexico.

Longer term, leading drilling firms will concentrate their fleets in deep waters and in remote and hostile locations. Those companies that can access hydrocarbons under the most difficult climatic and environmental conditions can command the highest day rates and utilization rates.

OIL (DOMESTIC INTEGRATED)

Definition. Domestic oil companies engage in exploration and production (also called "upstream" activities), as well as refining, marketing, and chemicals ("downstream"). Integrated means upstream activities are coordinated to downstream operations. Domestic oil firms differ from international oil companies in that the refining, marketing, and chemical businesses are for the most part contained within the United States. However, the exploration and production operations are located in both domestic and overseas oil and natural gas provinces.

Characteristics. Domestic refined product fundamentals are a function of crude oil costs, refined product prices, and sales of refined products; the principal cost is crude oil, the prices of which are a volatile combination of worldwide production and consumption. The primary U.S. refined product is gasoline. The price is mostly determined in highly competitive local markets. Sales of gasoline are dependent upon national and regional economic conditions. As the nation's GDP (gross domestic product) increases, motorists in general increase their travel. Regional influences also play a large role. Other refined products include diesel fuel, home heating oil, jet fuel, and petrochemicals. Domestic integrated oil companies, like international oil firms, have constructed diversified oil, natural gas, and refined product portfolios designed to limit market fluctuations while exploiting economic opportunities. Domestic firms restrict their portfolios to strategic U.S. retail markets, as opposed to overseas markets, because of capital constraints.

Related S&P 500 Industry Index:

Oil - Domestic Integrated
Month-End Price Performance
(As of 12/30/94)

Legend: Industry Index | 7-Month Moving Avg. | Relative Strength

Outlook. Domestic integrated oil stocks outperformed the overall market in 1994, reflecting mostly the rebounding chemical business. However, we don't anticipate the group's outperforming the market in 1995, as valuations have become excessive. The yield on S&P's domestic oil index is near a five-year low while earnings continue to be riddled with restructuring charges. Crude oil prices are weak and should continue to fall while natural gas prices have been battered by balmy winter weather. Lingering buying interest will remain, however, as investors look for the long-awaited recovery in refined product markets. In addition, gasoline markets should stabilize once the new reformulated gasoline becomes widely distributed. But we give domestic oil stocks a market weighting, as a recovery in gasoline fundamentals will be balanced out by the rich equity valuations.

Average oil prices, as measured by the U.S. light sweet futures contract, have been declining since 1990 and we expect this trend to continue for the balance of the decade. In 1994, oil prices averaged $17.00 a barrel. We foresee average oil prices in 1995 at $16.50 a barrel. North Sea production is surging while Latin American and Pacific Rim output is on the upswing. Exports from Russia are inching higher and OPEC (the Organization of Petroleum Exporting Countries) production discipline will be fleeting. Furthermore, oil prices will be undermined by less expensive competing fuels such as coal and natural gas, which are displacing oil in traditional energy applications.

Domestic integrated oil companies are heavily involved in U.S. natural gas development and production. Although natural gas markets in 1994 were weak, the long-term outlook is favorable. The Federal Energy Regulatory Commission implemented Order 636 in 1993. This order shifted the merchant or inventory function of natural gas from gas pipelines to gas distributors. As a result, we expect distributors to increase their consumption of natural gas. Natural gas supplies are abundant in North America, while the fuel is environmentally benign and priced at a discount to crude oil.

OIL (EXPLORATION & PRODUCTION)

Definition. Exploration and production companies search for crude oil and natural gas (hydrocarbons) worldwide. Larger exploration and production companies, such as Oryx Energy and Maxus Energy, engage in exploration projects in major overseas oil provinces such as the North Sea, the Pacific Rim, and Africa. Also, companies have begun searching for hydrocarbons in remote and previously inaccessible locations, including the former Soviet Union, western China and the South China Sea, and Colombia in South America.

Characteristics. Exploration and production companies generally have not integrated or diversified their operations with petroleum refining and marketing because of the significant costs associated with manufacturing and distribution. As a result, exploration and production fundamentals are highly leveraged to the price of crude oil. Exploration firms will diversify, or limit their sensitivity to crude oil prices through natural gas. Natural gas fundamentals differ from oil fundamentals in so much as oil is a world commodity and pricing is relatively homogeneous, whereas natural gas is a regional commodity and pricing is a function of local market conditions. There are three primary world gas markets: North America, where Canadian gas production and exports into the United States are accelerating; the North Sea; and the Pacific Rim. In the United States, growth of natural gas usage is exceeding the increase in crude oil consumption because of the environmentally benign qualities of gas and its plentiful North American supplies and supportive regulation. Natural gas is displacing crude oil in tradi-

Related S&P 500 Industry Index:
Oil - Exploration & Prod.
Month-End Price Performance
(As of 12/30/94)

Legend:
- Industry Index
- 7-Month Moving Avg.
- Relative Strength

tional industrial, commercial, residential, and power applications; it also is beginning to be used as a transport fuel. Because of favorable domestic natural gas fundamentals, exploration and production companies are shifting their development focus to gas.

Outlook.   Investors jettisoned exploration and production (E&P) stocks in 1994, owing to deteriorating oil and natural gas markets. Oil and gas prices buckled under the weight of oversupplied markets and sluggish consumption. As a result, the earnings power of E&P companies is highly suspect in 1995 and a fundamental recovery is not foreseen. This outlook does not preclude aggressive investors from trading altogether, however. There will continue to be a few E&P companies hitting the big strike as exciting oil and gas prospects remain to be discovered in the Gulf of Mexico, Alaska, the North Sea, Asia, and the former Soviet Union. Also, nimble investors could benefit from consolidation in the group as leveraged players are forced to seek deep-pocket partners.

Average oil prices, as measured by the U.S. light sweet futures contract, have been declining since 1990. Average prices in 1994 were about $17.00 a barrel. In 1995, we expect oil prices to average $16.50 a barrel, and to decline for the foreseeable future. Worldwide oil production has increased, owing to greater output in the North Sea, Latin America, and the Pacific Rim while exports from Russia are beginning to rise. And OPEC (the Organization of Petroleum Exporting Countries) production discipline is slipping as member states vie for increased production quotas. Worldwide oil consumption is only inching higher. Petroleum usage is being fueled by the economic recovery in the United States while the Japanese and European economies are just emerging from recession.

Low U.S. natural gas prices have taken a heavy toll on exploration and production equities. Prices have been battered by cheap imports from Canada. Also, natural gas projects have come on-line in the Gulf of Mexico while fuel oil stocks are high. Depending on the weather, we do not anticipate gas prices surging to levels of the past several years. Longer term, however, the outlook for natural gas markets is more favorable than crude oil, as gas replaces oil in industrial, commercial, residential, and utility applications.

OIL
(INTERNATIONAL
INTEGRATED)

Description. International integrated oil firms, like domestic integrated companies, are vertically integrated oil companies, engaging in exploration and production activities, as well as refining and marketing; they also produce chemicals in principal world markets. Integrated means upstream activities are coordinated to downstream operations. Historically, the two leading international oil companies were Standard Oil and Shell. The heirs to Standard Oil are Exxon, Mobil, Amoco and Chevron. Shell by most measures is the world's largest publicly held oil company. Privately held oil companies have as much impact and influence on world oil markets as publicly held firms. Most notable among the private oil companies is Aramco, the Arabian American Oil Co., which is entirely owned by the Kingdom of Saudi Arabia. Aramco is the largest of the 12-member oil consortium, OPEC (the Organization of Petroleum Exporting Countries).

Characteristics. Integrated oil companies build diversified portfolios of oil, natural gas, and refined product properties that limit the volatility of any one factor. Global oil markets are also highly sensitive and perhaps hinged upon geopolitics. For example, the 1991 Persian Gulf war and the 1991 collapse of the former Soviet Union reshaped the world oil industry and petroleum fundamentals. On a much smaller scale, rioting in Nigeria and civil war in Yemen, in 1994, influenced to a small degree oil market conditions.

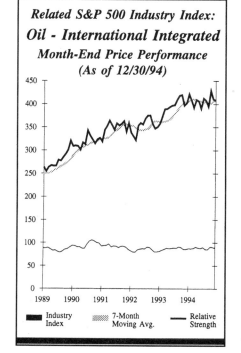

Related S&P 500 Industry Index:
Oil - International Integrated
Month-End Price Performance
(As of 12/30/94)

147

Outlook.   Investors in integrated oil stocks approach 1995 with mixed feelings. In 1994, the group outperformed the broad market, owing primarily to the stunning recovery in the chemical business. Also, to a lesser extent, years of cost cutting have started to boost profitability. With the new year, the outlook for chemicals remains promising while costs will continue to be reduced. And selected companies are foreseen to be hiking their common dividend. Yet, core petroleum operations will be weak, reflecting poor crude oil, natural gas, and refined product fundamentals. As a result, we are giving international integrated oil equities in general only a market weighting.

Oil prices, as measured by the U.S. light sweet contract, have on average declined since 1990 and are projected to continue falling. Average oil prices were $24.40 a barrel in 1990, when the world lunged toward war following Iraq's invasion of Kuwait. In 1991, oil prices fell with the liberation of Kuwait and average prices were $21.50 a barrel; in 1992 average prices were $18.90 a barrel; in 1993 average prices were $18.40 a barrel; and in 1994 average prices were about $17.00 a barrel. We estimate average oil prices will decline to some $16.50 a barrel in 1995 and will continue falling by about $1.00 a barrel per year through the decade. Fundamentally, oil supplies are ample. Output is accelerating in the North Sea, as completed projects are coming on-line. And a host of new production projects are scheduled for the next several years. We expect OPEC (the Organization of Petroleum Exporting Countries) production to exceed its 1995 quota, reflecting greater competition among oil producers. Oil exports from Russia are inching higher, as market reforms are stimulating new production projects. And increased capital spending is spurring production in Latin America and the Pacific Rim.

Consumption of petroleum products is robust in the United States. Yet, the upturn in interests rates should slow the growth of petroleum product sales in 1995. Europe and Japan are slowly emerging from recession and oil usage will be limited given their tentative economies. Longer term, the rate of growth of petroleum products will lag the rate of growth of real GDP, due to energy efficiencies and expanding use of natural gas. Oil companies will be shifting their capital spending and business projects to Pacific Rim and Latin American nations where growth opportunities exceed those in mature Western economies.

OIL WELL
EQUIPMENT
& SERVICES

Description. Oil service companies develop technologically sophisticated equipment, products, and services used in exploration and production of oil and natural gas. During drilling and production, the geology surrounding a well must be evaluated for changes. Wireline tools are utilized to detect the geological changes. Seismic evaluations, or shoots, amass data for geophysical scientists who assess the information for potential oil and natural gas deposits. Onshore vibrating equipment or offshore sonic equipment is used to send or shoot waves into the geology. The waves rebound and are recovered by data processing units that compile the seismic information. Once a potential oil and natural gas deposit is identified and an oil company commits to developing the field, a well is drilled.

Characteristics. As mentioned earlier, oil company earnings and equity valuations are a function of the price of commodities, the value of the dollar, refined product margins, and volumes. Each oil company has a unique sensitivity to these factors. Just like oil and gas drillers, oil service fundamentals are highly sensitive to oil and natural gas prices.

Outlook. Deteriorating oil markets in 1994 sent investors fleeing from oil service equities. Oil exploration budgets have been cut because of low crude oil prices and intensified competition. However, we remain neutral on the group as favorable natural gas exploration prospects should offset poor oil markets. Also, increased capital requirements and heightened technological competition will lead to industry consolidation.

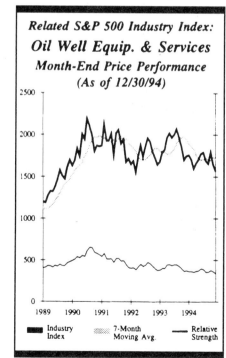

Related S&P 500 Industry Index:
Oil Well Equip. & Services
Month-End Price Performance
(As of 12/30/94)

Average oil prices, as measured by the U.S. light sweet futures contract, have been declining since 1990 and we expect this trend to continue for the balance of the decade. In 1994, average prices were $17.00 a barrel. In 1995, we estimate prices to average $16.50 a barrel. Oil output in the North Sea, Latin America, and the Pacific Rim is increasing while exports from Russia have begun to rise. And OPEC (the Organization of Petroleum Exporting Countries) production discipline is eroding. Worldwide petroleum growth will be limited by declining marginal energy consumption and environmental and conservation efforts. In a weak oil price environment, capital and exploration spending will decline, as evidenced by the downturn in overseas rig activity. The Hughes Christensen international rig count for December 1994 showed 735 rigs in operation, down from 788 rigs in the year-earlier period. We expect the Hughes Christensen count to trend lower for the foreseeable future. Oil service companies will maintain earnings, however, with the commercialization of new technologies. Major players will command greater pricing and margins with the development of proprietary products and services in such areas as drill bits, directional drilling, subsea well completions, coiled tubing, and seismic and logging services.

In 1994, natural gas prices fell, driving down the domestic rig count. The Baker Hughes rig count as of December 1994 fell to 827 units in operation, down from 876 units in the year-earlier period. Gas prices in late 1994 were pummeled by unseasonably mild winter weather and we think prices will rebound along with U.S. rig activity. Longer term, we expect the domestic rig count to trend higher.

PAPER & FOREST PRODUCTS

Description. This industry produces both paper and wood products. There are many types of paper, from newsprint to wrapping paper. Wood products consist mainly of lumber, plywood, and building panels.

Characteristics. Most paper and forest products companies are integrated from the tree to the customer. And since the highest value end use of the larger trees is lumber, most companies have large wood products operations. Although the paper and wood products markets are both highly cyclical, their cycles are often at variance, giving some protection to earnings. The most cyclical paper companies are those that primarily produce undifferentiated commodity paper products such as newsprint, linerboard, and market pulp. Companies that produce specialty papers tend to have much more stable earnings. Although most paper products are sold under long-term contracts, prices vary widely depending upon industry conditions, most notably upon the capacity utilization rate. Any excess capacity in the industry quickly translates into lower prices, and tight markets lead to rapidly rising prices.

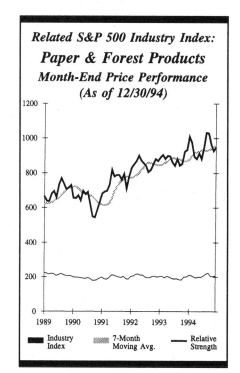

Related S&P 500 Industry Index:

Paper & Forest Products

Month-End Price Performance
(As of 12/30/94)

Industry Index   7-Month Moving Avg.   Relative Strength

Outlook. The investment outlook for the paper and forest products industry is mixed. Rising interest rates hurt construction markets as well as the pricing of wood products in 1994. Although prices will continue to be supported by restrictions on log harvesting, a sustained downturn in homebuilding activity would be a strong negative for the group, as nearly 70% of wood demand comes from the housing industry. As for paper markets, pricing has greatly benefited from economic growth in the United States and Europe, with the largest gains seen in the linerboard and pulp markets. Industry overcapacity, which plagued paper producers over the past few years, has now faded as a concern due to strong current demand. With pricing for major paper products continuing to surge, higher earnings could drive the shares of paper producers higher in 1995.

Intense competition has weighed on paper industry participants for the past several years, following large additions to production capacity in the late 1980s when demand was peaking. Economic weakness overseas, particularly in Europe, added to the industry's problems. But the corrugated box market has led the way to an accelerating industry recovery, as shipments of industrial and consumer goods have increased due to recovering economic conditions. Rebounding box shipments, combined with sharp price gains for most paper products, have boosted the share prices of forest products stocks.

The wood products supply/demand picture should continue to be very favorable, despite the recent pricing weakness related to higher interest rates and slower construction activity. Millions of acres of Pacific Northwest timberlands remain off limits to loggers due to environmental restrictions. Companies with large private timber holdings stand to gain from environmental concerns. Producers of alternative building materials, such as oriented strand board, will also benefit.

PERSONAL LOANS

Description. This group is comprised of a broad array of consumer-oriented financial service companies, offering, among other things, second mortgages and automobile loans.

Characteristics. The level and direction of interest rates is a key determinant of this industry's profitability. In addition, the slope of the yield curve (gap between the typically higher yield on 30-year bonds and lower-yielding 3-month Treasury bills) is an important determinant of financing spreads (the return on assets less the related cost of funds) for many financial firms. Other influencing factors include the level of unemployment, which correlates to the number of loan defaults, and the level of consumer confidence.

Outlook. The outlook for this interest-sensitive industry is slightly negative, because of the unfavorable impact on profit margins from projected higher interest rates. Interest rates have increased steadily since late 1993, reflecting the Fed's determination to prevent a resurgence of inflation. At the end of 1994, yields on 3-month bills were 5.84%, up from 3.68% in October 1993. The yield on 30-year bonds was 7.86%, versus 5.87%. We anticipate that long- and short-term rates will rise further to 8.25% and 6.25%, respectively, by mid-1995, as the Fed continues its efforts to dampen inflationary forces associated with an expanding economy. After mid-1995, both long- and short-term rates are expected to decline modestly. S&P projects the yield curve to narrow slightly until mid-1995.

A healthy economy is generally good for financial firms, in that it stimulates borrowing and leads to reduced credit losses. In a recession, borrowing slackens and credit losses rise. GDP grew at a 4.0% rate in the third and fourth quarters of 1994. In addition, consumers remain confident and are backing up that confidence with borrowing. The Conference Board's Consumer Confidence index ended 1993 at 79.8 and was reported at 101.6 for November.

PHOTOGRAPHY/
IMAGING

Description.   This group is involved in the reproduction of visual images, including both silver halide (traditional photography) or electronically-created images. Activities may include both recreational (e.g., vacation photos) and business applications (e.g., office copier machines).

Characteristics.   The factors that influence sales, earnings, and share prices include demographics, as the high birth rate in recent years should be favorable for picture taking; consumer confidence and personal income trends, which affect travel patterns, since lots of photos are taken during vacation; and finally the introduction of new technology and products—the convenience of disposable cameras has likely stimulated picture taking during the past few years. While the U.S. consumer film (noninstant) market is dominated by Eastman Kodak, and Polaroid dominates instant photography, the industry is moving toward more electronic imaging.

Outlook.   Our investment outlook for the photography group is modestly positive. Polaroid, one of the two major players we follow, is a speculative "buy" as we enter 1995, based on the earnings improvement estimated for 1994 and 1995, and the prospective success with the development of electronic and digital products. While we hold a favorable view toward Eastman Kodak's restructuring efforts, the shares are ranked "hold."

The conventional U.S. consumer photo industry is very mature, since most households already own a camera. Factors that should affect spending include consumer confidence, and related vacation travel. Also, the growing presence of camcorders—portable video cameras that enable users to see moving images almost immediately—has inevitably crimped the growth of still photography. Longer-term growth opportunities are likely to become stronger overseas, as affluence levels rise in other countries.

In the past decade, U.S. photo activity has been stimulated by the development and proliferation of relatively easy-to-use 35-mil-

155

limeter cameras, as well as quick-service photofinishing outlets. Recently, one of the fastest-growing segments has been single-use, pocket-size cameras, selling for $6 to $20. These cameras offer convenience for consumers who have forgotten to bring their more expensive, permanent equipment, or did not feel like carrying a larger camera.

The debut of Kodak's Photo CD, which integrates conventional photography with televisions and computers, has not become a hot item with consumers. Much of the initial demand is likely from government and corporate users. Photo CD allows home users and businesses to create electronic libraries of relatively high-quality still photographs for viewing on a TV or computer screen. Potential capabilities of Photo CD are expected to include manipulation of images, and combining pictures with graphics and sound. Longer-term, the accelerating sales of multimedia computers, with CD-ROM drives, could stimulate consumer interest in Photo-CD. If it catches on, Photo CD should boost future sales of conventional film. With Photo-CD, consumers would take 24 pictures with a 35-millimeter camera, and the images would then be transferred to a disk that can store about 100 images.

POLLUTION CONTROL

Description. Pollution control refers primarily to the collection, treatment, and disposal of wastes, which are commonly categorized as solid, hazardous, and nonhazardous. Treatments and disposal methods range from landfilling to incineration. Other major areas are recycling, remediation (the clean up of contaminated sites), air and water quality control, and waste-to-energy. In the last few years, the term "environmental control" has become the common industry title.

Characteristics. The three economic factors that influence industry stock prices are industrial production, as more wastes are generated in good economic times; capital spending, as the level of spending by companies on site remediation projects and air and water pollution control equipment is directly related to capital spending budgets of those corporations; and, finally, construction activity, as more wastes are generated when construction activity picks up. The industry is also regulation driven. Two pieces of legislation are the major factors that contribute to the industry's growth: the Resource Conservation and Recovery Act (RCRA), which regulates the treatment of current and future hazardous wastes; and the Comprehensive Environmental Response, Compensation and Liability Act (CERCLA), more commonly known as the Superfund, which established a fund to finance the clean up of sites that were abandoned prior to 1976.

Outlook. Stocks for the major pollution control companies retreated somewhat in the fourth quarter of 1994, reflecting the belief that the new

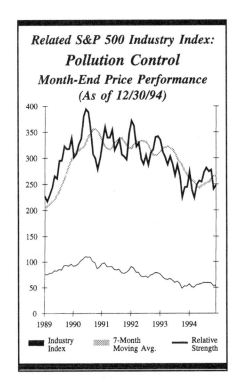

Related S&P 500 Industry Index:
Pollution Control
Month-End Price Performance
(As of 12/30/94)

Industry Index — 7-Month Moving Avg. — Relative Strength

157

Republican-controlled Congress will spend less on the environment than Democrats did. However, we think this is only a temporary setback since fundamentals for 1995 remain solid. We expect a near-term recovery for stocks in the solid waste group on rising earnings stemming from higher volumes in the wake of an improving economy and firmer prices. Industry consolidation is also taking place, as evidenced by the recent successful bid by Browning-Ferris for Attwoods, and the merger agreement between USA Waste Services and Chambers Development.

With economic growth continuing, we believe the solid waste area will show further improvement on higher volumes and modest price increases. Pricing has been aided by the passage of the Subtitle D regulations in 1993, which set higher landfill standards and forced the closure of those that fail to comply. We expect more industry consolidation in the near-term with major companies, as an avenue of growth, looking for acquisitions that will complement existing operations. Our long-term outlook for the group is for earnings growth of about 15% annually, with most of the gains coming from acquisitions and volume increases, partly offset by waste minimization efforts and growth for recycling.

In the hazardous waste area, incineration companies have received stiff competition from cement kilns, which are not as strictly regulated, resulting in lower prices to go along with reduced volumes of waste processed. However, regulators have begun to respond to the industry's cries for greater regulatory restraints on cement kiln operators. As a result, pricing should stabilize, while volumes have started to trend upward on a stronger economy. Though the near-term outlook has improved, long-term prospects remain questionable due to waste minimization efforts by customers and excess incineration capacity.

Air pollution control should see good long-term growth as contracts related to the Clean Air Act are awarded. However, activity in this area remains light as customers have delayed taking actions as they evaluate compliance options and the enforcement framework related to the act.

PROPERTY-CASUALTY INSURANCE

Description. Property insurance protects the physical property (like a home, factory, or auto) of the insured from loss due to theft or physical damage. Casualty insurance primarily protects the insured against legal liability that might arise from injuries and/or damage to others. Many casualty insurers also write surety insurance, which protects the insured against financial loss caused by the acts of others. The markets served are comprised of two major segments: personal and commercial. Homeowners' and automobile coverage constitute the majority of personal lines. On the commercial side, coverage ranges from "standard" lines, such as commercial auto, fire, and general liability, to more specialized lines like medical malpractice, officers and directors liability, architects and engineers professional liability.

Related S&P 500 Industry Index:
Prop./Casualty Insurance
Month-End Price Performance
(As of 12/30/94)

Industry Index | 7-Month Moving Avg. | Relative Strength

Characteristics. The demand for insurance is a function of economic growth, inflation rates, and the need to protect assets. The supply curve for insurance is interest-sensitive. When interest rates rise, the supply of insurance also rises as insurers are willing to provide more insurance at the same price since each premium dollar will generate a higher return. As a result, competition increases, and prices decline until additional demand is reduced or until it becomes unprofitable to provide coverage and insurers withdraw from the market. Even though weather-related catastrophe losses can occur at all times of the year, the storm-prone quarters are the first (winter storms) and third (hurricanes).

Outlook. After shunning this group amid concerns over rising interest rates and the adequacy of asbestos and environmental reserves,

159

investors have begun to focus on this downtrodden group's heretofore depressed valuations amid the likelihood that escalating losses from the 1994 California earthquake will exert increased upward pressure on premium rates.

Underwriting results for 1994's first nine months (latest available) continued to reflect the impact of catastrophes. Net written premiums inched up 3.6%, year to year, as growth in property lines offset ongoing price competition in most casualty lines. However, catastrophe losses surged to about $12.7 billion, which was more than the $5.7 billion of catastrophe losses incurred during all of 1993. As a result, the combined loss, expense, and dividend ratio climbed to 110.1% at the end of the first nine months, compared with 107.6% in the year-earlier period. To make matters worse, the bond market's retreat helped produce an 87% drop in total capital gains, which paced the 67% plunge in net income to $4.3 billion from $13.1 billion.

Industry surplus (or capital) rose 1.1% from year-end 1993 levels, to $184.3 billion at September 30, 1994. For the 12 months ended September 30, 1994, the net-premiums-written-to-surplus ratio (an indicator of underwriting capacity) equaled 1.35:1, versus a "typical" leverage ratio of about 2:1. But, much of this cushion could evaporate if catastrophe losses continue at their record pace, if the bond market retreats further, or if some heretofore inadequately reserved insurers fully account for their potential environmental claims.

Unlike the last cycle turn in the mid-1980s that was driven by an acute shortage of liability coverage, this recovery (albeit modest) will likely be paced by stronger property lines pricing. Net written premiums will rise about 4.5% to some $252.6 billion during 1994, versus written-premium growth of about 5.6% in 1993. Written premiums should advance about 6% during 1995.

PUBLISHING

Description. These companies publish books and magazines.

Characteristics. Book publishers' revenues are affected primarily by changes in the overall economy, consumer spending patterns, and demographic trends. Magazine revenues and earnings are directly affected by advertising expenditures and circulation; they are indirectly affected by growth in the economy. Profitability for both categories is also greatly affected by paper and postage costs, which together can account for some 25% of total expenses.

Outlook. Our investment outlook is mixed, as entertainment-oriented and specialty publishers should outperform the market in both the near and longer term, while book and magazine publishing stocks are, by and large, expected to keep pace with the general market.

Consumer magazine advertising pages in 1994 rose 5.3%, year to year. Ad revenues rose 12%. Among the top 10 advertising categories, automotive (the largest) continued to lead the pack with a double-digit page gain. Drugs and remedies (seventh largest) also rose sharply. Although toiletries and cosmetics (second largest), apparel (fifth), and food (sixth) were down, all categories have been gaining in recent months. A 12% advance for advertising revenues is projected for 1995.

Circulation revenues are rising slightly, boosted by higher newsstand sales. On the cost side, payroll expenses should continue to rise at less than 5%. Paper cost increases, under 5% most of 1994, are expected to accelerate in the months ahead. Postage costs will also advance roughly 10% in 1995. Heavier startups and promotions at some publishers are hurting margins, but on the

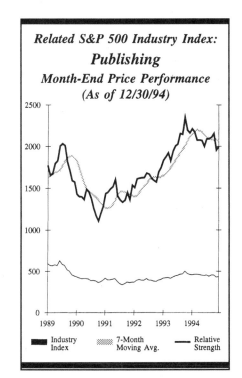

Related S&P 500 Industry Index:
Publishing
Month-End Price Performance
(As of 12/30/94)

Legend:
- Industry Index
- 7-Month Moving Avg.
- Relative Strength

161

whole, industry profits should continue to advance. Regional business, parenting, music/entertainment, and newspaper Sunday magazines are the only major publications where advertising remains lackluster.

The dollar value of publishers' book sales is projected to rise 6% in 1995 after an estimated rise of only 4% in 1994. The disappointment in 1994 stems from soft sales of grade school books and materials, which were down 8% in the nine months through September, reflecting the fact that 1994 is an off year in the state textbook adoption cycle. Adoptions should strengthen in 1995 and peak in 1996. Strong double-digit sales for adult trade books should continue, helped by discounting and a better economy. Juvenile book sales are likely to be flat in 1994 and up slightly in 1995. Mass-market paperback sales have also flattened. Professional and book club sales continue at a healthy 6–8% pace, while college sales should continue to recover.

PUBLISHING (NEWSPAPERS)

Description. These companies publish newspapers.

Characteristics. Newspaper revenues and earnings are directly affected by advertising expenditures and circulation, and are indirectly affected by growth in the economy. Personnel and newsprint are the major cost factors in a newspaper's operation. Newsprint pricing fluctuations directly impact margins.

Outlook. Newspaper publishing stocks underperformed the overall market in 1994, but have probably hit bottom. The stocks look like attractive candidates to outperform the market in the months ahead. In spite of healthy earnings gains in recent years, reflecting operating efficiencies, investors avoided the issues because of a very long advertising slump that persisted for newspapers longer than it did for other major media, particularly radio and television broadcasters. Concerns regarding the industry's ability to maintain its dominant position as an advertising medium also dampened ardor for the stocks. Now that newspaper advertising is advancing, a major stumbling block is out of the way. Strong double-digit earnings gains should continue in 1995 despite rising newsprint costs. It is generally common knowledge by now that the advent of broadband interactivity will not have a major impact on traditional media.

We expect classified advertising to continue to set the pace, gaining 11% in 1995 after a 12% rise expected for 1994. Retail advertising, the biggest sector, accounting for over 50% of total newspaper advertising, finally picked up steam in the third quarter and is expected to have risen

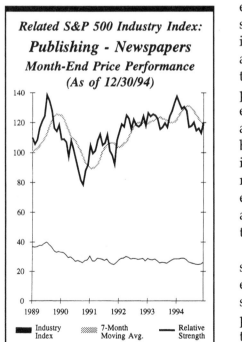

Related S&P 500 Industry Index:

Publishing - Newspapers

Month-End Price Performance
(As of 12/30/94)

| Industry Index | 7-Month Moving Avg. | Relative Strength |

163

roughly 4% in 1994. A 6.5% advance is likely for 1995. National advertising may advance nearly 13% in 1995 after a rise of 8% estimated for 1994. Thus, total newspaper advertising in 1995 could rise nearly 9%, compared to the 7.5% improvement that we estimated for 1994. Bolstered by continuing strength in the retail category, we expect to see strong advertising again in 1996.

Daily and Sunday newspaper circulation has been hurt by recent price hikes, severe winter weather, earthquakes, and flooding. In addition, an ongoing decline in readership is also behind the weak circulation numbers. Circulation revenues most likely rose no more than 2% in 1994. Gains of roughly 5% are projected for 1995.

Newsprint prices began to stabilize in the first half of 1994, and profit margins are beginning to be pressured by the slowly rising newsprint costs. The pressure should continue through 1995 as well, but rising revenues and ongoing cost controls elsewhere will be mitigating factors.

RAILROADS

Description. Railroads are primarily freight carriers (specializing in bulk commodities) that own and operate their own private rights of way.

Characteristics. The share prices of railroad companies are affected by the condition of the economy, exports, and the weather. Rail traffic, as measured by the product of tonnage and distance moved, tends to move in tandem with industrial production. With coal traffic now accounting for nearly half of the volume, weather patterns and the state of the export market can have an important bearing on rail traffic. Grain shipments are influenced by unpredictable overseas demand.

Outlook. Despite the poor performance by rail issues during 1994, we continue to believe the group will outperform the general market over the next 18 months. Investors have unjustifiably tarred railroads as cyclical plays, ignoring the fact that traffic levels actually advanced during the 1990–1991 recession. With economically insensitive coal and grain generating some 50% of rail traffic and intermodal growth at double-digit rates, we presently are not anticipating a drop in rail volume or profits in 1995 or 1996. Operating margins continue to benefit from the application of technology to boost productivity and, longer-term, additional efficiencies will be realized upon completion of proposed rail mergers. With capacity constraints in several traffic areas, railroads—for the first time since deregulation—are gaining power to lift rates. With most freight hauled under contract and only a small portion renewed in a given year, rates may rise only about 1.0% in 1995. Evidence that rail issues are deeply undervalued is the current bidding fren-

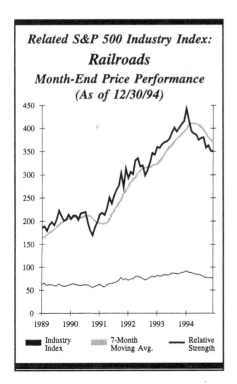

Related S&P 500 Industry Index:

Railroads

Month-End Price Performance
(As of 12/30/94)

| Industry Index | 7-Month Moving Avg. | Relative Strength |

zy for Santa Fe Pacific being waged by Burlington Northern and Union Pacific.

The rail industry's rejuvenation reflects several favorable developments. Deregulation has allowed carriers to recover costs in a timely manner and offer contracts. The energy crisis of the 1970s led to significant construction of coal-fired power plants, providing rails with a steady increase in profitable long-haul traffic. The industry's improved cash flow enabled it to buy out redundant workers and lift productivity through capital investment. Driver shortages in the trucking industry and the removal of restrictions in the 1994 Teamsters' contract will help rails recapture market share from trucks as motor carriers increase their use of rail piggyback. Near-term, investors are ignoring the improvement in the rail industry's fundamental picture, choosing instead to worry about interest rates and the business cycle.

In 1995 rails could post a 3.1% increase in traffic to 1185 billion ton-miles, following the 8.7% gain projected for 1994. Operating profits in 1995 are projected to rise 11.0% to $6.0 billion from the $5.4 billion for 1994. In 1995 the industry's return on investment could reach 8.5%, up from about the 2% ROI common in the 1970s.

RESTAURANTS

Description. These companies are basically food-service establishments located away from consumers' homes, offering both on-premise consumption of food and takeout service.

Characteristics. Influencing factors on revenues, earnings, and share prices include consumer spending and confidence; disposable income; cost pressures, such as commodities/food and labor (both direct wages and benefits); and individual restaurant unit sales comparisons. Among restaurant companies, there can be sizable variations in how well their operations are doing. Overall sales growth typically comes from three factors: the opening of new units, higher contributions from older restaurants, and acquisitions. Often, a good way to judge a business's overall health is to look at year-to-year sales comparisons among outlets that were open in both periods, particularly with menu price increases excluded.

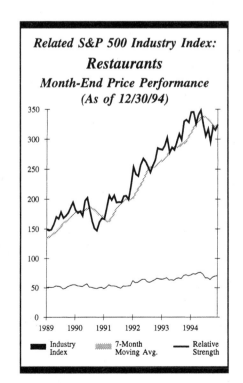

Related S&P 500 Industry Index:
Restaurants
Month-End Price Performance
(As of 12/30/94)

Outlook. Our investment outlook of restaurant or food-service stocks is moderately positive. Restaurants stocks were out of favor in 1994, reflecting concern about relatively soft sales levels and the prospect that competitive factors will be limiting the attractiveness of expansion opportunities. However, with various companies expected to post sizable profit increases in the year ahead, we are looking for at least a partial rebound in the prices of some of the industry stocks we follow.

In the past several years, industry profitability has generally been supported by an absence of significant food cost pressure. With such costs looking favorable, restaurant operators have been able to seek volume increases through lower menu prices and increased marketing efforts. Competitive conditions have led to an

167

increased industry emphasis on offering "value" to consumers. In part, this has meant an emphasis on lower-priced menu items, and in some cases, has resulted in lower prices for either single offerings or combinations of products. During the year ahead, we look for overall increases in food costs to be relatively modest. The industry's value emphasis is likely to continue. Other major industry themes will include an emphasis on lowering development costs of new restaurants. Reducing the cost of new units can both boost companies' return on investment and better enable them to enter smaller markets.

During the past two decades, an increasing portion of U.S. food dollars has gone to eating out. With a greater percentage of people working, particularly women, there has been less time available for at-home food preparation. Demographics will likely have a significant impact on future restaurant spending as well. As consumers get older, they are more likely to move away from fast-food outlets toward mid-scale restaurants.

RETAIL
(DEPARTMENT
STORES)

Description. These stores sell products allocated to particular departments, ranging from apparel to home furnishings. Some stores may be regional in nature, such as The Broadway, or national in scope, such as J.C. Penney.

Characteristics. The retail industry is directed by the factors that influence consumer spending: consumer confidence, disposable income, and job growth. Industry progress can be monitored through the monthly retail sales report.

Outlook. Personal consumption expenditures rose 3.5% in 1994, spurred by continued gains in sales of appliances and home furnishings of 8.3%. Nondurable expenditures (food, clothing, and shoes) advanced only about 3.0%; apparel sales began to pick up late in 1994. We believe that this trend will continue into 1995 as consumer purchases center around the home, and that the demographics of an older population and more casual dress will keep apparel sales advancing modestly for the balance of this decade.

Clearly, consumers are more upbeat these days. They are feeling better than at any time since the 1990–1991 recession ended. Unemployment has continued to drop and disposable income has been gaining ground. And while most industry observers agree that the consumer of the 1990s is going to be a more cautious spender than in the preceding decade, we believe Americans have not lost their acquisitive streak. S&P projects consumer consumption to

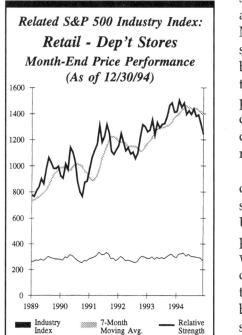

Related S&P 500 Industry Index:
Retail - Dep't Stores
Month-End Price Performance
(As of 12/30/94)

Industry Index — 7-Month Moving Avg. — Relative Strength

increase 3.0% in 1995, consisting of a 5.4% rise in consumer durables, a 2.2% advance in consumer nondurables, and a 2.7% gain in consumer services.

Slower growth in demand for apparel, an overabundance of selling space, and a value-conscious consumer have forced retailers to make cost-cutting a top priority. And they are responding by keeping mark-ups low, trimming inventories, and investing in technology to boost productivity. What's more, such companies as May Department Stores and Federated Department Stores have consolidated divisions in order to eliminate redundancies and have closed underperforming stores. The ultimate in department store consolidation occurred at the end of 1994 when Federated completed the acquisition of Macy's. In sum, retailers are putting the cost side of their business under a microscope. This, combined with improved apparel sales in 1994 and 1995, should boost earnings for this year and next.

RETAIL
(DRUG CHAINS)

Description. Retail drug chains are large drugstores that sell prescription drugs, over-the-counter products, and general merchandise.

Characteristics. Drug chains are regarded as more defensive than other stocks, as they are less susceptible to fluctuations in the growth of the economy than are other industries; one doesn't stop getting sick just because times are good or bad. Revenues can be influenced, however, by the rate of inflation, disposable income, and demographics.

Outlook. Strong sales volume continued in 1994; prescription and over-the-counter drug sales also advanced, and the uncertainties surrounding health care reform vanished. Chain drug stores' ability to post solid earnings gains in spite of lower drug price inflation and efforts to control costs have paid off.

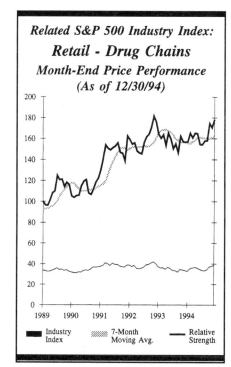

Related S&P 500 Industry Index:
Retail - Drug Chains
Month-End Price Performance
(As of 12/30/94)

| Industry Index | 7-Month Moving Avg. | Relative Strength |

Sales continue to be buoyed by consumers' fundamental interest in health and personal care; an aging population; the increased number of drugs coming off patent to more readily available over-the-counter (OTC) status; and an increasing use of drug therapies as an alternative to hospitalization. The baby boomer generation in particular is taking health matters into their own hands by adhering to vitamin therapies and home diagnostic testing. The long-term demographics of an aging society means that prescription usage increases. Although gross margins continue to be pressured by third party payment plans, generics have much higher margins and should slightly offset this trend.

The competition has also recognized the

longer-term plusses of this industry. Supermarkets (combination food/drug stores) and discount store operators have added pharmacies and beefed up their assortments of health and beauty aids departments (H&BA). Clearly, this has stiffened the competitive landscape. The combination of sharper pricing by the competition; increased low-margin, third-party payment plans; and lower drug price inflation is forcing chains to focus on generating more aggressive growth in their core businesses and finding ways to broaden into specialized areas. The challenge imposed by these competitors will, no doubt, intensify over time. As a result, the industry is fashioning a more proprietary identity based on comprehensive selections of basic H&BA items and OTC products and in-and-out shopping convenience. In addition, capital investments in retail technology and distribution efficiencies to keep costs in line have become a priority. As a result, we anticipate continued earnings growth of about 10% to 12% over the next few years, reflecting the strong underlying fundamentals of the industry.

RETAIL
(FOOD CHAINS)

Description. Retail food chains vary from supermarkets to convenience stores. Some establishments offer a large array of food products, whereas others offer a smaller, more focused assortment.

Characteristics. Food chains are regarded as more defensive than other stocks, as they are less susceptible to fluctuations in the growth of the economy than are other industries. Whether times are good or bad, one has to eat. Revenues can be influenced, however, by the rate of inflation, disposable income, and consumer confidence. The supermarket industry is a highly competitive, volume-driven business, which operates on low markup. Profits are made by increasing volume and reducing costs. Since the industry is labor intensive, efforts to cut costs include an emphasis on computer technology and taking a hard line on union negotiations.

Related S&P 500 Industry Index:
Retail - Food Chains
Month-End Price Performance
(As of 12/30/94)

Outlook. The outlook for supermarket chains is somewhat brighter than in the past two years. But even though the economy and consumer spending have improved, low food price inflation and sharp competition from discounters and warehouse clubs are still keeping a lid on sales and earnings growth.

The lowering of operating costs has become the key to success for supermarkets in the 1990s. By and large, they have been successful at balancing the pressures for immediate cost containment against the challenge to increase productivity over the longer term. Better inventory management and more efficient distribution have become important factors in this effort.

Companies are strengthening their merchandising and marketing efforts, and are investing in technology systems for accounting, ordering, receiving, and scheduling. In this business, where fixed costs are high but profit margins are razor thin, weak sales gains can translate into sharp profit declines as was seen last year. In short, chains are sharpening their prices, adding value, and attempting to build on their unique strengths. The goal has been to position the supermarket as the consummate convenience retailer—a provider of one-stop shopping. In addition, they are strengthening their value/price image by adding an array of private label products. These can sell at some 20% below branded goods and bring in heftier margins than branded goods.

Supermarket operators are wily competitors, and we believe that the industry is rising to the occasion with sales and earnings beginning an uptrend in late 1994, which will extend through 1995. The economy has strengthened, giving consumer spending a boost. Also, the consolidation in the warehouse club industry has slowed the building of clubs. Although supermarkets have not yet been declared the victors in their struggle to maintain marketshare against warehouse clubs and discounters, they are increasingly holding their own. But competition will remain tough. Always a new threat on the horizon, supercenters that sell food and general merchandise are being rolled out by Wal-Mart and Kmart. Over time, these powerhouse retailers could pose the next threat to traditional grocery stores.

RETAIL (GENERAL MERCHANDISE)

Description. These are stores that sell a variety of items, from apparel to household products to consumer electronics.

Characteristics. The retail industry is directed by the factors that influence consumer spending: consumer confidence, disposable income, and job growth. Industry progress can be monitored through the monthly retail sales report.

Outlook. The near-term investment outlook for the general merchandise retailers is more upbeat these days. Pent-up demand by consumers and easy comparisons with last year should boost gains in earnings. Apparel sales were weak in 1994, but we believe pent-up demand will boost sales in 1995. Home furnishings and more durable items, such as appliances and electronics, were strong performers in 1994 and should continue to experience healthy sales gains. As consumers continue to focus on their homes, products such as towels, sheets, and small appliances should experience sales gains.

Consumer spending picked up late last year as confidence in economic growth resumed. The unemployment rate continues to decline and, as a result, personal income has been rising all year. This has put more in consumers' pocketbooks and is likely to go into purchases previously deferred. Even so, consumers will remain somewhat more cost conscious. We expect discount retailers and mass merchandisers to continue to be the primary beneficiaries of increased spending. S&P projects consumer consumption to increase 3.0% in 1995, consisting of a 5.4% rise in

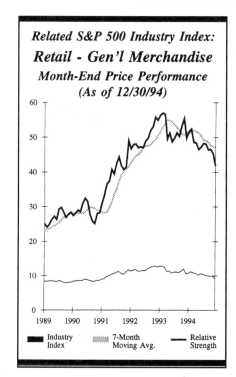

Related S&P 500 Industry Index:
Retail - Gen'l Merchandise
Month-End Price Performance
(As of 12/30/94)

| Industry Index | 7-Month Moving Avg. | Relative Strength |

consumer durables, a 2.2% advance in consumer nondurables, and a 2.7% gain in consumer services.

The longer-term investment outlook for general merchandise retailers is positive. Because of the highly competitive nature of retailing today, retailers are being forced to make cost-cutting a top priority. Major chains are eliminating redundancies and closing underperforming stores. Modest sales growth expectations, due to the proliferation of value-conscious consumers, have forced retailers to trim inventories and invest in cost-cutting technology to boost productivity. Investments in technology have helped many chains obtain better information about sales trends, which enables them to keep less merchandise in stock. And costs have been brought in line with sales growth. The leverage boosted earnings in 1994 and should extend into the first half of 1995.

RETAIL
(SPECIALTY)

Description.   These are stores that sell a narrow product assortment. While department stores and general merchandisers provide breadth of assortment, specialty retailers, dubbed "category killers," thrive on offering enormous selection in a single-product category at unbeatable prices. Large outlets or superstores, such as Circuit City, Toys "R" Us, and Home Depot, are gobbling up market share from "Mom and Pop" stores that cannot compete on price and assortment. Quick and convenient shopping add to the appeal of these specialty stores; they truly are customer friendly.

Characteristics.   The retail industry is directed by the factors that influence consumer spending: consumer confidence, disposable income, and job growth. Monthly results for the industry can be monitored through the retail sales report.

Outlook.   The near-term outlook for specialty retailers is upbeat. Consumer spending is on track to advance; consumer confidence is high; and unemployment is down. Although we see a resumption in apparel spending, reflecting pent-up demand, sales of home furnishings and appliances will continue to remain the consumer's main focus.

For the past year, consumer spending has been buoyed by solid gains in jobs and incomes. With consumer confidence relatively high, borrowing has increased. Spending cautiousness and price consciousness still abound, however. Consumer spending will not get the boost from lower interest rates that occurred last year. But we anticipate solid gains in retail sales during the important Christmas season—up 5% to 6%. These

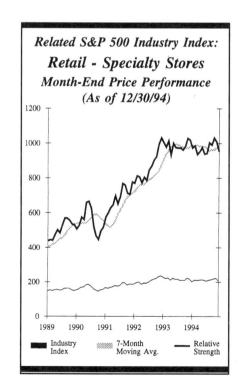

Related S&P 500 Industry Index:

Retail - Specialty Stores
Month-End Price Performance
(As of 12/30/94)

Industry Index | 7-Month Moving Avg. | Relative Strength

177

gains will be strong enough that, combined with better inventory management and careful attention to costs, overall profitability will be boosted.

Longer-term, we see a widening gap between the winners and the losers in retailing. Despite sharper competition from the department stores, as they lower prices to regain some lost marketshare, specialty stores will continue to have strong appeal. As America's households have become more diverse, so too have shopping patterns. This fragmentation of the marketplace has become a blight on mass-market retailing. As a result, becoming a specialist helps to establish a clear and unique identity in the mind of the consumer that can result in a destination store.

RETAIL
(SPECIALTY APPAREL)

Description.   These are stores that sell a variety of apparel items for men, women, and children through outlets and catalogs. While department stores and general merchandisers provide breadth of assortment, specialty retailers, dubbed "category killers," thrive on offering enormous selection in a single-product category at unbeatable prices. Large chains, such as The Gap, are gobbling up market share from "Mom and Pop" stores that cannot compete on price and assortment. Quick and convenient shopping add to the appeal of these stores.

Characteristics.   The retail industry is directed by the factors that influence consumer spending: consumer confidence, disposable income, and job growth. Monthly results for the industry can be monitored through the retail sales report.

Outlook.   The near-term outlook for specialty-apparel retailers is upbeat. Consumer spending is on track to advance; consumer confidence is high and unemployment down. We see a resumption in apparel spending, reflecting pent-up demand, behind the consumer's main focus on home furnishings and appliances. In addition, the demographics of an older population and more casual dress will keep apparel sales advancing modestly for the balance of this decade.

S&P Economics projects continued strength in consumer income and consumption during the next few years. Annualized personal income growth is forecast at 5.9% for 1995 and 5.3% in 1996. Consumer durable consumption is projected to rise 5.4% in 1995 and 2.8% in 1996. Annualized growth in consumer nondurable consumption is projected at 2.2% for 1995 and 1.7% for 1996.

Even though the 1980s-style mail order boom may be over, healthy sales gains continue in the mail order business, reflecting the popularity of this form of shopping. Consumers are tired of in-store shopping, and feel that walking the mall is no longer a favorite pastime. Shopping in the comfort of one's home is the ultimate in convenience. Mail order houses use the latest computer technology and data-gathering techniques to give customers information on merchandise specifics and to facilitate transactions. In 1994, it is estimated that well over 13 billion catalogs were mailed—an incredible 53 for every man, woman, and child in the country. To succeed in the face of such competition, marketers adopted a variety of tactics, from keeping better track of customers' buying patterns to reducing mail volume to cut expenses and build profitability. For catalog retailers, it is crucial to focus on that target customer niche and build loyalty. We attribute the strong sales gains at Lands' End to a succession of new catalogs for women's clothing.

SAVINGS & LOANS

Description. The nation's savings and loan industry, which is highly fragmented, offers a variety of transaction and savings products that fund the issuance of long-term fixed- and adjustable-rate mortgages.

Characteristics. S&Ls compete with banks, mortgage bankers, credit unions, and other financial institutions in making home mortgage loans and in accepting retail deposits. This commodity-like nature of the business results in weak profits for most participants. The level and direction of interest rates is a key determinant of this industry's profitability. In addition, the slope of the yield curve (the gap between the typically higher yield on 30-year bonds and lower-yielding 3-month Treasury bills) is an important determinant of financing spreads (the return on assets less the related cost of funds) for many financial firms. Other influencing factors include the level of unemployment, which correlates to the number of loan defaults and mortgage foreclosures, and housing prices, which also affect the volume of mortgages written and the losses from foreclosure resale.

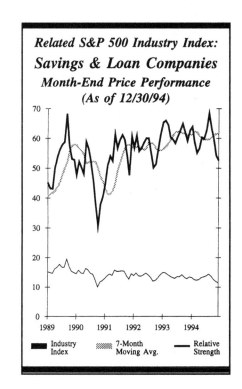

Related S&P 500 Industry Index:
Savings & Loan Companies
Month-End Price Performance
(As of 12/30/94)

| Industry Index | 7-Month Moving Avg. | Relative Strength |

Outlook. S&L stocks were weak in 1994 for two reasons. First, the increase in interest rates put pressure on interest rate spreads, which had negative implications for future profits. Second, takeover fever subsided. Based on our outlook for further hikes in short-term interest rates through mid-1995, interest rate spreads are likely to contract further. Therefore, the investment outlook for the industry as a whole is at best neutral.

Toward the end of 1994, the average publicly traded thrift was selling at a price-to-book-value ratio of 96%, up from 80% at the end of

181

December 1993. The industry also sold, on average, at a P/E ratio on trailing 12 months earnings per share of 12.0, up from the P/E of 10.5 at the end of December 1993.

Although takeover excitement has cooled, we still believe that longer-term industry consolidation will be a major theme for investors. There are approximately 2200 S&Ls nationwide and the industry is projected to experience a 38% shrinkage over the next five years. Reasons to expect a big pick up in takeovers include a large supply of companies up for sale, the industry's need to rationalize its cost structure, a number of well-capitalized suitor banks, and limited internal growth opportunities.

Absent other factors, S&L stocks generally trade on interest rates. Based on S&P's outlook for a slight rise in both short-term and long-term rates through mid-1995, the forecast is not favorable. Rising short-term rates will lead to an increase in funding costs, which will put pressure on profits. Higher long-term rates will choke off profits S&L's obtain from selling loans and mortgage-backed securities. The market, however, never valued income obtained from gains as highly as it did earnings from recurring sources.

The general perception that S&Ls are not investment grade is outmoded. Since 1989, the industry has rebuilt its capital considerably, and on an aggregate basis may now even be overcapitalized. The industry has reported 16 consecutive quarters of profits.

SHOES

Description. Shoe companies manufacture athletic footwear and nonrubber shoes.

Characteristics. This industry is cyclical and is dependent on consumer spending patterns. Share prices are subject to movements in consumer confidence and spending, interest rates, and disposable income.

Outlook. Shoe stocks significantly outperformed the market in 1994, following a 31% drop in 1993 on disappointing earnings. Thanks to an improved economy, consumers started buying shoes again in 1994, resulting in good earnings growth for most shoe companies, and expectations that earnings will continue to be robust into 1995. We currently recommend those shoe companies—such as Brown Group, Reebok, and Nike—that have large and growing market shares and a low-cost structure.

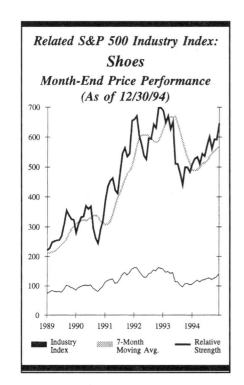

Related S&P 500 Industry Index:
Shoes
Month-End Price Performance
(As of 12/30/94)

Industry Index   7-Month Moving Avg.   Relative Strength

Following annual double-digit growth in the 1980s, shipments of athletic footwear have recently slowed to about 5% annually. We think many consumers are not wearing athletic footwear for casual purposes as much as they did in the 1980s. Instead, they are increasingly wearing nonrubber shoes. In response, market leaders Nike and Reebok have now entered into the nonathletic footwear market.

The nonathletic market is seeing increased demand after several years of declining volume, due to the recession, import growth, and the popularity of athletic shoes. While domestic producers of nonrubber shoes will continue to be plagued by imports, savvy producers, such as Brown Group, have moved most operating facilities offshore and should see substantial earnings improvement on higher volume and more efficient operations.

Over the longer term, domestic athletic footwear manufacturers should see renewed growth. There are niches that offer promising growth prospects, such as walking and all-purpose outdoor shoes. Overseas expansion offers the greatest long-term growth potential, however. Today, the international market, valued at $12 billion, is as untapped as the U.S. market was in the early 1970s.

SPECIALIZED
SERVICES

Description. Specialized service companies perform labor-intensive tasks for companies or households that choose not to maintain a full-time staff to perform these services. These services may range from temporary office help to lawn care.

Characteristics. The factors that influence the earnings and equity prices for these firms include (1) growth in the overall economy; (2) business and consumer confidence, as seen through the consumer confidence surveys and spending by advertising agencies; and (3) labor costs/capacity utilization, since companies will be less willing to hire full-time employees to perform these tasks during the early phase of an economic recovery as orders are just beginning to increase. Even with rising sales, companies can help keep overhead down and add to their nimbleness in responding to business conditions by using service firms to fill needs. Besides helping companies keep overhead costs low, a service firm also may be more experienced in certain functions, such as telephone marketing. Also, service firms may have economies of scale that their customers do not have, particularly if the customers are small businesses.

Outlook. The moderate improvement of the U.S. economy expected in the year ahead should continue to benefit a number of business service companies, which often fill needs for labor-intensive tasks. At recent share-price levels, our investment outlook for stocks in the commercial or business services group is, on average, modestly positive.

With the unemployment rate having moved lower, we expect that wage pressure on service

Related S&P 500 Industry Index:
Specialized Services
Month-End Price Performance
(As of 12/30/94)

| | Industry Index | 7-Month Moving Avg. | Relative Strength |

185

businesses will increase somewhat in the year ahead. However, the recent success of Republicans in Congressional elections suggests that passage of a sweeping national health plan has become even less likely, which eases the prospect that benefit costs for some employers could rise significantly.

A projected decline in the population of young adults in the next several years may add to the difficulty in attracting and retaining employees for these relatively low-paying jobs. However, even such longer-term wage pressure could be moderated, as employers turn to older people to fill more positions, and some people use service jobs for second-income or temporary situations.

SPECIALIZED PRINTING

Description. Companies in one of the newer industries within the S&P 500 print financial documents and personal checks, as well as directories and catalogs. Component companies are Deluxe Corp., R.R. Donnelley & Sons, and J.H. Harland.

Characteristics. These companies are influenced by interest rates, advertising spending trends, and paper prices.

Outlook. The year-ahead investment outlook for this small, yet diverse, group is neutral to slightly positive.

Deluxe Corp. is the largest U.S. concern engaged principally in printing bank checks. It also produces deposit tickets; makes computer forms and related products; provides software and services to financial institutions; and is a direct marketer of selected consumer products. A secular slowing in the check printing demand is being countered by strong growth in newer businesses, augmented by acquisitions. A small improvement in operating margins is anticipated in 1995, aided by significant operating economies and an expected slowing in startup and acquisition spending. A 1994 third-quarter dividend boost marked the thirty-fourth consecutive annual increase.

R. R. Donnelley & Sons is the largest commercial printer in the United States and produces catalogs, tabloids, directories, computer documentation, and other printed material. Sales and earnings are benefiting from strong marketing and business expansion efforts, improving business trends, and several publications.

John Harland is a leading supplier of checks, business documents, and forms to the financial industry. The company is continuing to take measures to counter a fundamental softening in check sales. These acquisitions include acquisitions, plant closings, faster growth in noncheck businesses, and efficiency measures. An aggressive stock repurchase program is also continuing. The dividend was increased for the forty-first consecutive year in 1994.

STEEL

Description.   There are two types of steel companies: integrated and mini mills. Integrated steel companies are vertically integrated and transform iron ore, limestone, and coal into carbon flat roll steel. Mini mills are not vertically integrated and use scrap steel to manufacture their output. Steel from both types of companies is used in the manufacture of durable goods such as cars, appliances, and a host of other products.

Characteristics.   The steel industry's health is closely linked to the growth in the overall economy. Therefore, such economic variables as interest rates, currency fluctuations, capital spending, and expenditures for consumer durables are important for the demand for steel. However, the strength or weakness of certain key industries such as autos and construction, as well the level of steel imports, can have a profound impact on industry shipments. Although shipments generally track the movements in the economy, sales and earnings tend to be more volatile. Sales and earnings for steel companies generally decline in the third quarter of every year due to seasonally lower auto production.

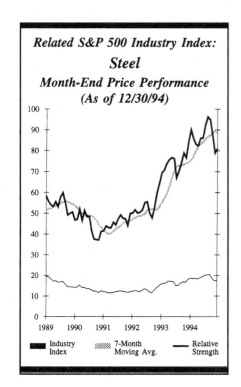

Related S&P 500 Industry Index:
Steel
Month-End Price Performance
(As of 12/30/94)

Industry Index | 7-Month Moving Avg. | Relative Strength

Outlook.   While steel stocks underperformed the S&P 500 in 1994, the shares should gain upside momentum in 1995 as it becomes apparent that price increases will hold and shipments maintain their strong pace. We expect that the group will outperform the "500" in 1995.

Based upon the S&P forecast for real GDP growth of 3.0% in 1995, flat auto sales, and a lower level of both carbon and stainless flat rolled imports, industry shipments should increase to about 93 million tons from 1994's estimated total of 91 million tons. Integrated steelmakers should be able to extend their gains into

1995 on higher volume and better pricing. The increase in shipments and volume will result from continued economic growth and reduced imports of flat rolled carbon products. Minimill profits will improve from 1994's levels based upon rising volume, higher prices, and less rapidly rising scrap costs. Specialty steelmakers should also achieve higher profits in 1995 because of a lower level of imports and higher prices.

As a result of our positive outlook, we have an "accumulate" ranking on Armco Inc., Carpenter Technology, Lukens Inc., U.S. Steel Group, and Worthington Industries. We rank Birmingham Steel "buy" based upon our expectation that earnings for fiscal 1995 should accelerate, aided by its acquisition of American Steel & Wire, greater highway spending, market share gains, and a shift toward higher margin products. Although the strike will hurt 1994's earnings, we are maintaining our "buy" on Allegheny Ludlum based upon its excellent long-term growth prospects which are enhanced by strong secular growth in stainless and an improved product mix. We rate newly public Rouge Steel (ROU, NYSE) a strong buy based upon its program to upgrade product mix and reduce costs, its rock solid business (some 45% of sales are tied to contracts with Ford Motor and Worthington Industries), and its strong finances.

TELECOMMUNICATIONS (LONG DISTANCE)

Description. Sometimes called interexchange carriers, these companies provide the transmission services for the long-haul portion of long-distance calls. However, they must rely on local operators for both the originating and terminating connection to customers.

Characteristics. The factors that influence share prices include GDP growth, as economic growth correlates with growth in demand for telephone services; inflation, since inflation rates are typically factored into regulators' formulas for determining local carriers' rates, which will impact long-distance carriers' costs to connect to local networks; inflation, through its impact on interest rates, also affects the carriers' cost of capital; and finally regulatory policy. Long-distance carriers are less heavily regulated than the local carriers, with no specific limits set on earnings (only AT&T is subject to price oversight). However, regulatory policy impacts the carriers in two ways. First, pro-competitive regulatory policy in the local market engenders lower costs to access local networks in completing long-haul calls (access costs are the long-distance carriers' largest expense). Second, legislative and regulatory actions can impact the competitive environment between the local and long-distance carriers. The industry is dominated by three national carriers but includes several hundred smaller carriers which operate regional networks or resell capacity leased from network-based carriers.

Outlook. The S&P telecommunications group sold-off late in 1994 on expectations that the new

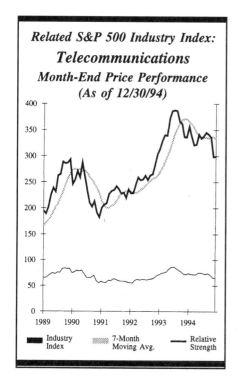

Related S&P 500 Industry Index:
Telecommunications
Month-End Price Performance
(As of 12/30/94)

Legend:
- Industry Index
- 7-Month Moving Avg.
- Relative Strength

Republican-controlled Congress will pass pro-competitive telecommunications legislation in 1995. Although legislation will likely allow the Baby Bells into the long-distance market, what restrictions will be placed on the Bells is unclear and the long-distance carriers may benefit from the opening of new market opportunities for themselves. We believe that at the current historically low multiple levels the group offers significant upside potential for selected stocks as the market begins to reassess the prospects of more competition and rewards those companies with sound long-term growth strategies.

Overall long-distance calling volume growth has slowed in recent years as industry pricing trends have stabilized. The top carriers have instituted price increases in recent periods. Over the near term we anticipate pricing to remain in a marginally upward trend, although discounting will continue in certain segments of the market; annual calling volume growth is seen in the 6% to 7% range for the foreseeable future. The major carriers are working to stimulate volume growth and round out service offerings by entering new markets. Aggressive moves to tap into demand for global advanced services by multinational corporations—an estimated $10 billion market growing at a 12% annual clip—are likely to help rein in the high costs of international calling and contribute to stronger volume growth.

The top carriers are also accelerating efforts to tap into the rapidly growing wireless market and encourage incremental usage growth of their own networks. AT&T has taken the lead with its acquisition of McCaw Cellular, while Sprint has formed a wireless venture with major cable operators, which will participate in the upcoming PCS (personal communications services) auctions. However, MCI believes it can participate in the wireless market through a reseller strategy and is focusing some incremental capital expenditures on entering the local telephone market. In addition to revenue growth, wireless and local ventures could also contribute to faster earnings growth by offering an alternative to the local telephone company in hooking up long haul calls; charges to access the local network account for the bulk of the carriers' costs.

TELEPHONES

Description. Sometimes referred to as local exchange carriers, these companies provide basic local telephone service, including dialtone and access to interexchange carriers for long-distance calls. Most of these companies also have significant cellular telephone service operations and related international telecommunications investments.

Characteristics. Economic growth correlates with growth in demand for phone services, specifically impacting growth in access lines and minutes of use. Because most local phone companies are regional, regional GDP growth is more significant than national GDP growth. Inflation impacts the local phone companies both through the impact on prices to customers and through the impact on interest rates. These companies typically have heavy capital expenditures, so higher interest rates, and therefore cost of capital, have an adverse impact on earnings. The industry is heavily regulated and protected from competition by the high cost of installing a phone network. The industry is divided into two major camps: the seven Bell regional holding companies (RHCs) and the more than 1000 "independent" local companies. The RHCs were spun-off from AT&T in January 1984 and consist of AT&T's former local telephone subsidiaries. The RHCs each operate in a separate region of the country. The independent companies range in size from GTE, which rivals the RHCs, down to small telephone companies handling only a couple of thousand access lines.

Outlook. Our near-term outlook is neutral as benefits from economic growth will be offset by the prospect of a tighter interest-rate environment and disappointment over the lack of telecommunications legislation. Over the longer

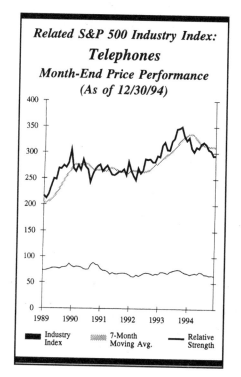

Related S&P 500 Industry Index:
Telephones
Month-End Price Performance
(As of 12/30/94)

Industry Index | 7-Month Moving Avg. | Relative Strength

193

term, the outlook is mixed as growing competition and the opening of new market opportunities offer both risks and rewards. Those companies whose corporate strategies have prepared them for the more competitive environment are likely to outperform the group and the market averages over time.

In the event of a market downturn, the group's above-average yields should provide support, as well as contribute to adequate total returns. However, the group's attractiveness as a yield play is diminishing as the companies look to redeploy resources to long-term growth opportunities rather than growing dividends at a rapid pace. The companies are facing a limited window of opportunity for investments in international telephone company privatizations and wireless spectrum licenses.

In the near term, regulation and competition will continue to be the primary forces impacting the industry. As competition in their markets increases, the companies are looking to leverage their investment in existing plant and advanced technologies by expanding into complementary businesses. However, the companies' efforts to enter the long-distance market were stymied by the Senate's inability to pass telecommunications legislation in 1994. Now the telephone companies must pursue their strategy through the court system. The Federal court has already paved the way for telcos to provide full cable television services, declaring restrictions on telephone company ownership of programming a violation of the first amendment.

The telephone companies have also benefited from a recent court ruling overturning an FCC decision requiring the telcos to allow competitors to bring their equipment onto telco premises to interconnect with the telcos' switching equipment. The court ruling will make it harder for alternative telephone service providers to compete for other-than-private-line services. But the telcos are also taking advantage of regulators' efforts to open the local markets by seeking to provide competitive telephone service within sister companies' operating territories.

TEXTILE/APPAREL MANUFACTURERS

Description. The major markets served by textile manufacturers are home furnishings (37% of all textiles), apparel fabrics (38%), and industrial fabrics (25%).

Characteristics. This industry is highly cyclical and is dependent on consumer spending patterns. Each cycle usually precedes an economic downturn by 6 to 12 months. The industry remains one of the most fragmented, with the majority of the players being small and privately held. Share prices are subject to movements in consumer confidence and spending, interest rates, and housing starts.

Outlook. We believe consumers are generally uninterested in buying clothing these days, partly reflecting the lack of any fashion trend, as well as changing demographics, which now incorporate an older population that prefers to stay at home. Consumers have also been spending more on appliances, furniture, and other household items, partly reflecting the strong housing market over the past few years. As such, our near-term investment outlook on those companies in the S&P Textiles index remains neutral.

There remain some apparel companies not included in the S&P Textile/Apparel index that we continue to favor, however. Shares of the moderately priced, brand-name apparel makers, including Kellwood Corp., Oxford Industries, and Phillips-Van Heusen, promise good earnings growth. Consumers increasingly buy this type of clothing through a variety of retail formats. A recent announcement by Wal-Mart, whose apparel sales alone have been estimated to total

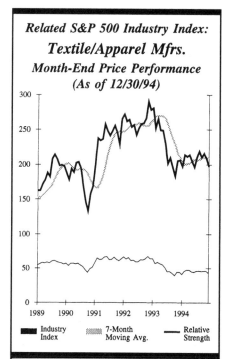

Related S&P 500 Industry Index:

Textile/Apparel Mfrs.

Month-End Price Performance
(As of 12/30/94)

Legend: Industry Index | 7-Month Moving Avg. | Relative Strength

195

$18 billion, that it would actively seek brand name apparel should also enhance appreciation of these stocks.

Longer term, we feel consumer demand for apparel will be healthy, although not as healthy as in the 1980s when annual growth averaged 7.4%. While fashion trends may periodically drive apparel sales in certain areas, overall demand for apparel is driven by the economy and personal income gains. Leading apparel manufacturers will also benefit from the passage of NAFTA. Not only does this agreement create a huge new market for apparel manufacturers, but it also will enable manufacturers to give retailers shorter lead times by sourcing production in Mexico instead of the Far East.

TOBACCO

Description.   This group includes cigarette manufacturers (Philip Morris, RJR Nabisco, American Brands) as well as tobacco traders (Universal Corp.), dealers (Dibrell Brothers, Standard Commercial), and nonsmoking tobacco products (UST).

Characteristics.   As defensive issues (those with earnings that are not generally tied to the overall health of the economy), any economic indicator that points to economic weakness will influence these issues favorably as it makes them more attractive to investors than the economically sensitive industries. Such indicators would include interest rates, consumer sentiment, and personal income growth. Investors should realize, however, that these issues respond much more to legislative actions, as they impact cigarette demand.

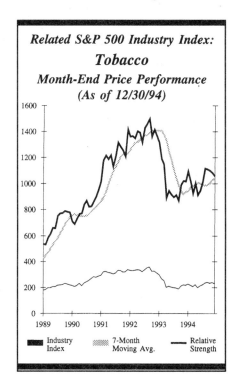

Related S&P 500 Industry Index:
Tobacco
Month-End Price Performance (As of 12/30/94)

Industry Index | 7-Month Moving Avg. | Relative Strength

Outlook.   The S&P Tobacco index significantly outperformed the S&P 500 in 1994. This principally reflects a more stable U.S. cigarette pricing environment, investor bottom-fishing in the wake of 1993's dramatic selloff (−25.6%), and the waning threat of a near-term sharp hike in cigarette federal excise taxes. Longer-term performance prospects are unfavorable, however, primarily due to increasing anti-smoking and other tobacco-use activity in both the United States and abroad. Also, industry risks continue to mount arising from pending class action liability lawsuits aimed at U.S. cigarette manufacturers, and declarations by the FDA citing the possibility of regulating the tobacco industry following allegations that producers may manipulate the level of nicotine in cigarettes.

Tobacco company earnings in 1994 continue to recover from 1993's depressed levels, owing to easy comparisons (due to the severe earnings hit incurred with 1993's cigarette price wars), and recent cost-cutting measures. Earnings prospects through early 1995 also have the benefit of easy comparisons, but longer-term prospects are unfavorable because price competition among the major producers will remain intense due to the steadily shrinking size (1–3% unit decline per annum) of the U.S. market.

United States cigarette companies have over the years pursued an aggressive expansion strategy both geographically and operationally in order to help alleviate their dependence upon a highly profitable, but also highly controversial, business in the United States. The actions were also an attempt to boost the valuations of their stocks, as investors generally do not assign generous price-earnings multiples to tobacco companies due to their greater perceived investment risk. Recently heightened anti-tobacco fervor and languishing stock prices are forcing cigarette companies to take action. In April 1994, American Brands agreed to sell its beleaguered American Tobacco unit to British-based B.A.T. Industries (the deal was challenged by the Federal Trade Commission in late October). RJR Nabisco Holdings in October said it will sell a 19% stake in its food business, and signaled that a total split from tobacco may not be far away. In late August 1994, Philip Morris tried to placate impatient shareholders by announcing a nearly 20% dividend hike and a whopping $6 billion, 3-year share buyback plan. The move should appease holders in the near term.

TOYS

Description: Toys are dolls, male action figures, board games, and other products of amusement for children. (Toys for grownups are found in the entertainment and leisure time industries.)

Characteristics. The share prices of toy companies are affected by consumer confidence and spending, as well as disposable income. Individual companies' fortunes are affected by the acceptance of new products. Share prices in general demonstrate strength leading up to the mid-February industry toy fair where new products are unveiled. These issues also show strength in late October when seasonally strong third-quarter earnings are reported. (Toy manufacturers sell their products to toy retailers in the third quarter, whereas the toy retailers show strongest earnings in the fourth quarter.)

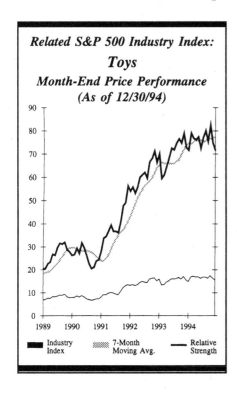

Related S&P 500 Industry Index:
Toys
Month-End Price Performance
(As of 12/30/94)

Industry Index | 7-Month Moving Avg. | Relative Strength

Outlook. Mattel attracted investors' attention immediately before Christmas 1994 when it announced that it would be implementing a restructuring to create efficiencies and eliminate redundancies caused by its recent acquisitions. The actions will result in the elimination of 1000 positions and result in a $70 million charge. In addition, the company predicted record earnings for 1994, announced a five-for-four stock spilt, and maintained its cash dividend, which effectively increased the payout by 25%. However favorable these actions were, the company also said that it expected to have a difficult first half due to higher resin and packaging costs and costs to invest in new technology. In addition, its cost reductions will only be partially implemented in the first half, although they should offset this margin pressure for the full year.

Acquisitions have continued to attract attention in the toy industry in recent months. In late

September 1994, Hallmark Cards announced that it had entered into a definitive agreement to acquire Revell-Monogram for $6.375 a share in cash for its 4.7 million common shares outstanding. Revell-Monogram, a leading model maker, lost $2.97 million on sales of $96 million in 1993. Earlier, Mattel had won a battle with Hasbro for control of J.W. Spear & Sons, a British company that holds the rights to Scrabble and other games outside the United States. This followed by several months its May acquisition of Kransco, a privately held toy company with revenues of approximately $175 million. Kransco is best known for the Power Wheels battery-powered, ride-on vehicles.

These acquisitions add to a distinct trend of consolidation in the industry over the past half-dozen years, including Mattel's purchase of number-four-ranked Fisher-Price in November 1993. Other well-known companies that have been purchased in recent years include Tonka, Universal Matchbox, View-Master Ideal Group, Coleco, and Kenner Parker Toys.

TRANSPORTATION (MISCELLANEOUS)

Description. This group includes truck leasing and air freight companies. Truck lessors provide vehicles under an operating lease and include a variety of services, including maintenance, licensing, fuel, and tax reporting. Air cargo companies may operate aircraft or purchase air cargo space to move documents, packages, or heavy cargo.

Characteristics. Both groups are influenced by general economic trends, such as industrial output, retail sales, and fuel costs.

Outlook. The near-term outlook for air-cargo stocks is positive. Following earlier gains, the majority of stocks have slumped since early summer, reflecting concern that the highly competitive domestic market would damage earnings. But volume growth has been strong. Freight and express traffic for the largest U.S. carriers experienced double-digit gains in 1994, with gains particularly strong for the international sector. We believe the economy's continued expansion should support traffic growth well into 1995. Domestic revenue gains probably will continue to be hampered by the industry's competitive pricing practices. Pressure on yields is continuing as carriers compete for larger corporate accounts. A focus on controlling costs and improving technical services to customers should be effective in countering the price cutting effects. Most industry forecasters see a pickup in international traffic growth in the 1990s. Supporting this outlook is the continuing growth expected in less-developed countries, the increasing acceptance by many industries of time-definite air transport for international goods distribution, and the growing geographical availability of such services.

The truck leasing segment of this industry should closely mirror the outlook for the heavy duty trucking/truckers industries which are both less than favorable as investors have shied away from these groups because of concerns with the longevity of the economic expansion. In addition, a growing glut of used vehicles by 1995 also will cause a shift in the decision process away from new trucks, either purchased or leased.

TRUCKERS

Description. The for-hire trucking industry is divided among two broad lines: full truckload carriers (TL) and less-than-truckload (LTL) companies. Each of the nearly 50,000 trucking firms hauls freight interstate over public roadways. Most companies own both the tractors and trailers used to perform their services.

Characteristics. Truckload carriers operate with few economies of scale and face considerable competition from railroads for shipments exceeding 750 miles. Increasingly, larger TL carriers have formed partnerships with railroads to feed them shipments for their piggyback services. LTL carriage, which includes about 25 major players plus a few hundred minor firms, is a much smaller market than the truckload segment. These issues are considered early cycle performers and will tend to rally once the economy, in particular industrial production, has bottomed. These stocks are also sensitive to changes in interest rates and, obviously, the price of oil.

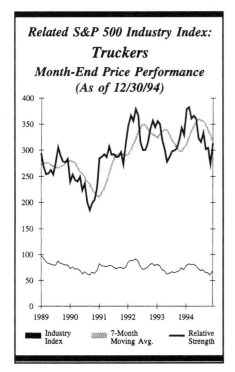

Related S&P 500 Industry Index:
Truckers
Month-End Price Performance
(As of 12/30/94)

Industry Index — 7-Month Moving Avg. — Relative Strength

Outlook. Trucking stocks have been in a broad trading range since 1992. Recently, they have moved to the lower end of that range participating in a general correction in transportation issues. Recent weakness primarily reflects investor concern with the longevity of the economic expansion. Also contributing to weakness in the S&P Trucking index is a slump in Roadway Services whose profits are being hurt by heavy startup costs for its new air freight business. Recently Consolidated Freightways has been under pressure as investors fear the strong gains posted at its Emery air freight unit will soon evaporate. While we see opportunities to trade these stocks, we would not make long-term commitments in the shares of LTL carriers at this time.

203

The truckload segment, the industry's largest, is expected to undergo a major consolidation over the next few years reflecting driver and capital shortages and competition from rail intermodal. Still, we see TL carriers posting higher profits in 1995, reflecting a projected 3.2% gain for industrial output. Though a driver shortage remains a concern, carriers have succeeded in passing through the higher wages needed to attract drivers to shippers via rate hikes.

LTL carriage, which includes about 25 major players plus about a hundred minor firms, is a much smaller market than the truckload segment. Profits for LTL lines are seen as doubling in 1995 after slipping an estimated 41% in 1994 due to the Teamster strike. Also aiding 1995 profits will be the new Teamsters contract that will let LTL truckers expand their use of rail piggyback and employ part-time workers for shorter periods. While most carriers are implementing a 4–4.5% rate hike for January 1, we think pressure from nontraditional players, including parcel service and air freight, will force truckers to pare the net rise to an amount below the inflation rate.

4

Buy, Sell, and Hold Recommendations

This chapter is made up of a "buy, sell, and hold" listing of more than 1000 companies arranged alphabetically by industry. The data for each company are as they stood on December 30, 1994 and include ticker symbol, share price, fiscal-year ending, sales/revenues, 1994 EPS (and footnotes), 1995 EPS (and footnotes), P/E (on estimated 1995 earnings), dividend yield, S&P common stock & dividend rank, and STARS.

The S&P common stock and dividend rank is an appraisal of the growth and stability of earnings and dividends over the past 10 years: **A+ = Highest; A = High; A − = Above average; B+ = Average; B = Below average; B − = Low; C = Lowest; D = In reorganization; and NR = Not ranked.** Quality rankings are not intended to predict stock price movements.

STARS stands for S&P's Stock Appreciation Ranking System. STARS evaluates the investment potential of the stocks it covers, with emphasis on performance over a 6-to-12-month period: **5 STARS = Buy** (expected to be among the best performing stocks); **4 STARS = Accumulate** (expected to be an above-average performer, relative to the S&P 500); **3 STARS = Hold** (expected to be an average performer); **2 STARS** = Avoid (below-average expectations, relative to the S&P 500); **1 STAR** = Sell (expected to be among the worst performers in all industries). Those investors who wish to keep abreast of STAR changes on a weekly basis (as well as periodic performance measures versus the market) should subscribe to S&P's *The Outlook.*

The footnotes for the letter codes found in the table are as follows:

*F-Y 1994 results.

d—Deficit.

e—Estimate.

f—Pro forma.

g—Fully diluted.

i—Foreign currency.

o—Combined earnings.

p—Preliminary.

s—Before tax-loss carryforward.

w—Excluding extraordinary income.

x—Including extraordinary income.

y—Excluding extraordinary charge.

z—Including extraordinary charge.

BE—Breakeven.

EUR—Estimate under review.

NE—No estimate.

NM—Not meaningful.

NR—Not ranked.

Readers should also be aware that earnings for fiscal years ending March 31 or earlier are shown in the column of the preceding calendar year.

Peer Comparisons

										S&P Com. Stk. & Div. Rank	STARS 5=Buy 1=Sell
Industry Company	SYM	12/94 Price	Fiscal Year End	Sales	EPS ('94)	EPS ('95)	PE ('95)	Yield			

Industry / Company	SYM	12/94 Price	Fiscal Year End	Sales	EPS ('94)	EPS ('95)	PE ('95)	Yield	S&P Com. Stk. & Div. Rank	STARS 5=Buy 1=Sell
Aerospace										
AAR Corp	AIR	13	MY	408 *	0.60 wy	0.70 e	19	3.5	B+	1
BE Aerospace	BEAV	7	FB	203	0.35 e	0.80 e	9	Nil	NR	2
• Boeing Co	BA	47	DC	25,438	2.45 e	1.95 e	24	2.1	A	4
§ GenCorp	GY	12	NV	1,905	0.90 e	0.90 e	13	5.0	B	3
• Genl Dynamics	GD	44	DC	3,187	3.45 e	3.55 e	12	3.2	B	3
Genl Motors Cl'H'	GMH	35	DC	13,518	2.65 e	2.85 e	12	2.2	B+	4
• Lockheed Corp	LK	73	DC	13,071	7.00 e	7.35 e	10	3.1	B+	4
• Martin Marietta	ML	44	DC	9,436	4.96 e	4.55 e	10	2.1	A	4
• McDonnell Douglas	MD	142	DC	14,487	14.00 e	15.00 e	9	1.6	B+	3
• Northrop Grumman	NOC	42	DC	5,063	4.50 e	4.90 e	9	3.8	B-	3
§ OEA Inc	OEA	25	JL	110 *	0.88	1.15 e	21	0.8	B+	3
§ Precision Castparts	PCP	20	MR	420	1.50 e	1.70 e	12	1.1	A-	3
• Raytheon Co	RTN	64	DC	9,201	5.70 e	6.40 e	10	2.3	A+	4
• Rockwell Intl	ROK	36	SP	11,123 *	2.87	3.15 e	11	3.0	A-	4
§ Rohr Inc	RHR	10	JL	918 *	0.38	0.65 e	16	Nil	B-	3
§ Sequa Corp Cl'A'	SQA.A	26	DC	1,697	0.50 e	2.50 e	10	Nil	C	3
§ Sundstrand Corp	SNS	46	DC	1,383	2.85 e	3.40 e	13	2.6	B	3
§ Teleflex Inc	TFX	36	DC	667	2.35 e	2.75 e	13	1.5	A+	4
§ Thiokol Corp	TKC	28	JE	1,044 *	3.02 y	3.10 e	9	2.4	NR	3
• United Technologies	UTX	63	DC	21,081	4.70 e	5.25 e	12	3.1	B	4
Airlines										
§ Alaska Air Group	ALK	15	DC	1,128	1.00 e	1.40 e	11	Nil	C	3
• AMR Corp	AMR	53	DC	15,816	4.00 e	7.00 e	8	Nil	C	4
§ Atlantic So'east Air	ASAI	16	DC	288	1.60 e	1.85 e	8	2.0	B+	3
British Airways ADS	BAB	57	MR	9,328	4.95 e	5.40 e	10	3.3	NR	3
Comair Holdings	COMR	18	MR	297	1.70 e	1.90 e	9	1.8	B+	3
Contl Airlines'B'	CAI.B	9	DC	3,907	d5.20 e	1.50 e	6	Nil	NR	3
• Delta Air Lines	DAL	51	JE	12,359 *	d10.32	2.00 e	25	0.3	B-	3
KLM Royal Dutch Air	KLM	25	MR	4,613	1.50 e	3.00 e	8	Nil	NR	3
• Southwest Airlines	LUV	17	DC	2,297	1.15 e	1.40 e	12	0.2	B+	4
UAL Corp(New)	UAL	87	DC	14,511	4.00 e	9.00 e	10	Nil	C	4
• USAir Group	U	4	DC	7,083	d9.50 e	d3.00 e	NM	Nil	C	2
Aluminum										
• Alcan Aluminium Ltd	AL	25	DC	7,307	BE e	1.60 e	16	1.1	B-	3
§ Alumax Inc	AMX	28	DC	2,347	BE e	1.80 e	16	Nil	NR	2
• Aluminum Co of Amer	AA	87	DC	9,056	1.20 e	3.80 e	23	2.0	B-	3
Kaiser Aluminum	KLU	11	DC	1,719	d1.75 e	d0.25 e	NM	Nil	NR	1
§ MAXXAM Inc	MXM	31	DC	2,031	d7.15 e	EUR	NM	Nil	C	2
• Reynolds Metals	RLM	49	DC	5,269	d0.75 ze	2.75 e	18	2.0	B-	3
Auto Parts After Market										
§ Arvin Indus	ARV	23	DC	1,939	1.90 e	2.30 e	10	3.2	B	4
Bandag, Inc	BDG	61	DC	590	3.40 e	3.65 e	17	1.3	A+	2
§ Carlisle Cos	CSL	36	DC	611	2.25 e	2.40 e	15	2.2	B	3
• Cooper Tire & Rubber	CTB	24	DC	1,194	1.50 e	1.72 e	14	1.0	A	4
• Echlin Inc	ECH	30	AU	2,229 *	2.06 w	2.50 e	12	2.5	B+	5
§ Federal-Mogul	FMO	20	DC	1,576	1.55 e	1.80 e	11	2.3	B-	3
• Genuine Parts	GPC	36	DC	4,384	2.32 e	2.55 e	14	3.1	A+	4

• An S&P 500 Company
§ An S&P Mid-Cap 400 Company

Peer Comparisons (*Continued*)

•	Goodyear Tire & Rub	GT	34	DC	11,643	3.75 e	4.00 e	8	2.3	B	3
	Magna Intl Cl'A'	MGA	38	JL	3,569 *	4.18 i	4.80 ei	8	2.0	B	4
§	Mark IV Industries	IV	20	FB	1,244	1.42 e	1.55 e	13	0.5	B	3
§	Modine Mfg	MODI	29	MR	670	2.00 e	2.30 e	13	1.8	A-	5
	Monro Muffler Brake	MNRO	17	MR	94	1.14 e	1.35 e	13	Nil	NR	4
	Orbital Engine ADS	OE	8	JE	13 *	d0.71	0.15 e	53	Nil	NR	5
	Simpson Indus	SMPS	9	DC	262	0.87 e	1.13 e	8	4.3	B	4
	Spartan Motors	SPAR	13	DC	167	1.00 e	1.35 e	10	0.3	B+	4
•	SPX Corp	SPW	17	DC	756	1.15 e	1.25 e	13	2.4	B-	1
§	Superior Indus Intl	SUP	27	DC	393	1.80 e	2.15 e	12	0.6	A	5
	TBC Corp	TBCC	9	DC	569	0.69 e	0.80 e	12	Nil	B+	4
	Tower Automotive	TWER	9	DC	195	1.05 e	1.25 e	7	Nil	NR	4

Automobiles

•	Chrysler Corp	C	49	DC	43,600	9.40 e	10.75 e	5	3.2	B-	5
•	Ford Motor	F	28	DC	108,521	5.00 e	6.50 e	4	3.7	B-	4
•	Genl Motors	GM	42	DC	138,220	6.35 e	8.50 e	5	1.8	B-	5
	Honda Motor ADR	HMC	36	MR	37,448	0.80 e	1.00 e	36	0.6	NR	2

Beverages-(Alcoholic)

•	Anheuser-Busch Cos	BUD	51	DC	11,505	3.85 e	4.25 e	12	3.1	A+	3
•	Brown-Forman Cl'B'	BF.B	31	AP	1,401 *	2.04 yo	2.10 e	15	3.2	A	2
•	Coors (Adolph)Cl'B'	ACCOB	17	DC	1,582	1.15 e	1.20 e	14	2.9	B-	2
•	Seagram Co. Ltd	VO	30	JA	6,038	2.20 e	2.60 e	11	2.0	A-	5

Beverages-(Soft Drinks)

•	Coca-Cola Co	KO	52	DC	13,957	2.00 e	2.30 e	22	1.5	A+	3
§	Coca-Cola Enterprises	CCE	18	DC	5,465	0.40 e	0.55 e	33	0.2	NR	3
	Dr Pepper/Seven-Up Cos	DPS	26	DC	707	1.15 e	1.35 e	19	Nil	NR	3
•	PepsiCo Inc	PEP	36	DC	25,021	2.15 e	2.35 e	15	1.9	A+	3

Broadcast Media

	British Sky Broadcstg Gp ADS	BSY	24	JE	860 *	0.67 f	1.25 e	19	1.3	NR	4
	Cablevision Sys'A'	CVC	51	DC	667	d10.80 e	d9.50 e	NM	Nil	C	4
•	Capital Cities/ABC	CCB	85	DC	5,674	4.25 e	4.80 e	18	0.2	A	3
•	CBS Inc	CBS	55	DC	3,510	3.50 e	3.75 e	15	0.7	B	4
§	Chris-Craft Indus	CCN	35	DC	440	2.50 e	2.90 e	12	Nil	B-	3
•	Comcast Cl'A'Spl(non-vtg)	CMCSK	16	DC	1,338	d0.26 e	d0.33 e	NM	0.5	B-	4
	Gaylord Entertainment 'A'	GET	23	DC	623	0.90 e	0.95 e	24	1.2	NR	3
§	Multimedia Inc	MMEDC	29	DC	635	2.25 e	2.20 e	13	Nil	B	3
§	TCA Cable TV	TCAT	22	OC	152	0.92 e	1.10 e	20	2.2	B+	4
•	Tele-Communicns'A'	TCOMA	22	DC	4,153	0.23 e	0.35 e	62	Nil	C	4
	Turner Broadcast'B'	TBS.B	16	DC	1,922	0.20 e	0.45 e	36	0.4	B-	3

Building Materials

§	CalMat Co	CZM	17	DC	348	0.75 e	1.15 e	15	2.3	B	3
	Centex Construction Prod	CXP	12	MR	137	1.00 e	1.40 e	9	Nil	NR	4
•	Masco Corp	MAS	23	DC	3,886	1.75 e	2.15 e	11	3.1	B+	4
•	Owens-Corning	OCF	32	DC	2,944	1.80 e	4.00 e	8	Nil	NR	3
•	Sherwin-Williams	SHW	33	DC	2,949	2.16 e	2.45 e	14	1.6	A	3
	USG Corp(New)	USG	20	DC	1,325	d1.75 e	d0.30 e	NM	Nil	NR	3
	Vulcan Materials	VMC	51	DC	1,133	2.45 e	3.00 e	17	2.6	A-	4
§	York International	YRK	37	DC	2,032	2.35 e	2.55 e	14	0.4	NR	3

Chemicals

•	Air Products & Chem	APD	45	SP	3,485 *	2.06 w	3.00 e	15	2.1	A	4
	ARCO Chemical	RCM	44	DC	3,192	2.80 e	3.00 e	15	5.6	NR	3
§	CBI Indus	CBH	26	DC	1,672	1.10 e	1.55 e	17	1.8	B	3
•	Dow Chemical	DOW	67	DC	18,060	3.75 e	5.50 e	12	3.8	B	4
•	duPont(EI)deNemours	DD	56	DC	37,098	3.90 e	4.50 e	12	3.3	B+	4

Peer Comparisons (*Continued*)

	Company	Ticker									
•	Eastman Chemical	EMN	51	DC	3,903	4.00 e	4.50 e	11	3.1	NR	4
§	Freeport McMoRan	FTX	18	DC	1,611	0.30 e	0.48 e	37	7.0	B	4
	Geon Co	GON	27	DC	973	1.90 e	2.25 e	12	1.8	NR	4
§	Georgia Gulf Corp	GGC	39	DC	769	2.72 e	4.40 e	9	Nil	NR	5
•	Goodrich (B.F.)	GR	43	DC	1,818	2.00 e	2.40 e	18	5.0	B-	3
•	Hercules, Inc	HPC	115	DC	2,773	6.00 e	7.00 e	16	2.1	B	3
§	IMC Global	IGL	44	JE	1,442 *	d0.14 y	3.00 e	15	0.9	NR	3
	Imperial Chem Ind ADR	ICI	47	DC	15,735	2.20 e	3.00 e	16	3.8	B+	3
§	Lyondell Petrochem	LYO	26	DC	3,850	2.25 e	3.00 e	9	3.4	NR	4
•	Monsanto Co	MTC	71	DC	7,902	5.00 e	5.75 e	12	3.5	A-	4
•	Praxair Inc	PX	21	DC	2,438	1.40 e	1.55 e	13	1.3	NR	4
•	Rohm & Haas	ROH	57	DC	3,269	3.75 e	4.00 e	14	2.5	B+	4
§	Sterling Chemicals	STX	13	SP	701 *	0.34	1.20 e	11	Nil	NR	3
•	Union Carbide	UK	29	DC	4,640	2.00 e	2.50 e	12	2.5	NR	3
	Vigoro Corp	VGR	30	JE	727 *	2.43	2.80 e	11	2.8	NR	4
§	Wellman Inc	WLM	28	DC	842	1.70 e	2.00 e	14	0.8	NR	3
§	Witco Corp	WIT	25	DC	2,143	1.90 e	2.20 e	11	4.5	B	4

Chemicals (Diversified)

	Company	Ticker									
•	Avery Dennison Corp	AVY	36	DC	2,609	1.90 e	2.20 e	16	3.0	A-	4
•	Engelhard Corp	EC	22	DC	2,151	1.25 e	1.45 e	15	2.1	B	3
•	FMC Corp	FMC	58	DC	3,754	4.45 e	5.00 e	12	Nil	NR	3
•	First Mississippi	FRM	25	JE	508 *	0.88 w	2.50 e	10	1.4	B-	3
§	Olin Corp	OLN	52	DC	2,423	3.55 e	5.00 e	10	4.2	B	4
•	PPG Indus	PPG	37	DC	5,754	2.35 e	3.25 e	11	3.1	A-	4

Chemicals (Specialty)

	Company	Ticker									
§	Albemarle Corp	ALB	14	DC	903	0.80 e	0.80 e	17	1.4	NR	2
§	Cabot Corp	CBT	28	SP	1,680 *	1.96	2.25 e	13	1.9	B	4
§	Crompton & Knowles	CNK	16	DC	558	1.00 e	1.05 e	15	2.9	A+	3
§	Dexter Corp	DEX	22	DC	887	1.56 e	1.75 e	12	4.0	B	3
§	Ethyl Corp	EY	10	DC	1,938	0.80 e	0.90 e	11	5.1	NR	3
§	Ferro Corp	FOE	24	DC	1,066	1.50 e	1.85 e	13	2.2	B+	3
§	Fuller (HB)	FULL	34	NV	975	2.20 e	2.50 e	14	1.6	B+	3
•	Grace (W.R.)	GRA	39	DC	4,408	0.85 e	3.40 e	11	3.6	B	4
•	Great Lakes Chemical	GLK	57	DC	1,828	4.00 e	4.50 e	13	0.7	A	5
§	Hanna (M.A.)Co	MAH	24	DC	1,520	1.50 e	1.75 e	14	2.2	B-	4
§	Loctite Corp	LOC	47	DC	613	2.15 e	2.50 e	19	1.8	A	3
§	Lubrizol Corp	LZ	34	DC	1,526	2.65 e	2.45 e	14	2.7	B+	2
•	Morton International	MII	29	JE	2,878 *	1.51	1.75 e	16	1.5	B+	5
•	Nalco Chemical	NLC	34	DC	1,389	1.30 e	2.10 e	16	2.8	A	3
§	RPM, Inc	RPOW	19	MY	816 *	0.93	1.10 e	17	2.9	A+	3
§	Schulman (A.)	SHLM	28	AU	749 *	1.19	1.40 e	20	1.0	A	4
	Valspar Corp	VAL	34	OC	787 *	2.08 p	2.20 e	15	1.7	A+	4

Computer Software & Services

	Company	Ticker									
§	Adobe Systems	ADBE	30	NV	313	1.40 e	1.75 e	17	0.6	B	3
•	Autodesk, Inc	ACAD	40	JA	406	1.40 e	1.70 e	23	0.6	B+	4
•	Automatic Data Proc	AUD	59	JE	2,469 *	2.37 y	2.75 e	21	1.0	A+	5
	Banyan Systems	BNYN	18	DC	128	0.90 e	1.15 e	16	Nil	NR	4
§	BMC Software	BMCS	57	MR	289	4.00 e	4.80 e	12	Nil	B+	4
§	Borland Intl	BORL	6	MR	394	d1.85 e	0.20 e	31	Nil	NR	3
§	Cadence Design Sys	CDN	21	DC	369	0.70 e	1.08 e	19	Nil	B-	5
•	Ceridian Corp	CEN	27	DC	886	1.40 e	1.60 e	17	Nil	C	3
§	Comdisco, Inc	CDO	23	SP	2,098 *	2.25 py	2.50 e	9	1.5	B	5
•	Computer Assoc Intl	CA	49	MR	2,148	2.25 e	3.70 e	13	0.4	B+	4
•	Computer Sciences	CSC	51	MR	2,583	2.05 e	2.45 e	21	Nil	B+	3
	Comshare, Inc	CSRE	14	JE	97 *	0.04	0.75 e	19	Nil	C	2
	Continuum Co	CNU	31	MR	243	1.30 e	1.60 e	19	Nil	B	4
	Electronic Arts	ERTS	19	MR	418	1.05 e	1.20 e	16	Nil	B+	4

Peer Comparisons (*Continued*)

•	First Data	FDC	47	DC	1,490	1.90 e	2.25 e	21	0.2	NR	2
§	Genl Motors CI'E'	GME	38	DC	8,562	1.70 e	1.95 e	20	1.2	NR	4
§	Informix Corp	IFMX	32	DC	353	0.95 e	1.25 e	26	Nil	B	4
§	LEGENT Corp	LGNT	29	SP	502 *	1.44 pw	2.30 e	13	Nil	B+	3
•	Lotus Development	LOTS	41	DC	981	d0.30 e	2.00 e	21	Nil	B	3
•	Microsoft Corp	MSFT	61	JE	4,649 *	1.88	2.15 e	28	Nil	B+	5
•	Novell Inc	NOVL	17	OC	1,998 *	0.56 p	1.05 e	16	Nil	B+	4
•	Oracle Systems	ORCL	44	MY	2,001 *	0.96	1.45 e	30	Nil	B	5
§	Parametric Technology	PMTC	35	SP	244 *	1.14 p	1.50 e	23	Nil	NR	4
	PLATINUM technology	PLAT	23	DC	62	0.11 e	0.82 e	28	Nil	NR	3
§	Policy Mgmt Systems	PMS	42	DC	453	1.50 e	2.20 e	19	Nil	NR	3
•	Shared Medical Sys	SMED	33	DC	501	1.50 e	1.70 e	19	2.5	B+	3
	SHL Systemhouse	SHKIF	5	AU	1,161 *	0.29 i	0.55 ei	9	Nil	C	4
	Sierra On-Line	SIER	34	MR	63	d0.30 e	1.00 e	34	Nil	C	1
	Software Publishing	SPCO	5	SP	62 *	d0.40	0.25 e	18	Nil	C	4
	Sterling Software	SSW	37	SP	473 *	2.54	2.50 e	15	Nil	B-	4
§	Structural Dynamics Res	SDRCE	5	DC	186	0.08 e	0.52 e	10	Nil	B+	2
	Sybase Inc	SYBS	52	DC	427	1.20 e	1.85 e	28	Nil	NR	4
§	Symantec Corp	SYMC	18	MR	268	0.75 e	1.15 e	15	Nil	C	3

Computer Systems

	3Com Corp	COMS	52	MY	827 *	d0.46	2.10 e	25	Nil	B-	4
•	Amdahl Corp	AMH	11	DC	1,681	0.40 e	0.50 e	22	Nil	C	2
§	Amer Power Conversion	APCC	16	DC	250	0.75 e	0.93 e	18	Nil	B	3
•	Apple Computer	AAPL	39	SP	9,189 *	2.61	3.20 e	12	1.2	B+	3
	Artisoft Inc	ASFT	8	JE	107 *	0.89	0.70 e	11	Nil	NR	3
§	AST Research	ASTA	15	JE	2,367 *	1.64	d1.50 e	NM	Nil	B-	2
§	Bay Networks	BNET	30	JE	384 *	1.06 f	1.45 e	20	Nil	NR	3
	C-Cube Microsystems	CUBE	19	DC	24	0.25 e	0.70 e	27	Nil	NR	4
§	Cabletron Systems	CS	47	FB	598	2.25 e	2.75 e	17	Nil	B	4
	Chipcom Corp	CHPM	50	DC	150	1.05 e	1.90 e	26	Nil	NR	2
•	Compaq Computer	CPQ	40	DC	7,191	3.28 e	4.00 e	10	Nil	B	4
§	Conner Peripherals	CNR	10	DC	2,152	1.55 e	2.00 e	5	Nil	NR	3
§	Convex Computer	CNX	8	DC	193	d2.05 e	0.20 e	39	Nil	C	2
•	Cray Research	CYR	16	DC	895	2.25 e	1.90 e	8	Nil	B	3
•	Data General	DGN	10	SP	1,121 *	d2.45	0.20 e	50	Nil	C	1
§	Dell Computer Corp	DELL	41	JA	2,873	2.95 e	3.95 e	10	Nil	NR	3
§	Diebold, Inc	DBD	41	DC	623	2.10 e	2.45 e	17	2.1	B+	3
•	Digital Equipment	DEC	33	JE	13,451 *	d15.43 y	d0.60 e	NM	Nil	C	2
§	Exabyte Corp	EXBT	21	DC	310	1.45 e	1.65 e	13	Nil	NR	4
•	Intergraph Corp	INGR	8	DC	1,050	d1.25 ze	d0.10 e	NM	Nil	B-	3
•	Intl Bus. Machines	IBM	74	DC	62,716	4.35 e	6.00 e	12	1.3	B-	4
	Komag Inc	KMAG	26	DC	385	2.55 e	2.90 e	9	Nil	B-	4
	Maxtor Corp	MXTR	6	MR	1,153	d1.65 e	0.10 e	55	Nil	C	2
§	Mentor Graphics	MENT	15	DC	340	0.42 e	0.72 e	21	Nil	C	4
	NetFRAME Systems	NETF	8	DC	67	0.65 e	0.80 e	10	Nil	NR	3
	Pyramid Technology	PYRD	13	SP	219 *	d1.66	0.35 e	37	Nil	C	3
§	Quantum Corp	QNTM	15	MR	2,131	3.70 e	4.00 e	4	Nil	B-	4
§	Seagate Technology	SEG	24	JE	3,500 *	3.08	3.00 e	8	Nil	B	4
§	Sequent Computer Sys	SQNT	20	DC	354	1.10 e	1.45 e	14	Nil	C	4
§	Silicon Graphics	SGI	31	JE	1,482 *	0.91	1.25 e	25	Nil	B-	4
§	Storage Technology	STK	29	DC	1,405	1.35 e	2.50 e	12	Nil	C	4
§	Stratus Computer	SRA	38	DC	514	2.70 e	3.10 e	12	Nil	B+	3
•	Sun Microsystems	SUNW	36	JE	4,690 *	2.02	2.75 e	13	Nil	B	4
§	Symbol Technologies	SBL	31	DC	360	1.31 e	1.45 e	21	Nil	B-	4
•	Tandem Computers	TDM	17	SP	2,108 *	1.50	1.75 e	10	Nil	C	4
•	Unisys Corp	UIS	9	DC	7,743	0.86 e	1.25 e	7	Nil	B-	3

Conglomerates

•	ITT Corp	ITT	89	DC	22,762	7.50 e	8.50 e	10	2.2	B+	4

Peer Comparisons (*Continued*)

•	Teledyne Inc	TDY	20	DC	2,492	d0.05 e	1.50 e	13	Nil	NR	3
•	Tenneco Inc	TGT	43	DC	13,255	3.30 e	3.95 e	11	3.7	B-	5
•	Textron, Inc	TXT	50	DC	9,078	4.80 e	5.35 e	9	2.7	A	5
	Containers (Metals & Glass)										
•	Ball Corp	BLL	32	DC	2,441	1.35 e	1.40 e	23	1.9	B+	2
•	Crown Cork & Seal	CCK	38	DC	4,163	1.45 e	2.40 e	16	Nil	B+	3
	Owens-Illinois	OI	11	DC	3,535	1.00 e	1.05 e	10	Nil	NR	3
	Containers (Paper)										
•	Bemis Co	BMS	24	DC	1,203	1.35 e	1.50 e	16	2.2	A	3
	Sealright Co	SRCO	18	DC	276	1.25 e	1.40 e	13	2.5	B+	4
•	Stone Container	STO	17	DC	5,060	d2.10 e	d0.25 e	NM	Nil	C	3
•	Temple-Inland	TIN	45	DC	2,736	2.15 e	2.75 e	16	2.3	B+	3
	Cosmetics										
•	Alberto-Culver Cl'B'	ACV	27	SP	1,216 *	1.57 o	1.75 e	16	1.0	A	3
•	Avon Products	AVP	60	DC	4,008	3.85 e	4.40 e	14	3.3	B+	4
§	Carter-Wallace	CAR	13	MR	665	d0.85 e	0.80 e	16	2.5	A	3
•	Gillette Co	G	75	DC	1,503 *	3.10 e	3.60 e	21	1.3	A	4
•	Intl Flavors/Fragr	IFF	46	DC	1,189	2.00 e	2.25 e	21	2.6	A+	4
	Maybelline Inc	MAY	18	DC	347	1.25 e	1.80 e	10	1.5	NR	3
§	Tambrands Inc	TMB	39	DC	611	2.50 e	2.70 e	14	4.3	B+	2
	Distributors (Consumer Products)										
•	Fleming Cos	FLM	23	DC	13,092	1.55 e	2.40 e	10	5.1	B+	1
	FoxMeyer Health	FOX	15	MR	5,409	0.70 e	1.15 e	13	Nil	B-	3
•	Supervalu Inc	SVU	24	FB	15,937	0.60 e	2.50 e	10	3.8	A	1
•	Sysco Corp	SYY	26	JE	10,943 *	1.18	1.40 e	18	1.7	A+	4
	Electric Companies										
§	Allegheny Power Sys	AYP	22	DC	2,332	1.95 e	2.00 e	11	7.5	A-	3
•	Amer Electric Pwr	AEP	33	DC	5,269	2.80 e	2.85 e	12	7.3	B+	3
§	Atlantic Energy	ATE	18	DC	866	1.75 e	1.80 e	10	8.7	A-	2
•	Baltimore Gas & El	BGE	22	DC	2,669	1.90 e	2.05 e	11	6.8	A	3
§	Black Hills Corp	BKH	21	DC	139	1.65 e	1.65 e	13	6.1	A	3
	Boston Edison	BSE	24	DC	1,482	2.40 e	2.50 e	10	7.5	B+	3
•	Carolina Pwr & Lt	CPL	27	DC	2,895	2.20 e	2.30 e	12	6.6	A-	3
	Centerior Energy	CX	9	DC	2,474	1.45 e	1.55 e	6	9.0	B-	1
•	Central & So. West	CSR	23	DC	3,688	2.10 e	2.15 e	11	7.5	A-	3
§	Central La Elec	CNL	23	DC	382	2.05 e	2.10 e	11	6.2	A-	3
§	Central Maine Power	CTP	14	DC	894	1.20 e	1.20 e	11	6.6	B	2
•	CINergy Corp	CIN	24	DC	1,752	1.90 e	2.05 e	11	7.3	B	3
§	CMS Energy	CMS	23	DC	3,482	2.10 e	2.20 e	10	3.6	B	3
•	Consolidated Edison	ED	26	DC	6,265	2.90 e	2.65 e	10	7.7	A	3
§	Delmarva Pwr & Lt	DEW	18	DC	971	1.60 e	1.80 e	10	8.4	B+	3
•	Detroit Edison	DTE	26	DC	3,555	2.60 e	2.65 e	10	7.8	A-	3
•	Dominion Resources	D	36	DC	4,434	3.15 e	3.20 e	11	7.1	A	3
	DPL Inc	DPL	21	DC	1,151	1.50 e	1.55 e	13	5.7	B+	3
	DQE	DQE	30	DC	1,196	2.85 e	3.00 e	10	5.9	B+	3
•	Duke Power	DUK	38	DC	4,282	3.00 e	3.05 e	13	5.1	A-	3
	Eastern Util Assoc	EUA	22	DC	566	2.50 e	2.40 e	9	7.0	B+	4
•	Entergy Corp(New)	ETR	22	DC	4,485	1.85 e	2.35 e	9	8.2	B	3
§	Florida Progress	FPC	30	DC	2,449	2.25 e	2.50 e	12	6.7	A-	4
•	FPL Group	FPL	35	DC	5,316	2.90 e	3.05 e	12	4.7	B	4
	Genl Public Util	GPU	26	DC	3,596	1.40 e	2.90 e	9	6.8	B	3
§	Hawaiian Elec Indus	HE	32	DC	1,142	2.50 e	2.65 e	12	7.2	A-	3
•	Houston Indus	HOU	36	DC	4,324	3.45 e	3.25 e	11	8.4	B+	3
§	Idaho Power	IDA	24	DC	540	1.85 e	2.05 e	11	7.9	B	3

Peer Comparisons (*Continued*)

	Company	Ticker									
§	Illinova Corp	ILN	22	DC	1,581	2.00 e	2.10 e	10	4.5	B	3
§	Iowa-Ill Gas & Elec	IWG	20	DC	545	1.90 e	2.00 e	10	8.7	B+	3
§	IPALCO Enterprises	IPL	30	DC	664	2.55 e	2.60 e	12	7.0	B+	3
§	Kansas City Pwr & Lt	KLT	23	DC	857	1.65 e	1.95 e	12	6.5	B+	3
§	LG&E Energy	LGE	37	DC	900	1.65 e	2.85 e	13	5.8	B+	3
	Long Island Light'g	LIL	15	DC	2,881	2.15 e	2.10 e	7	11.5	B	2
§	Magma Power	MGMA	38	DC	167	2.55 e	2.65 e	14	Nil	B	2
	MDU Resources Group	MDU	27	DC	440	2.10 e	2.20 e	12	5.8	B+	3
§	Minnesota Pwr & Lt	MPL	25	DC	506	2.25 e	2.30 e	11	8.0	A-	3
§	Montana Power	MTP	23	DC	1,076	2.05 e	2.15 e	11	6.9	B+	4
§	Nevada Power	NVP	20	DC	652	1.80 e	1.75 e	12	7.8	B+	3
§	New England El Sys	NES	32	DC	2,234	3.15 e	3.20 e	10	7.1	A-	3
§	New York State E&G	NGE	19	DC	1,800	2.10 e	2.30 e	8	7.3	B	3
•	Niagara Mohawk Pwr	NMK	14	DC	3,933	0.90 e	1.50 e	10	7.8	B	2
§	NIPSCO Industries	NI	30	DC	1,678	2.45 e	2.55 e	12	5.2	B	4
§	Northeast Utilities	NU	22	DC	3,629	2.25 e	2.30 e	9	8.1	B	3
•	Northern States Pwr	NSP	44	DC	2,404	3.45 e	3.50 e	13	6.0	A-	3
•	Ohio Edison	OEC	19	DC	2,370	1.95 e	2.00 e	9	8.1	B	3
§	Oklahoma Gas & Elec	OGE	33	DC	1,447	3.15 e	3.20 e	10	8.0	A-	3
•	Pacific Gas & Elec	PCG	24	DC	10,582	2.55 e	2.85 e	9	8.0	B	2
•	PacifiCorp	PPW	18	DC	3,412	1.45 e	1.65 e	11	5.9	B+	5
•	PECO Energy	PE	25	DC	3,988	1.85 e	2.60 e	9	6.6	B	3
§	Pinnacle West Capital	PNW	20	DC	1,719	1.95 e	2.00 e	10	4.5	B	4
§	Portland Genl Corp	PGN	19	DC	947	2.00 e	2.00 e	10	6.2	B	2
§	Potomac Electric Pwr	POM	18	DC	1,725	1.85 e	1.90 e	10	9.0	A-	3
§	Public Svc Colorado	PSR	29	DC	1,999	2.25 e	2.50 e	12	6.8	B+	3
•	Public Svc Enterpr	PEG	27	DC	5,706	2.75 e	2.80 e	9	8.1	B+	3
§	Public Svc New Mexico	PNM	13	DC	874	1.65 e	1.35 e	10	Nil	B	3
§	Puget Sound P&L	PSD	20	DC	1,113	1.63 e	1.90 e	11	9.1	B+	3
	San Diego Gas & El	SDO	19	DC	1,980	1.15 e	1.90 e	10	7.8	A	2
§	SCANA Corp	SCG	42	DC	1,264	3.40 e	3.65 e	12	6.6	A-	4
•	SCEcorp	SCE	15	DC	7,821	1.55 e	1.60 e	9	6.8	B+	3
	Sierra Pacific Resources	SRP	19	DC	528	1.75 e	1.80 e	10	5.9	B	3
•	Southern Co	SO	20	DC	8,489	1.50 e	1.60 e	13	5.9	A-	3
§	Southwestern Pub Sv	SPS	27	AU	843 *	2.38	2.45 e	11	8.3	A-	2
§	TECO Energy	TE	20	DC	1,284	1.30 e	1.55 e	13	4.9	A	3
•	Texas Utilities	TXU	32	DC	5,435	2.55 e	2.80 e	11	9.6	B+	2
•	Unicom Corp	UCM	24	DC	5,260	1.50 e	2.40 e	10	6.6	B	3
•	Union Electric	UEP	35	DC	2,066	2.95 e	3.00 e	12	6.8	A-	3
	United Illuminating	UIL	30	DC	653	3.30 e	3.40 e	9	9.3	B	3
§	UtiliCorp United	UCU	27	DC	1,572	2.15 e	2.25 e	12	6.4	A-	3
	Western Resources	WR	29	DC	1,909	2.89 e	2.64 e	11	6.9	A-	3
§	Wisconsin Energy Corp	WEC	26	DC	1,644	1.65 e	2.10 e	12	5.4	A	3
§	WPL Holdings	WPH	27	DC	773	2.45 e	2.30 e	12	7.0	A	3

Electrical Equipment

	Company	Ticker									
•	AMP Inc	AMP	73	DC	3,451	3.50 e	4.00 e	18	2.3	A-	4
•	Emerson Electric	EMR	62	SP	8,607 *	4.04 y	3.85 e	16	2.7	A+	4
•	Genl Electric	GE	51	DC	60,562	3.30 e	3.85 e	13	3.2	A+	5
•	Genl Signal	GSX	32	DC	1,530	2.30 e	2.60 e	12	3.0	B-	4
•	Grainger (W.W.)	GWW	58	DC	2,628	3.35 e	3.80 e	15	1.3	A+	4
•	Honeywell, Inc	HON	32	DC	5,963	2.15 e	2.50 e	13	3.1	B	3
•	Raychem Corp	RYC	36	JE	1,462 *	0.04	0.16 e	223	0.8	B-	4
§	Sensormatic Elect	SRM	36	JE	656 *	1.16	1.44 e	25	0.6	B+	4
•	Thomas & Betts	TNB	67	DC	1,076	3.50 e	4.00 e	17	3.3	B+	4
•	Westinghouse Elec	WX	12	DC	8,875	0.65 e	0.80 e	15	1.6	B	4

Electronics (Defense)

	Company	Ticker									
	Alliant Techsystems	ATK	41	MR	775	0.84 e	3.65 e	11	Nil	NR	3
•	E G & G Inc	EGG	14	DC	2,698	d0.25 e	1.20 e	12	3.9	A	2

Peer Comparisons (*Continued*)

•	E-Systems	ESY	42	DC	2,097	2.96 e	4.00 e	10	2.8	A	3
•	Loral Corp	LOR	38	MR	4,008	3.30 e	3.70 e	10	1.5	A+	5
	Watkins-Johnson	WJ	30	DC	286	2.45 e	2.80 e	11	1.6	B	4

Electronics (*Instruments*)

§	AMETEK, Inc	AME	17	DC	732	1.05 e	1.35 e	13	1.4	B	4
§	Beckman Instruments	BEC	28	DC	876	1.60 e	2.40 e	12	1.4	NR	4
•	Hewlett-Packard	HWP	100	OC	24,991 *	6.14 p	7.35 e	14	1.2	A	4
•	Perkin-Elmer	PKN	26	JE	1,024 *	1.14	2.00 e	13	2.6	B-	4
•	Tektronix Inc	TEK	34	MY	1,318 *	2.00	2.45 e	14	1.7	B-	4
§	Thermo Electron	TMO	45	DC	1,250	2.10 e	2.55 e	18	Nil	B+	5
§	Varian Associates	VAR	35	SP	1,552 *	2.22	2.50 e	14	0.6	B+	3

Electronics (*Semiconductors*)

•	Advanced Micro Dev	AMD	25	DC	1,648	3.50 e	3.60 e	7	Nil	B-	4
§	Altera Corp	ALTR	42	DC	140	1.57 e	1.75 e	24	Nil	B-	1
§	Analog Devices	ADI	35	OC	773 *	1.45 p	1.70 e	21	Nil	B-	2
§	Applied Materials	AMAT	42	OC	1,660 *	2.51 w	3.15 e	13	Nil	B	3
§	Arrow Electronics	ARW	36	DC	2,536	2.90 e	3.60 e	10	Nil	B-	3
§	Atmel Corp	ATML	34	DC	222	1.30 e	1.55 e	22	Nil	NR	2
§	Avnet, Inc	AVT	37	JE	3,548 *	2.16 y	2.90 e	13	1.6	A-	4
	Brooktree Corp	BTRE	9	SP	109 *	0.12 p	0.35 e	24	Nil	NR	3
	Chips/Technologies	CHPS	7	JE	73 *	0.16	0.40 e	18	Nil	NR	4
§	Cirrus Logic	CRUS	23	MR	544	1.93 e	2.39 e	9	Nil	B-	4
§	Cypress Semiconductor	CY	23	DC	305	1.20 e	1.35 e	17	Nil	B	2
	Exar Corp	EXAR	25	MR	162	1.45 e	1.70 e	14	Nil	B-	4
	GenRad, Inc	GEN	6	DC	159	0.27 e	0.50 e	12	Nil	C	4
	Integrated Circuit Sys	ICST	8	JE	94 *	1.11	1.25 e	6	Nil	NR	4
•	Intel Corp	INTC	64	DC	8,782	5.95 e	6.25 e	10	0.3	B	4
	Intl Rectifier	IRF	24	JE	329 *	0.78	1.35 e	18	Nil	B-	3
§	Linear Technology Corp	LLTC	50	JE	201 *	1.51	2.00 e	25	0.5	B+	2
§	LSI Logic	LSI	40	DC	719	1.87 e	2.20 e	18	Nil	C	2
	Maxim Integrated Prod	MXIM	35	JE	154 *	0.75	0.97 e	36	Nil	B	1
•	Micron Technology	MU	44	AU	1,629 *	3.83	5.00 e	9	0.4	B-	1
•	Motorola, Inc	MOT	58	DC	16,963	2.50 e	3.00 e	19	0.6	A	4
•	Natl Semiconductor	NSM	20	MY	2,295 *	1.98 w	1.90 e	10	Nil	B-	3
	Solectron Corp	SLR	28	AU	1,457 *	1.32	1.54 e	18	Nil	B	4
§	Teradyne Inc	TER	34	DC	555	1.88 e	2.35 e	14	Nil	B-	2
•	Texas Instruments	TXN	75	DC	8,523	7.30 e	8.10 e	9	1.3	B-	3
	VLSI Technology	VLSI	12	DC	516	0.85 e	1.25 e	10	Nil	C	4
§	Xilinx Inc	XLNX	59	MR	256	2.00 e	2.77 e	21	Nil	NR	1

Engineering & Construction

•	Fluor Corp	FLR	43	OC	8,485 *	2.32 p	2.70 e	16	1.3	B	4
•	Foster Wheeler	FWC	30	DC	2,583	1.80 e	2.05 e	15	2.4	A-	4
§	Granite Construction	GCCO	20	DC	570	1.10 e	1.35 e	15	0.9	NR	3
§	Jacobs Engr Group	JEC	19	SP	1,166 *	0.75	1.40 e	13	Nil	B	4
•	Morrison Knudsen	MRN	13	DC	2,723	d0.95 e	0.80 e	16	6.2	B-	2
•	Zurn Indus	ZRN	18	MR	786	0.90 e	1.20 e	15	4.8	A-	3

Entertainment

	Acclaim Entertainment	AKLM	14	AU	481 *	1.00	1.10 e	13	Nil	NR	4
•	Disney (Walt) Co	DIS	46	SP	10,055 *	2.04	2.40 e	19	0.6	A	2
•	King World Prod'ns	KWP	35	AU	481 *	2.33	2.95 e	12	Nil	B+	3
•	Time Warner Inc	TWX	35	DC	14,544	d0.10 e	0.15 e	234	1.0	B-	4
•	Viacom Inc Cl'B'	VIA.B	41	DC	2,005	d1.00 e	1.00 e	41	Nil	NR	3

Financial Miscellaneous

	Alliance Cap Mgmt L.P.	AC	19	DC	500	1.73 e	1.95 e	10	8.8	NR	4
•	Amer Express	AXP	30	DC	14,173	2.75 e	3.20 e	9	3.0	B	5

Peer Comparisons (*Continued*)

•	Amer General	AGC	28	DC	4,829	3.00 e	3.25 e	9	4.1	B+	4
	Eaton Vance	EAVN	28	OC	218 *	3.00 pwo	3.40 e	8	2.2	A-	4
•	Federal Home Loan	FRE	51	DC	5,456	5.35 e	5.85 e	9	2.0	NR	4
•	Federal Natl Mtge	FNM	73	DC	16,053	7.85 e	8.90 e	8	3.2	A-	4
§	First Financial Mgmt	FFM	62	DC	1,670	2.55 e	3.05 e	20	0.1	B+	5
§	Franklin Resources	BEN	36	SP	827 *	3.00 p	3.20 e	11	1.1	A	4
	Student Loan Mktg	SLM	33	DC	2,417	5.15 e	5.25 e	6	4.5	A	2
	SunAmerica Inc	SAI	36	SP	884	3.58 y	4.35 e	8	1.6	B+	5
	T.Rowe Price Assoc	TROW	30	DC	310	2.00 e	2.25 e	13	2.1	B+	4
•	Transamerica Corp	TA	50	DC	4,833	4.95 e	5.65 e	9	4.0	B	3
•	Travelers Inc(New)	TRV	32	DC	6,797	3.95 e	4.50 e	7	1.8	B+	4
	United Asset Mgmt	UAM	37	DC	450	2.10 e	2.30 e	16	2.8	B+	5

Foods

•	Archer-Daniels-Midland	ADM	21	JE	11,374 *	0.93	1.25 e	17	0.4	A+	4
	Borden, Inc	BN	12	DC	5,506	d0.20 e	0.55 e	22	Nil	B-	2
•	Campbell Soup	CPB	44	JL	6,690 *	2.51	2.80 e	16	2.8	B	4
•	ConAgra Inc	CAG	31	MY	23,512 *	1.81	2.05 e	15	2.6	A+	4
•	CPC Intl	CPC	53	DC	6,738	2.25 e	3.55 e	15	2.7	A+	4
§	Dean Foods	DF	29	MY	2,431 *	1.78 w	2.10 e	14	2.3	A	3
§	Dole Food Co	DOL	23	DC	3,431	1.35 e	1.95 e	12	1.7	B	3
§	Dreyer's Gr Ice Cr	DRYR	25	DC	471	0.11 e	0.45 e	55	0.9	B	2
	Eskimo Pie	EPIE	19	DC	66	1.50 e	1.64 e	11	1.0	NR	2
§	Flowers Indus	FLO	18	JE	990 *	0.80	1.10 e	16	4.4	B+	2
•	Genl Mills	GIS	57	MY	8,517 *	2.95	3.70 e	15	3.2	A	3
	Grand Metropolitan ADS	GRM	25	SP	12,367	1.95 e	2.10 e	12	3.7	NR	3
•	Heinz (H.J.)	HNZ	37	AP	7,047 *	2.35	2.35 e	16	3.9	A+	3
•	Hershey Foods	HSY	48	DC	3,488	3.00 e	3.30 e	15	2.6	A+	3
	Hormel (Geo A)	HRL	25	OC	3,065 *	1.54 p	1.70 e	15	2.3	A+	4
§	IBP, Inc	IBP	30	DC	11,671	3.45 e	3.65 e	8	0.6	NR	4
	Interstate Bakeries	IBC	14	MY	1,143 *	0.78	1.25 e	11	3.6	NR	3
§	Intl Multifoods	IMC	18	FB	2,225	2.90 e	1.70 e	11	4.3	B+	3
•	Kellogg Co	K	58	DC	6,295	3.15 e	3.40 e	17	2.4	A+	3
§	Lance, Inc	LNCE	18	DC	473	0.95 e	1.00 e	18	5.3	A-	2
§	McCormick & Co	MCCRK	18	NV	1,557	1.35 e	1.50 e	12	2.8	A	4
§	Michael Foods	MIKL	10	DC	475	0.79 e	0.95 e	10	2.0	NR	3
•	Pet Inc	PT	20	JE	1,582 *	0.86 y	1.15 e	17	1.8	NR	3
•	Quaker Oats	OAT	31	JE	5,955 *	1.68	2.00 e	15	3.7	A-	3
•	Ralston-Purina Group	RAL	45	SP	7,705 *	2.12 py	2.80 e	16	2.6	B+	4
•	Sara Lee Corp	SLE	25	JE	15,536 *	0.44 y	1.65 e	15	2.6	A	4
§	Smucker (J.M.) Cl'A'	SJM.A	24	AP	512 *	1.05 o	1.35 e	18	2.0	A	2
§	Tyson Foods Cl'A'	TYSNA	21	SP	5,110 *	d0.01 o	1.55 e	14	0.3	A	4
§	Univl Foods	UFC	28	SP	930 *	1.95	2.15 e	13	3.4	A	5
•	Wrigley, (Wm) Jr	WWY	49	DC	1,429	1.98 we	2.00 e	25	1.1	A+	3

Gold Mining

	Amax Gold Inc	AU	6	DC	82	d0.25 e	d0.06 e	NM	Nil	C	4
•	Amer Barrick Res	ABX	22	DC	668	0.78 e	0.90 e	25	0.4	B+	5
§	Battle Mtn Gold	BMG	11	DC	193	0.10 e	0.20 e	55	0.4	NR	5
•	Echo Bay Mines	ECO	11	DC	367	d0.15 e	0.25 e	43	0.7	B-	4
	Hecla Mining	HL	10	DC	82	d0.25 e	0.10 e	101	Nil	C	5
•	Homestake Mining	HM	17	DC	722	0.65 xe	0.85 e	20	1.1	B-	5
	Newmont Gold	NGC	36	DC	602	0.75 e	1.17 e	30	1.3	B+	4
•	Newmont Mining	NEM	36	DC	634	0.75 e	1.08 e	33	1.3	B	4
•	Placer Dome Inc	PDG	22	DC	917	0.40 e	0.55 e	40	1.3	B-	4

Hardware & Tools

•	Black & Decker Corp	BDK	24	DC	4,882	1.30 e	1.60 e	15	1.6	B-	4
•	Snap-On Inc	SNA	33	DC	1,132	2.30 e	2.45 e	14	3.2	B+	3
•	Stanley Works	SWK	36	DC	2,273	2.75 e	3.15 e	11	3.9	B+	4

Peer Comparisons (*Continued*)

Health Care (Diversified)											
•	Abbott Laboratories	ABT	33	DC	8,408	1.85 e	2.05 e	16	2.3	A+	4
•	Allergan, Inc	AGN	28	DC	859	1.70 e	1.85 e	15	1.5	NR	3
•	Amer Home Products	AHP	63	DC	8,305	4.90 e	4.60 e	14	4.7	A+	3
•	Bristol-Myers Squibb	BMY	58	DC	11,413	4.60 e	4.80 e	12	5.1	A+	3
•	Johnson & Johnson	JNJ	55	DC	14,138	3.05 e	3.35 e	16	2.1	A+	4
•	Mallinckrodt Group	MKG	30	JE	1,940 *	1.33	2.40 e	12	1.8	B	3
•	Warner-Lambert	WLA	77	DC	5,794	5.15 e	5.60 e	14	3.1	A-	4
	Health Care (Drugs)										
	Glaxo Hldg plc ADR	GLX	20	JE	8,484 *	1.29	1.45 e	14	4.3	NR	3
	Immunex Corp	IMNX	15	DC	95	d0.90 e	d0.50 e	NM	Nil	C	3
§	IVAX Corp	IVX	19	DC	645	1.16 e	1.30 e	15	0.3	B-	3
•	Lilly (Eli)	LLY	66	DC	6,452	4.76 e	4.48 e	15	3.9	A	3
	Marion Merrell Dow	MKC	20	DC	2,818	1.50 e	1.30 e	16	4.9	A	3
•	Merck & Co	MRK	38	DC	10,498	2.40 e	2.65 e	14	3.1	A+	4
§	Mylan Labs	MYL	27	MR	252	1.35 e	1.55 e	17	0.7	A-	4
•	Pfizer, Inc	PFE	77	DC	7,478	4.15 e	4.80 e	16	2.4	A-	5
	Rhone-Poulenc Rorer	RPR	37	DC	4,019	2.40 e	3.30 e	11	3.0	B+	3
•	Schering-Plough	SGP	74	DC	4,341	4.80 e	5.40 e	14	2.7	A+	4
	SmithKline Beecham ADS	SBH	36	DC	8,939	2.30 e	2.50 e	14	2.8	NR	3
•	Upjohn Co	UPJ	31	DC	3,611	2.70 e	2.50 e	12	4.8	A	3
	Health Care (Miscellaneous)										
•	ALZA Corp	AZA	18	DC	234	1.05 e	1.20 e	15	Nil	B	3
•	Amgen Inc	AMGN	59	DC	1,374	3.05 e	3.60 e	16	Nil	B-	4
•	Beverly Enterprises	BEV	14	DC	2,871	0.85 e	1.00 e	14	Nil	B-	3
§	Biogen Inc	BGEN	42	DC	149	0.35 e	0.03 e	NM	Nil	B-	4
§	Chiron Corp	CHIR	80	DC	318	1.00 e	1.65 e	49	Nil	C	3
	Genentech Inc	GNE	46	DC	650	1.05 e	1.30 e	35	Nil	NR	4
•	Manor Care	MNR	27	MY	1,163 *	1.29	1.45 e	19	0.3	A-	4
	PacifiCare Health Sys'A'	PHSYA	65	SP	2,893 *	3.02 wo	3.80 e	17	Nil	B+	3
•	U.S. HealthCare	USHC	41	DC	2,645	2.40 e	2.95 e	14	2.0	B+	4
•	United Healthcare	UNH	45	DC	2,527	1.75 e	2.25 e	20	Nil	B	4
	Wellpoint Hlth Networks'A'	WLP	29	DC	2,449	2.11 e	2.50 e	12	Nil	NR	4
	Heavy Duty Trucks & Parts										
•	Cummins Engine	CUM	45	DC	4,248	6.00 e	6.25 e	7	2.2	B-	3
•	Dana Corp	DCN	24	DC	5,460	2.20 e	2.45 e	10	3.5	B-	2
•	Eaton Corp	ETN	50	DC	4,401	4.20 e	4.65 e	11	2.4	B	3
§	Federal Signal	FSS	20	DC	565	0.99 e	1.15 e	18	2.0	A+	3
•	Navistar Intl	NAV	15	OC	5,337 *	0.72 p	1.45 e	10	Nil	C	3
•	PACCAR Inc	PCAR	44	DC	3,379	5.15 e	5.35 e	8	4.5	B+	4
	Wabash National	WNC	39	DC	360	1.40 e	1.73 e	23	0.2	NR	3
	Homebuilding										
•	Centex Corp	CTX	23	MR	3,214	3.20 e	2.20 e	10	0.8	B+	3
•	Kaufman & Broad Home	KBH	13	NV	1,238	1.15 e	1.35 e	10	2.3	B+	3
	Lennar Corp	LEN	16	NV	667	1.93 e	2.20 e	7	0.6	A-	5
•	Pulte Corp	PHM	23	DC	1,633	2.35 e	2.60 e	9	1.0	B+	3
	Ryland Group	RYL	15	DC	1,474	1.60 e	1.90 e	8	4.0	B+	5
	U.S. Home	UH	16	DC	799	2.80 e	3.15 e	5	Nil	NR	5
	Hospital Management										
•	Columbia/HCA Hlthcare	COL	37	DC	10,252	2.40 e	2.80 e	13	0.3	NR	4
•	Community Psych Ctrs	CMY	11	NV	336	0.20 e	0.50 e	22	Nil	B	3
§	FHP Int'l Corp	FHPC	26	JE	2,473 *	1.71	1.85 e	14	Nil	NR	3
•	Natl Medical Entpr	NME	14	MY	2,967 *	d2.90 w	1.35 e	10	Nil	NR	4

Peer Comparisons (*Continued*)

Hotel-Motel											
	Aztar Corp	AZR	6	DC	519	0.45 e	0.45 e	13	Nil	NR	4
	Boomtown Inc	BMTN	16	SP	103 *	d0.89 p	1.10 e	14	Nil	NR	4
§	Caesars World	CAW	67	JL	1,016 *	3.19	3.60 e	19	Nil	B	3
§	Circus Circus Enterp	CIR	23	JA	955	1.60 e	1.95 e	12	Nil	B+	3
•	Hilton Hotels	HLT	68	DC	1,394	2.50 e	3.10 e	22	1.7	B+	3
	Host Marriott	HMT	10	DC	1,354	d0.10 e	d0.05 e	NM	Nil	B-	4
§	Intl Game Technology	IGT	16	SP	674 *	1.07 p	1.20 e	13	0.7	B	4
•	Marriott International	MAR	28	DC	8,062	1.50 e	1.75 e	16	0.9	NR	3
§	Mirage Resorts	MIR	21	DC	953	1.30 e	1.35 e	15	Nil	B-	4
	Prime Hospitality	PDQ	8	DC	109	0.35 e	0.55 e	14	Nil	NR	5
•	Promus Cos	PRI	31	DC	1,252	1.30 e	1.65 e	19	Nil	NR	3
Household Furnishings & Appliances											
•	Armstrong World Indus	ACK	39	DC	2,525	4.75 e	5.30 e	7	3.3	B+	4
•	Bassett Furniture	BSET	29	NV	511 *	1.75 p	1.90 e	15	2.8	B	3
	Ethan Allen Interiors	ETH	24	JE	437 *	1.53	1.88 e	13	Nil	NR	4
	Fedders Corp	FJQ	7	AU	232 *	0.61 w	0.77 e	9	Nil	C	4
§	Heilig-Meyers	HMY	25	FB	864	1.38 e	1.65 e	15	0.9	A+	5
	La-Z Boy Chair	LZB	32	AP	805 *	1.90 w	2.20 e	14	2.1	A-	4
	LADD Furniture	LADF	7	DC	521	0.40 e	0.65 e	10	1.8	B-	4
§	Leggett & Platt	LEG	35	DC	1,527	2.68 e	3.05 e	11	1.8	A	4
•	Maytag Corp	MYG	15	DC	2,987	1.55 e	1.55 e	10	3.3	B-	4
	Mohawk Industries	MOHK	13	DC	1,195	1.40 e	1.65 e	8	Nil	NR	1
§	Natl Presto Indus	NPK	42	DC	119	2.48 e	2.65 e	16	4.5	B+	2
§	Shaw Indus	SHX	15	DC	2,321	1.00 e	1.10 e	14	1.4	A	4
•	Whirlpool Corp	WHR	50	DC	7,533	4.45 e	5.00 e	10	2.4	B+	4
•	Zenith Electronics	ZE	12	DC	1,228	0.30 e	1.50 e	8	Nil	C	4
Household Products											
§	Church & Dwight	CHD	18	DC	508	0.35 e	0.60 e	30	2.4	A	1
•	Clorox Co	CLX	59	JE	1,837 *	3.94	3.75 e	16	3.2	A	4
•	Colgate-Palmolive	CL	63	DC	7,141	3.80 e	4.35 e	15	2.5	B+	4
•	Kimberly-Clark	KMB	50	DC	6,973	3.60 e	4.10 e	12	3.4	A+	3
•	Procter & Gamble	PG	62	JE	30,296 *	3.09	3.65 e	17	2.2	A-	4
•	Scott Paper	SPP	69	DC	4,749	2.50 e	4.40 e	16	1.1	B	4
§	Stanhome Inc	STH	32	DC	751	2.58 e	2.80 e	11	3.3	A-	3
	Unilever ADR	UL	73	DC	41,168	4.60 e	5.20 e	14	2.2	NR	3
•	Unilever N.V.	UN	117	DC	39,865	8.10 e	9.00 e	13	2.3	A-	3
Housewares											
•	Newell Co	NWL	21	DC	1,645	1.25 e	1.40 e	15	1.9	A+	3
•	Premark Intl	PMI	45	DC	3,097	3.20 e	3.50 e	13	1.7	NR	4
•	Rubbermaid, Inc	RBD	29	DC	1,960	1.45 e	1.65 e	17	1.7	A+	4
Insurance Brokers											
•	Alexander & Alex Sv	AAL	19	DC	1,342	0.45 e	0.50 e	37	0.5	B-	3
•	Marsh & McLennan	MMC	79	DC	3,163	5.35 e	6.05 e	13	3.6	A+	4
Leisure Time											
•	Bally Entertainment	BLY	6	DC	1,320	BE e	0.40 e	15	Nil	C	3
•	Brunswick Corp	BC	19	DC	2,207	1.30 e	1.60 e	12	2.3	B	4
	Carnival Corp'A'	CCL	21	NV	1,806 *	1.35 p	1.62 e	13	1.4	B+	4
	Discovery Zone	ZONE	12	DC	59	0.40 e	0.65 e	18	Nil	NR	2
•	Handleman Co	HDL	11	AP	1,067 *	0.83	1.15 e	10	3.8	A-	3
§	Harley-Davidson	HDI	28	DC	1,217	1.35 e	1.60 e	18	0.5	B+	4
•	Outboard Marine	OM	20	SP	1,078 *	2.42	2.70 xe	7	2.0	B-	3

Peer Comparisons (*Continued*)

Life Insurance											
§	AFLAC Inc	AFL	32	DC	5,001	2.80 e	3.25 e	10	1.4	A	4
	Conseco Inc	CNC	43	DC	2,636	7.00 e	7.50 e	6	1.1	B+	3
•	Jefferson-Pilot	JP	52	DC	1,247	4.10 e	4.50 e	12	3.3	A-	3
•	Lincoln Natl Corp	LNC	35	DC	8,297	3.25 e	4.25 e	8	4.9	B+	3
§	Provident Life and Accid'B'	PVB	22	DC	2,938	3.10 e	3.35 e	6	4.7	B	4
•	Providian Corp	PVN	31	DC	2,884	3.65 e	4.00 e	8	2.9	A	4
•	Torchmark Corp	TMK	35	DC	2,177	3.90 e	4.50 e	8	3.2	A+	3
•	UNUM Corp	UNM	38	DC	3,397	2.25 e	4.25 e	9	2.5	NR	3
•	USLIFE Corp	USH	35	DC	1,600	4.25 e	4.65 e	7	3.7	B+	3
Machine Tools											
•	Cincinnati Milacron	CMZ	24	DC	1,029	1.30 e	1.76 e	13	1.5	B-	4
•	Giddings & Lewis	GIDL	15	DC	517	1.00 e	1.20 e	12	0.8	NR	4
Machinery (Diversified)											
	AMTROL, Inc	AMTL	17	DC	164	1.50 e	1.80 e	9	1.1	NR	2
•	Briggs & Stratton	BGG	33	JE	1,286 *	3.54 y	3.50 e	9	3.0	B+	3
	BW/IP Inc	BWIP	17	DC	427	1.15 e	1.45 e	12	2.3	NR	3
	Case Corp	CSE	22	DC	3,890	1.40 e	1.70 e	13	0.9	NR	4
•	Caterpillar Inc	CAT	55	DC	11,615	4.37 e	5.25 e	11	1.8	B-	3
•	Clark Equipment	CKL	54	DC	875	2.70 e	7.65 e	7	Nil	C	3
•	Cooper Indus	CBE	34	DC	6,274	2.05 e	2.20 e	15	3.8	A	3
•	Deere & Co	DE	66	OC	9,030 *	7.01 p	8.50 e	8	3.3	B	4
§	Donaldson Co	DCI	24	JL	594 *	1.17 w	1.35 e	18	1.1	A	3
§	Duriron Co	DURI	18	DC	314	1.00 e	1.20 e	15	2.3	B+	3
§	Goulds Pumps	GULD	22	DC	556	1.00 e	1.40 e	15	3.6	B+	3
•	Harnischfeger Indus	HPH	28	OC	1,140 *	0.70 yp	1.25 e	23	1.4	B	3
•	Ingersoll-Rand	IR	32	DC	4,021	1.96 e	2.40 e	13	2.3	B+	3
§	Keystone Intl	KII	17	DC	516	0.95 e	1.10 e	16	4.2	B+	4
§	Lawson Products	LAWS	26	DC	196	1.45 e	1.65 e	16	1.8	A-	3
	Lindsay Mfg	LINZ	30	AU	113 *	2.31 w	2.35 e	13	Nil	NR	3
•	NACCO Indus Inc Cl'A'	NC	48	DC	1,549	4.05 e	5.10 e	9	1.4	B+	4
§	Pentair, Inc	PNTA	43	DC	1,328	2.50 e	2.85 e	15	1.6	B+	4
§	Stewart & Stevenson	SSSS	35	JA	982	2.05 e	2.40 e	14	0.8	B	3
§	Tecumseh Products Cl'A'	TECUA	45	DC	1,314	5.20 e	5.60 e	8	2.2	B+	4
•	Timken Co	TKR	35	DC	1,709	2.00 e	2.70 e	13	2.8	B-	3
•	Varity Corp	VAT	36	JA	2,726	2.40 e	2.75 e	13	Nil	B-	4
§	Watts Industries'A'	WATTA	21	JE	519 *	1.38 o	1.55 e	14	1.0	A-	4
Major Regional Banks											
•	Banc One Corp	ONE	25	DC	7,227	2.60 e	3.40 e	7	4.8	A+	3
§	Bancorp Hawaii	BOH	25	DC	938	2.75 e	3.50 e	7	4.0	A+	2
•	Bank of Boston	BKB	26	DC	7,396	3.60 e	4.00 e	6	4.1	B-	4
	Bank South Corp	BKSO	18	DC	467	1.55 e	1.75 e	10	2.9	B-	3
•	Barnett Banks Inc	BBI	39	DC	3,130	4.75 e	5.35 e	7	4.2	A-	3
	BayBanks Inc	BBNK	53	DC	789	4.95 e	5.90 e	9	3.4	B+	4
•	Boatmen's Bancshares	BOAT	27	DC	2,107	3.40 e	3.60 e	8	5.0	A	3
§	City National	CYN	11	DC	216	0.85 e	0.95 e	11	1.8	C	3
	Commerce Bancshares	CBSH	27	DC	582	2.86 e	3.00 e	9	2.3	A+	3
•	CoreStates Financial	CFL	26	DC	2,014	1.80 e	3.40 e	8	5.2	A-	3
§	Crestar Financial	CF	38	DC	1,081	4.45 e	5.05 e	7	4.2	B+	4
§	Fifth Third Bancorp	FITB	48	DC	954	3.80 e	4.35 e	11	2.5	A+	4
§	First Bank System	FBS	33	DC	2,231	3.50 e	3.95 e	8	3.4	B-	4
	First Commerce	FCOM	22	DC	496	2.80 e	3.90 e	6	5.4	B+	4
	First Empire State	FES	136	DC	851	15.95 e	18.30 e	7	1.7	A+	4
•	First Fidelity Bancorp	FFB	45	DC	2,429	5.20 e	5.70 e	8	4.4	B	4
	First Hawaiian	FHWN	24	DC	512	2.45 e	2.70 e	9	4.9	A	3
•	First Interstate Bancorp	I	68	DC	3,898	8.60 e	10.80 e	6	4.4	B-	4
§	First of America Bk	FOA	30	DC	1,857	4.10 e	4.70 e	6	5.6	A	4
§	First Security	FSCO	23	DC	812	2.90 e	3.19 e	7	4.5	A-	3

Peer Comparisons (*Continued*)

§	First Tenn Natl	FTEN	41	DC	857	1.14 e	5.00 e	8	4.6	A-	4
•	First Union Corp	FTU	41	DC	5,755	5.30 e	5.65 e	7	4.4	A	4
§	First Virginia Banks	FVB	32	DC	587	3.55 e	3.80 e	8	4.1	A	4
•	Fleet Financial Group	FLT	32	DC	4,677	3.80 e	4.85 e	7	4.9	B+	4
	Hibernia Corp Cl'A'	HIB	8	DC	367	0.90 e	1.10 e	7	3.0	C	3
	Huntington Bancshares	HBAN	17	DC	1,542	1.95 e	2.05 e	8	4.6	A-	4
	Integra Finl Corp	ITG	41	DC	1,084	5.00 e	5.25 e	8	4.3	NR	3
•	KeyCorp(New)	KEY	25	DC	5,216	3.50 e	3.75 e	7	5.1	A+	3
§	Marshall & Ilsley	MRIS	19	DC	787	1.05 e	2.10 e	9	3.1	A	2
•	Mellon Bank Corp	MEL	31	DC	3,622	2.50 e	4.45 e	7	5.8	B-	3
§	Mercantile Bancorp	MTL	31	DC	893	3.75 e	4.05 e	8	3.5	B+	4
§	Mercantile Bankshares	MRBK	20	DC	455	1.90 e	2.10 e	9	4.0	A	3
§	Meridian Bancorp	MRDN	27	DC	1,247	2.75 e	3.35 e	8	5.1	A-	3
	Midlantic Corp	MIDL	27	DC	1,012	3.80 e	3.00 e	9	2.5	B-	3
•	NationsBank Corp	NB	45	DC	10,392	6.30 e	6.90 e	7	4.4	A-	3
•	Natl City Corp	NCC	26	DC	2,702	2.70 e	3.00 e	9	4.6	A-	4
•	NBD Bancorp	NBD	27	DC	3,208	3.40 e	3.60 e	8	4.8	A	3
§	Northern Trust	NTRS	35	DC	1,259	3.35 e	3.80 e	9	2.9	B+	5
•	Norwest Corp	NOB	23	DC	5,277	2.45 e	2.85 e	8	3.5	A-	4
	Old Kent Finl	OKEN	30	DC	802	3.50 e	3.60 e	8	4.0	A+	4
•	PNC Bank Corp	PNC	21	DC	4,146	3.20 e	2.80 e	8	6.6	B+	3
§	Regions Financial	RGBK	31	DC	688	3.40 e	3.77 e	8	3.8	A+	4
	Republic New York	RNB	45	DC	2,328	5.60 e	6.10 e	7	2.9	B+	3
•	Shawmut Natl	SNC	16	DC	1,931	1.85 e	3.00 e	5	5.3	B-	3
	Signet Banking	SBK	29	DC	1,169	2.80 e	1.40 e	20	3.4	B	4
	Star Banc Corp	STB	36	DC	631	3.90 e	4.15 e	9	3.8	A+	4
§	State Str Boston	STBK	29	DC	1,532	2.70 e	3.00 e	10	2.2	A+	1
	Summit Bancorp'n	SUBN	19	DC	304	1.73 e	1.91 e	10	4.3	A	3
•	SunTrust Banks	STI	48	DC	3,089	4.35 e	4.70 e	10	3.0	A+	3
	Synovus Financial	SNV	18	DC	615	1.30 e	1.50 e	12	2.4	A+	4
	U.S. Trust	USTC	64	DC	446	4.70 e	5.00 e	13	3.1	A	4
§	UJB Financial	UJB	24	DC	1,062	2.45 e	3.08 e	8	4.3	A-	4
	Union Bank	UBNK	27	DC	1,266	1.70 e	3.25 e	8	5.2	A-	3
	Union Planters	UPC	21	DC	483	2.60 e	3.10 e	7	4.4	B+	3
	Valley Natl Bancorp	VLY	27	DC	249	2.30 e	2.50 e	11	3.7	A	4
•	Wachovia Corp	WB	32	DC	2,750	3.10 e	3.40 e	9	4.0	A-	3
•	Wells Fargo	WFC	145	DC	4,854	14.70 e	16.00 e	9	2.7	B+	3
§	Wilmington Trust Corp	WILM	23	DC	405	2.40 e	2.65 e	9	4.7	A+	4
	Zions Bancorp	ZION	36	DC	346	4.40 e	5.05 e	7	3.3	B+	4
	Manufactured Housing										
§	Clayton Homes	CMH	16	JE	628 *	0.94 w	1.12 e	14	0.5	B+	5
•	Fleetwood Enterpr	FLE	19	AP	2,369 *	1.46 y	2.15 e	9	2.9	B+	5
	Oakwood Homes	OH	24	SP	579 *	1.54	1.90 e	13	0.3	B+	4
•	Skyline Corp	SKY	19	MY	580 *	1.34	1.60 e	12	2.5	B+	4
	Manufacturing (Diversified)										
•	AlliedSignal Inc	ALD	34	DC	11,827	2.65 e	3.00 e	11	1.9	B+	4
•	Crane Co	CR	27	DC	1,310	1.80 e	2.10 e	13	2.7	B+	3
§	Danaher Corp	DHR	52	DC	1,076	2.50 e	2.80 e	19	0.3	B	3
•	Dover Corp	DOV	52	DC	2,484	3.45 e	3.90 e	13	2.0	A-	3
	Hanson plc ADR	HAN	18	SP	17,660 *	1.66	1.50 e	12	5.3	NR	4
§	Harsco Corp	HSC	41	DC	1,422	2.95 e	3.30 e	12	3.6	B+	3
•	Illinois Tool Works	ITW	44	DC	3,159	2.35 e	2.90 e	15	1.3	A+	2
	Ionics Inc	ION	63	DC	175	2.20 e	2.50 e	25	Nil	B	3
•	Johnson Controls	JCI	49	SP	6,871 *	3.80	4.30 e	11	3.1	B+	3
§	Kennametal, Inc	KMT	25	JE	803 *	0.45 y	1.75 e	14	2.4	A	4
§	Litton Indus	LIT	37	JL	3,446 *	d2.69 y	2.85 e	13	Nil	B	3
•	Millipore Corp	MIL	48	DC	445	2.55 e	3.05 e	16	1.2	B+	3
•	Pall Corp	PLL	19	JL	701 *	0.86	1.00 e	19	1.9	A	3

Peer Comparisons (*Continued*)

	Company	Ticker									
•	Parker-Hannifin	PH	46	JE	2,576 *	1.07 y	3.55 e	13	2.1	B+	3
	PRI Automation	PRIA	16	SP	19	0.71 p	0.90 e	18	Nil	NR	4
•	TRINOVA Corp	TNV	29	DC	1,644	2.30 e	2.60 e	11	2.3	B-	3
•	Tyco International	TYC	48	JE	3,263 *	2.70	3.10 e	15	0.8	B+	4

Medical Products & Supplies

	Company	Ticker									
§	Acuson Corp	ACN	16	DC	295	0.65 e	0.75 e	22	Nil	B	3
	AMSCO Intl	ASZ	9	DC	503	0.54 e	0.85 e	11	Nil	NR	4
•	Bard (C.R.)	BCR	27	DC	971	1.85 e	2.10 e	13	2.2	A-	4
•	Bausch & Lomb	BOL	34	DC	1,872	2.70 e	3.25 e	10	2.8	A	3
•	Baxter International	BAX	28	DC	8,879	2.15 e	2.35 e	12	3.7	B+	3
•	Becton, Dickinson	BDX	48	SP	2,559 *	3.05	3.25 e	15	1.7	A+	3
•	Biomet, Inc	BMET	14	MY	373 *	0.61	0.70 e	20	Nil	B+	4
§	Cordis Corp	CORD	61	JE	337 *	2.27 w	2.95 e	21	Nil	B-	4
	Hillenbrand Indus	HB	28	NV	1,448	1.25 e	2.40 e	12	2.0	A+	4
	IGEN Inc	IGEN	5	MR	23	0.25 e	0.37 e	15	Nil	NR	4
•	Medtronic, Inc	MDT	56	AP	1,391 *	2.02	2.50 e	22	0.7	A+	4
§	Nellcor Inc	NELL	33	JE	235 *	1.22	1.95 e	17	Nil	B	4
§	SciMed Life Systems	SMLS	51	FB	265	3.15 e	3.70 e	14	Nil	B-	3
•	St. Jude Medical	STJM	40	DC	253	2.20 e	2.50 e	16	Nil	B+	4
§	Stryker Corp	STRY	37	DC	557	1.42 e	1.71 e	21	0.1	A-	3
•	U.S. Surgical	USS	19	DC	1,037	0.20 e	0.75 e	25	0.4	A-	3

Metals Miscellaneous

	Company	Ticker									
•	ASARCO Inc	AR	29	DC	1,736	d1.00 xe	2.00 e	14	1.4	B-	2
§	Brush Wellman	BW	17	DC	295	1.00 e	1.30 e	13	1.8	B-	4
§	Cleveland-Cliffs	CLF	37	DC	356	3.15 e	3.40 e	11	3.5	B	3
	Coeur d'Alene Mines	CDE	16	DC	84	d0.20 e	0.01 e	1638	0.9	B-	4
•	Cyprus Amax Minerals	CYM	26	DC	1,764	1.35 e	2.50 e	10	3.0	NR	2
	Freep't McMoRan Copper&Gold'A'	FCX	21	DC	926	0.35 e	0.80 e	27	2.8	NR	4
•	Inco Ltd	N	29	DC	2,130	d0.50 ze	0.50 e	57	1.3	B-	1
	Nord Resources	NRD	7	DC	94	d0.15 e	0.10 e	65	Nil	C	3
•	Phelps Dodge	PD	62	DC	2,596	4.50 xe	6.25 e	10	2.9	B	3

Miscellaneous

	Company	Ticker									
•	AirTouch Communications	ATI	29	DC	988	0.26 e	0.40 e	73	Nil	NR	4
•	Amer Greetings Cl'A'	AGREA	27	FB	1,781	2.01 e	2.30 e	12	2.0	B+	4
•	Corning Inc	GLW	30	DC	4,039	2.05 e	2.30 e	13	2.4	A-	3
•	Dial Corp	DL	21	DC	3,000	1.60 e	1.85 e	11	2.8	B+	4
§	Gibson Greetings	GIBG	15	DC	547	d1.00 e	1.40 e	11	2.7	B+	2
•	Harcourt General	H	35	OC	3,154 *	2.22 p	2.05 e	17	1.8	B+	5
•	Harris Corp	HRS	43	JE	3,336 *	3.07 y	3.80 e	11	2.9	B+	3
•	Jostens Inc	JOS	19	JE	827 *	d0.36	1.00 e	19	4.6	B+	4
•	Minnesota Min'g/Mfg	MMM	53	DC	14,020	3.14 e	3.60 e	15	3.2	A+	4
•	Pioneer Hi-Bred Intl	PHYB	35	AU	1,479 *	2.40	2.30 e	15	1.9	B+	3
•	TRW Inc	TRW	66	DC	7,948	4.75 e	5.50 e	12	3.0	B+	4
•	Whitman Corp	WH	17	DC	2,530	1.01 e	1.30 e	13	1.9	B	3

Money Center Banks

	Company	Ticker									
§	Bank of New York	BK	30	DC	3,822	3.85 e	4.25 e	7	4.3	B	4
•	BankAmerica Corp	BAC	40	DC	15,900	5.35 e	5.95 e	7	4.0	B	4
•	Bankers Trust NY	BT	55	DC	7,800	7.70 e	10.25 e	5	7.2	A-	4
•	Chase Manhattan	CMB	34	DC	11,417	5.90 e	6.25 e	6	4.6	B-	3
•	Chemical Banking Corp	CHL	36	DC	12,427	4.60 e	5.90 e	6	4.9	B-	3
•	Citicorp	CCI	41	DC	32,196	6.30 e	6.80 e	6	1.4	B-	5
•	First Chicago	FNB	48	DC	4,827	6.80 e	7.10 e	7	4.6	B-	3
•	Morgan (J.P.)	JPM	56	DC	11,941	6.05 e	6.75 e	8	5.3	B+	3

Multi-Line Insurance

	Company	Ticker									
•	Aetna Life & Casualty	AET	47	DC	17,118	4.50 e	6.00 e	8	5.8	B-	2

Peer Comparisons (*Continued*)

•	Amer Intl Group	AIG	98	DC	20,130	6.60 e	7.70 e	13	0.4	A+	5
§	Aon Corp	AOC	32	DC	3,844	3.15 e	3.35 e	10	4.0	A-	4
•	CIGNA Corp	CI	64	DC	18,402	6.00 e	6.50 e	10	4.7	B	2
	CNA Financial	CNA	65	DC	11,011	1.75 e	4.00 e	16	Nil	B	3
§	Kemper Corp	KEM	38	DC	1,549	3.50 e	4.25 e	9	2.4	B	4

Natural Gas (Distibutors & Pipelines)

§	Atlanta Gas Light	ATG	30	SP	1,200 *	2.34	1.20 e	25	6.9	A-	3
	British Gas ADS	BRG	49	DC	15,371	2.50 e	2.70 e	18	4.9	NR	1
§	Brooklyn Union Gas	BU	22	SP	1,339 *	1.85	1.90 e	12	6.2	A-	3
•	Coastal Corp	CGP	26	DC	10,136	2.05 e	2.35 e	11	1.5	B+	4
•	Columbia Gas System	CG	24	DC	3,391	4.80 e	5.45 e	4	Nil	D	3
•	Consolidated Nat Gas	CNG	36	DC	3,184	2.15 e	2.35 e	15	5.4	B+	3
•	Eastern Enterprises	EFU	26	DC	1,100	1.95 e	2.15 e	12	5.3	B	3
§	El Paso Natural Gas	EPG	31	DC	909	2.45 e	2.95 e	10	3.9	NR	4
•	Enron Corp	ENE	31	DC	7,972	1.90 e	2.20 e	14	2.6	B	5
•	ENSERCH Corp	ENS	13	DC	1,902	0.35 e	0.65 e	20	1.5	B	3
	Equitable Resources	EQT	27	DC	1,095	2.05 e	2.35 e	12	4.3	B+	3
§	Indiana Energy	IEI	21	SP	475 *	1.53	1.55 e	13	5.1	B+	3
§	MAPCO, Inc	MDA	51	DC	2,715	2.75 e	5.55 e	9	1.9	A-	4
§	MCN Corp	MCN	18	DC	1,470	1.37 e	1.50 e	12	4.9	NR	4
§	Natl Fuel Gas	NFG	26	SP	1,141 *	2.23 w	2.25 e	11	6.1	B+	3
•	NICOR Inc	GAS	23	SP	1,674	2.10 e	2.20 e	10	5.5	B	3
•	Noram Energy	NAE	5	DC	2,950	0.35 e	0.50 e	11	5.2	B-	4
	Northern Border Ptnrs L.P.	NBP	21	DC	205	2.00 e	2.00 e	10	10.6	NR	3
	Nova Corp	NVA	9	DC	3,274	1.10 ie	1.40 ie	7	1.8	B-	3
•	ONEOK Inc	OKE	18	AU	792 *	1.34	1.35 e	13	6.2	B	3
•	Pacific Enterprises	PET	21	DC	2,899	1.85 e	1.90 e	11	6.0	B-	3
•	Panhandle East'n	PEL	20	DC	2,121	1.75 e	1.90 e	10	4.2	B	4
•	Peoples Energy	PGL	26	SP	1,279 *	2.13	2.20 e	12	6.8	B+	3
§	Questar Corp	STR	28	DC	660	2.05 e	2.25 e	12	4.1	A-	3
§	Seagull Energy	SGO	19	DC	377	0.50 e	0.90 e	21	Nil	B	3
•	Sonat, Inc	SNT	28	DC	1,741	1.90 e	2.00 e	14	3.8	B	3
	Southwest Gas	SWX	14	DC	690	1.00 e	1.20 e	12	5.8	B ·	3
	TransCanada P.L.	TRP	12	DC	4,242	1.59 ei	1.65 ei	7	5.8	B	3
•	Transco Energy	E	17	DC	2,922	0.85 e	1.10 e	15	3.6	B	3
	UGI Corp	UGI	20	SP	762 *	1.40 p	1.25 e	16	6.7	B+	2
	Washington Energy	WEG	14	SP	432 *	d1.97 p	0.90 e	15	7.4	B	3
§	Washington Gas Lt	WGL	34	SP	915 *	2.83	2.85 e	12	6.6	A	3
	WICOR, Inc	WIC	28	DC	850	2.30 e	2.40 e	12	5.6	B	3
•	Williams Cos	WMB	25	DC	2,438	1.60 e	1.75 e	14	3.3	B	4

Office Equipment & Supplies

•	Alco Standard	ASN	63	SP	7,996 *	1.10	3.00 e	21	1.6	B+	3
§	Ennis Business Forms	EBF	13	FB	133	1.25 e	EUR	NM	4.6	A	3
•	Moore Corp Ltd	MCL	19	DC	2,329	1.20 e	3.00 e	6	4.9	B-	2
•	Pitney Bowes	PBI	32	DC	3,543	2.40 e	2.70 e	12	3.2	A+	3
§	Reynolds & Reynolds 'A'	REY	25	SP	809 *	1.51	1.90 e	13	1.6	B+	5
§	Standard Register	SREG	18	DC	722	1.52 e	1.75 e	10	4.1	A	3
§	Wallace Computer Svc	WCS	29	JL	588 *	2.13 wy	2.30 e	13	2.5	A	4
•	Xerox Corp	XRX	99	DC	14,601	6.65 e	8.00 e	12	3.0	B-	4

Oil (Domestic Integrated)

•	Amerada Hess	AHC	46	DC	5,852	0.70 e	1.00 e	46	1.3	B-	3
•	Ashland Oil	ASH	35	SP	9,457 *	2.94	3.45 e	10	3.1	B	4
•	Atlantic Richfield	ARC	102	DC	17,189	5.05 e	5.45 e	19	5.4	B+	3
•	Kerr-McGee	KMG	46	DC	3,281	1.70 e	1.95 e	24	3.2	B	3
•	Louisiana Land/Exp	LLX	36	DC	815	BE e	BE e	NM	2.7	B-	3
§	Murphy Oil	MUR	43	DC	1,671	2.70 e	3.00 e	14	3.0	B	3
•	Occidental Petrol'm	OXY	19	DC	8,116	d0.25 e	0.25 e	77	5.1	B-	3

Peer Comparisons (*Continued*)

	Company	Ticker									
•	Pennzoil Co.	PZL	44	DC	2,782	d6.60 e	1.00 e	44	6.7	B-	3
•	Phillips Petroleum	P	33	DC	11,933	1.65 e	1.95 e	17	3.4	B-	3
§	Quaker State Corp	KSF	14	DC	759	0.50 e	1.10 e	13	2.8	B-	5
•	Sun Co	SUN	29	DC	7,297	1.00 e	2.30 e	13	6.2	NR	5
§	Tosco Corp	TOS	29	DC	3,559	2.55 e	3.35 e	9	2.1	B-	4
•	Unocal Corp	UCL	27	DC	8,344	d1.15 e	1.25 e	22	2.9	B	3
•	USX-Marathon Grp	MRO	16	DC	11,962	1.10 e	0.30 e	55	4.1	NR	3
§	Valero Energy	VLO	17	DC	1,222	0.55 e	1.00 e	17	3.0	B	3

Oil & Gas Drilling
	Company	Ticker									
•	Helmerich & Payne	HP	26	SP	329 *	0.86 w	0.75 e	34	1.9	B	3
§	Parker Drilling	PKD	5	AU	152 *	d0.53	0.06 e	79	Nil	C	3
•	Rowan Cos	RDC	6	DC	353	d0.10 e	d0.25 e	NM	Nil	C	5

Oil (Exploration & Production)
	Company	Ticker									
§	Anadarko Petroleum	APC	39	DC	476	0.90 e	0.85 e	45	0.7	B	3
§	Apache Corp	APA	25	DC	467	0.75 e	1.10 e	23	1.1	B-	4
•	Burlington Resources	BR	35	DC	1,249	1.20 e	1.50 e	23	1.5	NR	3
•	Maxus Energy	MXS	3	DC	787	d0.45 e	d1.45 e	NM	Nil	C	3
	Mesa Inc	MXP	5	DC	222	d1.80 e	d2.00 e	NM	Nil	C	3
§	Noble Affiliates	NBL	25	DC	287	0.40 e	0.75 e	33	0.6	B	3
•	Oryx Energy Co	ORX	12	DC	1,080	d2.80 e	d2.45 e	NM	Nil	NR	3
§	Parker & Parsley Petrol	PDP	21	DC	329	0.05 e	0.60 e	34	0.4	B	3
•	Santa Fe Energy Res	SFR	8	DC	437	0.10 e	0.20 e	40	Nil	NR	3
	Sceptre Resources	SRL	6	DC	209	0.45 ie	0.50 ie	13	Nil	C	4

Oil (International Integrated)
	Company	Ticker									
•	Amoco Corp	AN	59	DC	25,336	3.35 e	3.40 e	17	3.7	B	3
	British Petrol ADS	BP	80	DC	52,425	5.00 e	4.50 e	18	2.3	NR	3
•	Chevron Corp	CHV	45	DC	33,014	2.40 e	3.00 e	15	4.1	B	3
	Elf Aquitaine ADS	ELF	35	DC	37,197	0.95 e	1.25 e	28	2.5	NR	3
•	Exxon Corp	XON	61	DC	97,828	3.80 e	4.35 e	14	4.9	B+	4
	Imperial Oil Ltd	IMO	33	DC	8,903	2.00 ei	2.25 ei	15	3.8	B	3
•	Mobil Corp	MOB	84	DC	63,474	4.25 e	5.50 e	15	4.0	B+	3
	Norsk Hydro A.S. ADS	NHY	39	DC	8,291	2.50 e	2.00 e	20	1.0	NR	3
	Repsol S.A. ADS	REP	27	DC	15,485	2.25 e	2.70 e	10	2.5	NR	3
•	Royal Dutch Petrol	RD	108	DC	0	5.90 e	6.75 e	16	3.8	A	3
	Shell Transp/Trad ADR	SC	65	DC	38,650	3.15 e	3.55 e	18	3.7	A-	3
•	Texaco Inc	TX	60	DC	33,245	3.00 e	4.25 e	14	5.3	B	3
	TOTAL 'B' ADS	TOT	30	DC	22,889	1.30 e	1.50 e	20	1.7	NR	3
	YPF Sociedad Anonima ADS	YPF	21	DC	3,960	1.80 e	2.10 e	10	3.7	NR	4

Oil Well Equipment & Services
	Company	Ticker									
•	Baker Hughes Inc	BHI	18	SP	2,505 *	0.85 y	0.50 e	37	2.5	B	4
•	Dresser Industries	DI	19	OC	5,310 *	1.98 p	1.25 e	15	3.6	B	3
•	Halliburton Co	HAL	33	DC	6,351	0.75 e	1.00 e	33	3.0	B-	3
•	McDermott Intl	MDR	25	MR	3,060	0.05 e	1.35 e	18	4.0	B-	3
	Oceaneering Intl	OII	10	MR	230	0.75 e	0.85 e	12	Nil	B-	3
•	Schlumberger Ltd	SLB	50	DC	6,705	2.10 e	2.30 e	22	2.3	B+	4
	SEACOR Holdings	CKOR	20	DC	74	1.35 e	1.50 e	13	Nil	NR	3
§	Tidewater Inc	TDW	19	MR	522	0.85 e	1.05 e	18	2.1	B-	2
§	Varco Int'l	VRC	6	DC	193	0.30 e	0.40 e	16	Nil	B-	3
•	Western Atlas	WAI	38	DC	2,212	1.50 e	1.50 e	25	Nil	NR	3

Paper & Forest Products
	Company	Ticker									
•	Boise Cascade	BCC	27	DC	3,958	d3.80 e	d1.75 e	NM	2.2	B-	3
§	Bowater, Inc	BOW	27	DC	1,354	d0.80 e	1.20 e	22	2.2	B-	3
•	Champion Intl	CHA	37	DC	5,069	d0.30 e	d1.35 e	NM	0.5	B-	2
§	Chesapeake Corp	CSK	33	DC	885	1.60 e	2.40 e	14	2.1	B-	3
§	Consolidated Papers	CDP	45	DC	947	1.80 e	2.35 e	19	2.8	B+	3

Peer Comparisons (*Continued*)

•	Federal Paper Board	FBO	29	DC	1,386	0.80 e	1.45 e	20	4.1	B	3
•	Georgia-Pacific	GP	72	DC	12,330	2.70 e	3.85 e	19	2.2	B-	3
§	Glatfelter (P. H.)	GLT	16	DC	474	0.15 e	0.70 e	22	4.5	B+	3
•	Intl Paper	IP	75	DC	13,685	3.05 e	4.00 e	19	2.2	B+	3
•	James River Corp	JR	20	DC	4,650	d0.40 e	0.35 e	58	2.9	B-	1
	Jefferson Smurfit	JJSC	17	DC	2,948	0.05 e	1.00 e	17	Nil	NR	3
§	Longview Fibre	LFB	16	OC	791 *	0.64 p	1.15 e	14	3.2	B	3
•	Louisiana Pacific	LPX	27	DC	2,511	3.20 e	3.80 e	7	1.8	B+	4
•	Mead Corp	MEA	49	DC	4,790	2.30 e	2.70 e	18	2.0	B-	3
	Pope & Talbot	POP	16	DC	629	1.70 e	1.70 e	9	4.7	B	3
•	Potlatch Corp	PCH	37	DC	1,369	1.30 e	1.75 e	21	4.2	B+	3
§	Rayonier Inc	RYN	31	DC	936	2.35 e	2.65 e	12	2.3	NR	3
§	Sonoco Products	SONO	22	DC	1,947	1.35 e	1.55 e	14	2.5	A-	3
•	Union Camp	UCC	47	DC	3,120	1.25 e	2.40 e	20	3.3	B	3
§	Wausau Paper Mills	WSAU	23	AU	427 *	1.42 w	1.30 e	18	1.0	A	3
•	Westvaco Corp	W	39	OC	2,607 *	1.55	2.90 e	14	2.8	B	5
•	Weyerhaeuser Co	WY	38	DC	9,545	2.60 e	3.25 e	12	3.2	B+	5
§	Willamette Indus	WMTT	48	DC	2,622	2.45 e	3.05 e	16	2.0	B+	3
	Personal Loans										
•	Beneficial Corp	BNL	39	DC	1,958	3.30 e	4.55 e	9	4.4	B+	4
	Capstead Mortgage	CMO	17	DC	642	3.05 e	2.50 e	7	17.1	NR	1
	Countrywide Credit Indus	CCR	13	FB	756	1.20 e	1.40 e	9	2.4	B+	2
	Green Tree Finl	GNT	30	DC	367	2.55 e	2.90 e	10	0.8	B+	3
•	Household Intl	HI	37	DC	4,455	3.50 e	4.15 e	9	3.3	B+	3
	Lomas Financial	LFC	4	JE	271 *	d9.07	BE e	NM	Nil	NR	3
	Mercury Finance	MFN	13	DC	194	0.74 e	0.95 e	14	2.4	B+	4
	Photography/Imaging										
•	Eastman Kodak	EK	48	DC	16,364	2.60 e	3.20 e	15	3.3	B	3
•	Polaroid Corp	PRD	33	DC	2,245	2.45 e	2.85 e	11	1.8	B	5
	Pollution Control										
§	Amer Waste Svcs'A'	AW	2	DC	87	0.05 e	0.07 e	23	Nil	NR	2
•	Browning-Ferris Indus	BFI	28	SP	4,315 *	1.52 y	1.80 e	16	2.3	A-	4
§	Calgon Carbon	CCC	10	DC	269	0.35 e	0.55 e	18	1.6	NR	2
	Chambers Devel Cl'A'(1/10vtg)	CDV.A	4	DC	288	d1.08 e	0.15 e	26	Nil	C	3
	Chemical Waste Mgmt	CHW	9	DC	2,130	0.30 e	0.40 e	23	Nil	NR	3
	Groundwater Technology	GWTI	14	AP	171 *	d0.03	0.80 e	17	Nil	B	4
	Gundle Environmental Sys	GUN	5	MR	119	0.55 e	0.65 e	8	Nil	NR	3
§	Intl Technology	ITX	3	MR	393	d0.08 e	0.20 e	16	Nil	B-	3
§	Laidlaw Inc Cl'B'	LDW.B	8	AU	2,128 *	0.33 o	0.45 e	18	1.4	B+	3
§	Mid-American Waste Sys	MAW	7	DC	170	0.45 e	0.55 e	12	Nil	NR	3
•	Rollins Environ Sv	REN	5	SP	181 *	d0.17 pw	0.15 e	33	Nil	B	4
	Sanifill Inc	FIL	25	DC	121	1.10 e	1.35 e	19	Nil	NR	4
	Waste Mgmt Intl plc ADS	WME	11	DC	1,412	0.80 e	0.85 e	13	Nil	NR	2
	Wheelabrator Tech	WTI	15	DC	1,142	1.00 e	1.20 e	12	0.6	NR	4
•	WMX Technologies	WMX	26	DC	9,136	1.64 e	1.90 e	14	2.2	A-	4
	Property-Casualty Insurance										
	20th Century Indus	TW	11	DC	1,104	d9.55 e	1.00 e	11	Nil	A	2
	AMBAC Inc	ABK	37	DC	328	4.10 e	5.00 e	7	1.4	NR	3
	Berkley (W.R.)	BKLY	38	DC	582	2.50 e	2.70 e	14	1.1	B+	3
	Capital Guaranty	CGY	14	DC	35	1.80 e	2.05 e	7	1.4	NR	4
•	Chubb Corp	CB	77	DC	5,500	5.65 e	8.00 e	10	2.3	A	5
•	Contl Corp	CIC	19	DC	5,174	d7.00 e	1.35 e	14	Nil	C	3
	GEICO Corp	GEC	49	DC	2,638	3.00 e	3.50 e	14	2.0	A	3
•	Genl Re Corp	GRN	124	DC	3,560	7.50 e	9.00 e	14	1.5	A	4
§	Hartford Stm Boiler Ins	HSB	40	DC	636	2.50 e	3.00 e	13	5.5	B+	3
	Loews Corp	LTR	87	DC	13,687	7.50 e	8.00 e	11	1.1	A-	2

Peer Comparisons (*Continued*)

	Company	Ticker									
	MBIA Inc	MBI	56	DC	429	6.00 e	6.50 e	9	2.2	NR	4
	Ohio Casualty	OCAS	28	DC	1,670	1.20 e	2.50 e	11	5.1	B+	3
§	Progressive Corp,Ohio	PGR	35	DC	1,955	2.75 e	3.00 e	12	0.6	B+	2
•	SAFECO Corp	SAFC	52	DC	3,517	4.60 e	5.75 e	9	3.7	A	3
•	St. Paul Cos	SPC	45	DC	4,460	4.25 e	4.85 e	9	3.3	A-	4
§	Transatlantic Holdings	TRH	56	DC	720	4.00 e	5.00 e	11	0.7	NR	4
•	USF&G Corp	FG	14	DC	3,249	0.95 e	1.35 e	10	1.4	B-	3

Publishing

	Company	Ticker									
•	Dun & Bradstreet	DNB	55	DC	4,710	3.70 e	4.15 e	13	4.7	A	4
	Gartner Group'A'	GART	39	SP	169 *	0.65	1.07 e	36	Nil	NR	3
§	Houghton Mifflin	HTN	45	DC	463	3.75 e	3.20 e	14	1.9	A-	4
	Marvel Entertainment Grp	MRV	14	DC	415	0.60 e	0.72 e	20	Nil	NR	5
•	McGraw-Hill Inc	MHP	67	DC	2,195	NE	NE	NM	3.5	NR	NR
•	Meredith Corp	MDP	47	JE	800 *	1.91	2.05 e	23	1.5	B	5
	Reader's Digest Assn'A'	RDA	49	JE	2,806 *	2.34 yo	2.55 e	19	3.2	B+	3
	Reuters Hldgs ADS	RTRSY	44	DC	2,774	1.85 e	2.10 e	21	1.5	NR	3
	Scholastic Corp	SCHL	51	MY	632 *	2.04 yo	2.25 e	23	Nil	NR	2
§	Western Publishing	WPGI	10	JA	617	d0.50 e	0.90 e	11	Nil	NR	3

Publishing (Newspaper)

	Company	Ticker									
	Amer Publishing 'A'	AMPC	11	DC	452	0.60 e	0.85 e	13	0.9	NR	4
§	Belo (A.H.)Cl'A'	BLC	57	DC	545	3.25 e	3.70 e	15	1.0	B	4
•	Dow Jones & Co	DJ	31	DC	1,932	1.80 e	2.10 e	15	2.7	A	3
•	Gannett Co	GCI	53	DC	3,642	3.25 e	3.55 e	15	2.5	A	4
•	Knight-Ridder Inc	KRI	51	DC	2,451	3.30 e	3.90 e	13	2.9	A-	5
	McClatchy Newspapers'A'	MNI	22	DC	449	1.58 e	1.70 e	13	1.5	B	4
§	Media General Cl'A'	MEG.A	28	DC	601	4.50 e	1.65 e	17	1.5	B	5
•	New York Times Cl'A'	NYT.A	22	DC	2,020	2.03 e	1.30 e	17	2.5	B+	3
	News Corp Ltd ADS	NWS	16	JE	7,985 *	1.76 w	2.07 e	8	0.5	NR	5
•	Times Mirror	TMC	31	DC	3,714	0.85 e	1.05 e	30	3.4	B-	1
•	Tribune Co.	TRB	55	DC	1,953	3.35 e	3.85 e	14	1.8	B+	4
§	Washington Post'B'	WPO	243	DC	1,498	14.85 e	16.25 e	15	1.7	B+	4

Railroads

	Company	Ticker									
•	Burlington Northern	BNI	48	DC	4,699	4.30 e	5.30 e	9	2.4	NR	4
	Canadian Pacific, Ord	CP	15	DC	6,579	1.25 ei	1.50 ei	10	1.5	B-	3
	Chicago & No. West'n Transp	CNW	20	DC	1,043	1.95 e	2.30 e	8	Nil	NR	5
•	Conrail Inc	CRR	51	DC	3,453	3.45 e	4.85 e	10	2.9	B-	4
•	CSX Corp	CSX	70	DC	8,940	5.75 e	7.00 e	10	2.5	B	4
§	GATX Corp	GMT	44	DC	1,087	3.70 e	4.25 e	10	3.4	A-	4
§	Illinois Central Corp	IC	31	DC	565	2.50 e	2.90 e	11	3.2	NR	4
	ITEL Corp	ITL	35	DC	1,909	1.25 e	1.45 e	24	Nil	C	3
§	Kansas City So. Ind	KSU	31	DC	961	2.65 e	3.05 e	10	0.9	B	4
•	Norfolk Southern	NSC	61	DC	4,460	4.85 e	5.35 e	11	3.1	A-	4
•	Santa Fe Pacific	SFX	18	DC	2,726	1.00 e	1.10 e	16	0.5	B-	3
	Southern Pacific Rail	RSP	18	DC	2,919	0.95 e	1.35 e	13	Nil	NR	3
§	Trinity Indus	TRN	32	MR	1,785	2.25 e	2.85 e	11	2.1	B+	3
•	Union Pacific	UNP	45	DC	7,561	4.65 e	4.75 e	10	3.7	A-	4

Restaurants

	Company	Ticker									
§	Brinker Intl	EAT	18	JE	878 *	0.83	1.05 e	17	Nil	B+	3
§	Buffets Inc	BOCB	10	DC	335	0.75 e	0.85 e	12	Nil	B+	3
	Consolidated Products	COPI	10	SP	159 *	0.88 p	0.64 e	15	Nil	NR	4
§	Cracker Brl Old Ctry	CBRL	19	JL	641 *	0.94 w	1.10 e	17	0.1	A	2
	DAKA Intl	DKAI	15	JE	250 *	1.55	1.15 ge	13	Nil	B-	5
§	Intl Dairy Queen 'A'	INDQA	17	NV	311	1.28 e	1.35 e	13	Nil	B+	5
•	Luby's Cafeterias	LUB	22	AU	391 *	1.45 w	1.60 e	14	2.9	A	3
•	McDonald's Corp	MCD	29	DC	7,408	1.67 e	1.90 e	15	0.8	A+	3
§	Morrison Restaurants	RI	25	MY	1,213 *	1.20	1.75 e	14	1.4	A	3

Peer Comparisons (*Continued*)

	Company	Ticker										
	Outback Steakhouse	OSSI	24	DC	271	0.85 e	1.15 e	20	Nil	NR	2
	Piccadilly Cafeterias	PIC	8	JE	276 *	0.70	0.85 e	9	6.0	B+	3
	Quantum Restaurant Group	KRG	12	DC	119	0.85 e	1.05 e	11	Nil	NR	4
•	Ryan's Family Stk Hse	RYAN	8	DC	394	0.55 e	0.60 e	13	Nil	B+	5
§	Sbarro Inc	SBA	26	DC	266	1.60 e	1.83 e	14	2.4	B+	4
•	Shoney's Inc	SHN	13	OC	1,166 *	1.52 pyw	1.45 e	9	Nil	B	4
§	Sizzler International	SZ	6	AP	488 *	d3.26	0.30 e	20	2.6	NR	2
	VICORP Restaurants	VRES	18	OC	413 *	d0.69 p	0.80 e	22	Nil	B-	2
•	Wendy's Intl	WEN	14	DC	1,320	0.94 e	1.10 e	13	1.6	B	4
	Retail (Department Stores)										
•	Dillard Dept Str'A'	DDS	27	JA	5,131	2.30 e	2.80 e	10	0.4	A+	3
	Federated Department Stores	FD	19	JA	7,229	1.80 e	1.35 e	14	Nil	NR	4
•	May Dept Stores	MA	34	JA	11,529	3.00 e	3.40 e	10	3.0	A+	4
•	Mercantile Stores	MST	40	JA	2,730	2.70 e	3.00 e	13	2.5	B+	5
	Neiman-Marcus Group	NMG	14	JL	2,093 *	d0.35	0.70 e	19	1.4	NR	3
•	Nordstrom, Inc	NOBE	42	JA	3,590	2.50 e	2.80 e	15	0.9	A+	3
•	Penney (J.C.)	JCP	45	JA	18,983	4.25 e	4.65 e	10	3.7	A-	5
	Retail (Drug Stores)										
	Eckerd Corp	ECK	30	JA	4,191	2.25 e	2.55 e	12	Nil	NR	2
	Genovese Drug Str'A'	GDX.A	11	JA	489	0.94 e	1.05 e	11	2.1	A-	3
•	Longs Drug Stores	LDG	32	JA	2,499	2.65 e	2.90 e	11	3.5	A-	3
	Medicine Shoppe Intl	MSII	27	SP	51 *	1.84 p	2.05 e	13	2.0	B+	5
	Revco D.S.	RXR	24	MY	2,504 *	0.77	0.95 e	25	Nil	NR	5
•	Rite Aid	RAD	23	FB	4,059	1.65 e	1.85 e	13	2.5	A-	4
•	Walgreen Co	WAG	44	AU	9,235 *	2.28	2.55 e	17	1.7	A+	3
	Retail (Food Chains)										
•	Albertson's, Inc	ABS	29	JA	11,284	1.60 e	1.80 e	16	1.5	A+	4
•	Amer Stores	ASC	27	JA	18,763	2.30 e	2.25 e	12	1.7	B+	4
•	Bruno's, Inc	BRNO	8	JE	2,835 *	0.52 y	0.60 e	14	3.1	A	3
	Food Lion Inc Cl'B'	FDLNB	5	DC	7,610	0.32 e	0.40 e	13	1.7	A-	3
•	Giant Food Cl'A'	GFS.A	22	FB	3,567	1.55 e	1.70 e	13	3.3	A-	3
•	Great Atl & Pac Tea	GAP	18	FB	10,384	d3.95 e	1.45 e	13	1.1	B-	2
•	Kroger Co	KR	24	DC	22,384	2.50 e	2.80 e	9	Nil	B	4
•	Winn-Dixie Stores	WIN	51	JE	11,082 *	2.90	3.25 e	16	3.0	A+	3
	Retail (General Merchandise)										
	Caldor Corp	CLD	22	JA	2,414	2.80 e	3.40 e	7	Nil	NR	5
•	Dayton Hudson	DH	71	JA	19,233	5.70 e	6.60 e	11	2.3	A	3
§	Family Dollar Stores	FDO	13	AU	1,428 *	1.10 w	1.05 e	12	2.7	A-	2
•	K mart	KM	13	JA	34,557	1.15 e	1.40 e	9	7.3	A-	3
§	MacFrugals Bargains Closeouts	MFI	20	JA	627	1.20 e	1.40 e	14	Nil	B	4
•	Sears,Roebuck	S	46	DC	50,838	3.40 e	5.25 e	9	3.4	B	4
•	Wal-Mart Stores	WMT	21	JA	67,345	1.20 e	1.45 e	15	0.8	A+	4
	Retail (Specialty)										
	AutoZone Inc	AZO	24	AU	1,508 *	0.78	0.97 e	25	Nil	NR	3
	Barnes & Noble	BKS	31	JA	1,337	0.80 e	1.20 e	26	Nil	NR	3
•	Circuit City Stores	CC	22	FB	4,130	1.55 e	1.85 e	12	0.4	A	4
§	Cross (A.T.) Cl'A'	ATX.A	14	DC	165	0.55 e	0.70 e	19	4.6	B	3
	Dart Group Cl'A'	DARTA	77	JA	1,377	2.50 e	3.75 e	21	0.1	B-	4
	Hi-Lo Automotive	HLO	10	DC	205	0.84 e	0.92 e	11	Nil	NR	2
•	Home Depot	HD	46	JA	9,239	1.35 e	1.70 e	27	0.3	A-	4
§	Home Shopping Network	HSN	10	DC	1,047	0.30 e	0.50 e	20	Nil	B-	3
§	Intelligent Electronics	INEL	8	JA	2,646	0.90 e	1.85 e	4	5.0	NR	3
•	Lowe's Cos	LOW	35	JA	4,538	1.45 e	1.80 e	19	0.5	A-	4
•	Melville Corp	MES	31	DC	10,435	3.20 e	3.60 e	9	4.9	A	3
	MicroAge Inc	MICA	12	OC	2,221 *	1.22 p	1.50 e	8	Nil	B+	3

Peer Comparisons (*Continued*)

	Company	Ticker									
	Payless Cashways	PCS	9	NV	2,606	1.25 e	1.20 e	8	Nil	NR	3
•	Pep Boys-Man,Mo,Ja	PBY	31	JA	1,241	1.30 e	1.48 e	21	0.5	A+	3
•	Price/Costco Inc	PCCW	13	AU	16,481 *	d0.51	1.05 e	12	Nil	NR	3
	QVC Inc	QVCN	42	JA	1,222	1.45 e	1.83 e	23	Nil	NR	3
•	Tandy Corp	TAN	50	DC	4,103	2.89 e	3.40 e	15	1.4	B	4
•	Toys R Us	TOY	31	JA	7,946	1.90 e	2.25 e	14	Nil	B+	4
	Tractor Supply	TSCO	21	DC	279	1.30 e	1.55 e	14	Nil	NR	4
•	Woolworth Corp	Z	15	JA	9,626	0.75 e	1.45 e	10	4.0	B+	5

Retail (Specialty Apparel)

	Company	Ticker									
§	AnnTaylor Stores	ANN	34	JA	502	1.35 e	1.75 e	20	Nil	NR	4
•	Charming Shoppes	CHRS	7	JA	1,254	0.55 e	0.70 e	9	1.3	A-	2
	Designs Inc	DESI	7	JA	241	0.90 e	1.05 e	7	Nil	NR	4
•	Gap Inc	GPS	31	JA	3,296	2.20 e	2.60 e	12	1.5	A	4
§	Lands' End	LE	14	JA	870	1.15 e	1.35 e	10	Nil	NR	3
•	Limited Inc	LTD	18	JA	7,245	1.30 e	1.55 e	12	1.9	A+	4
	Petrie Stores	PST	22	JA	1,480	0.25 e	0.45 e	50	0.8	B-	4
	Talbots Inc	TLB	31	JA	737	1.55 e	1.80 e	17	0.6	NR	4
•	TJX Companies	TJX	16	JA	3,627	1.25 e	1.60 e	10	3.5	B	3
§	Waban Inc	WBN	18	JA	3,589	1.75 e	1.95 e	9	Nil	NR	4

Savings & Loans

	Company	Ticker									
•	Ahmanson (H F) & Co	AHM	16	DC	3,329	d1.85 e	2.20 e	7	5.4	B	4
	Calif Federal Bank'A'	CAL	11	DC	1,084	d3.90 e	1.25 e	9	Nil	C	3
	Charter One Finl	COFI	19	DC	385	2.90 e	3.05 e	6	3.5	NR	4
	Coast Svgs Finl	CSA	15	DC	576	0.05 e	1.20 e	12	Nil	NR	4
	G P Financial	GNPT	21	DC	561	2.40 e	2.60 e	8	3.8	NR	4
	Glendale Federal Bank	GLN	10	JE	1,145	d6.48 wp	1.20 e	8	Nil	NR	5
•	Golden West Finl	GDW	35	DC	1,932	3.85 e	4.35 e	8	0.9	A-	3
•	Great Westn Finl	GWF	16	DC	2,883	1.75 e	2.25 e	7	5.7	B-	5
	Standard Fedl Bank	SFB	24	DC	769	3.75 e	4.10 e	6	2.6	NR	4
	Wash Fed S&L Seattle	WFSL	17	SP	296 *	2.32	2.45 e	7	5.0	A	4
	Washington Mutual	WAMU	17	DC	1,180	2.65 e	2.90 e	6	4.5	B	4

Shoes

	Company	Ticker									
•	Brown Group	BG	32	JA	1,598	2.25 e	3.15 e	10	5.0	B-	5
	L.A. Gear, Inc	LA	5	NV	398	d0.40 e	0.11 e	45	Nil	C	2
•	NIKE, Inc Cl'B'	NKE	75	MY	3,790 *	3.96 o	5.00 e	15	1.3	A-	4
•	Reebok Intl	RBK	40	DC	2,894	3.10 e	3.50 e	11	0.7	B+	4
•	Stride Rite	SRR	11	NV	583	0.50 e	0.90 e	12	3.4	A-	2
§	U.S. Shoe	USR	19	JA	2,626	0.85 e	1.70 e	11	1.7	B-	5
	Wolverine World Wide	WWW	26	DC	333	1.40 e	1.75 e	15	0.6	B	3

Specialized Services

	Company	Ticker									
§	Angelica Corp	AGL	28	JA	427	1.44 e	1.65 e	17	3.4	B+	3
•	Block (H & R)	HRB	37	AP	1,239 *	1.88	1.90 e	20	3.3	A+	4
§	Cintas Corp	CTAS	36	MY	523 *	1.12	1.35 e	26	0.4	A+	4
•	Ecolab Inc	ECL	21	DC	1,042	1.25 e	1.55 e	13	2.3	B	4
§	Flightsafety Intl	FSI	41	DC	297	2.20 e	2.45 e	17	1.1	A	3
•	Interpublic Grp Cos	IPG	32	DC	1,794	1.85 e	2.15 e	15	1.7	A+	4
§	Kelly Services'A'	KELYA	28	DC	1,955	1.55 e	1.80 e	15	2.6	A	4
•	Natl Service Indus	NSI	26	AU	1,882 *	1.67	1.80 e	14	4.3	A	3
•	Ogden Corp	OG	19	DC	2,039	1.65 e	1.80 e	10	6.6	B+	3
§	Rollins Inc	ROL	23	DC	576	1.40 e	1.60 e	14	2.1	A-	4
•	Safety-Kleen	SK	15	DC	796	0.85 e	1.00 e	15	2.4	B+	3
•	Service Corp Intl	SRV	28	DC	899	1.55 e	1.75 e	16	1.5	A-	3
	ServiceMaster L.P.	SVM	24	DC	2,759	1.80 e	2.00 e	12	3.7	A+	3

Specialty Printing

	Company	Ticker									
§	Banta Corp	BNTA	30	DC	691	2.30 e	2.60 e	12	1.8	B+	3

Peer Comparisons (*Continued*)

Bowne & Co	BNE	17	OC	381 *	1.80 p	2.00 e	9	2.0	B+	3
• Deluxe Corp	DLX	26	DC	1,582	1.85 e	2.15 e	12	5.6	A	4
• Donnelley(RR)& Sons	DNY	30	DC	4,388	1.77 e	2.10 e	14	2.1	A-	4
• Harland (John H.)	JH	20	DC	519	1.70 e	1.85 e	11	4.9	A	3

Steel

§ Allegheny Ludlum	ALS	19	DC	1,100	0.19 e	1.20 e	16	2.5	NR	5
• Armco Inc	AS	7	DC	1,664	0.20 e	0.80 e	8	Nil	C	4
• Bethlehem Steel	BS	18	DC	4,323	0.70 e	3.29 e	5	Nil	C	3
Birmingham Steel	BIR	20	JE	703 *	0.86 w	2.00 e	10	2.0	NR	5
§ Carpenter Technology	CRS	56	JE	629 *	4.55 y	4.50 e	12	4.2	B+	4
Chaparral Steel Co	CSM	7	MY	462 *	0.41	0.60 e	12	2.7	NR	4
• Inland Steel Indus	IAD	35	DC	3,888	1.65 e	2.25 e	16	Nil	C	3
J & L Specialty Steel	JL	20	DC	649	1.40 e	1.60 e	12	1.8	NR	4
§ Lukens Inc	LUC	29	DC	862	1.40 e	2.10 e	14	3.4	B	4
• Nucor Corp	NUE	55	DC	2,254	2.55 e	3.20 e	17	0.3	A-	4
§ Oregon Steel Mills	OS	16	DC	680	0.40 e	1.10 e	14	3.5	B	3
Quanex Corp	NX	23	OC	699 *	0.96 p	1.80 e	13	2.4	B	4
Rouge Steel 'A'	ROU	29	DC	1,077	3.57 e	4.28 e	7	0.2	NR	5
Steel Technologies	STTX	13	SP	241 *	0.87	0.95 e	14	0.6	B+	4
Texas Indus	TXI	35	MY	707 *	2.29	3.45 e	10	0.5	B-	4
• USX-U.S. Steel Group	X	36	DC	5,612	2.05 e	4.50 e	8	2.8	NR	4
• Worthington Indus	WTHG	20	MY	1,285 *	0.94	1.20 e	17	2.0	A-	4

Communication Equipment Manufacturers

§ ADC Telecommunications	ADCT	50	OC	449 *	1.46 y	1.72 e	29	Nil	B	4
Allen Group	ALN	24	DC	280	0.90 e	1.05 e	23	0.8	B	2
• cisco Systems	CSCO	35	JL	1,243 *	1.19	1.70 e	21	Nil	NR	5
Compression Labs	CLIX	8	DC	141	BE e	0.40 e	20	Nil	C	3
• DSC Communications	DIGI	36	DC	731	1.20 e	1.55 e	23	Nil	B	4
Dynatech Corp	DYTC	33	MR	458	1.95 e	2.30 e	14	Nil	B	5
• Northern Telecom Ltd	NT	33	DC	8,148	1.35 e	1.70 e	20	1.0	B	1
§ Octel Communications	OCTL	21	JE	406 *	0.54	1.50 e	14	Nil	B	4
QUALCOMM Inc	QCOM	24	SP	272 *	0.28 p	0.65 e	37	Nil	NR	2
• Scientific-Atlanta	SFA	21	JE	812 *	0.45	0.85 e	25	0.2	B+	3

Telephones

• ALLTEL Corp	AT	30	DC	2,342	1.62 e	1.85 e	16	3.1	A	4
• Ameritech Corp	AIT	40	DC	11,710	2.10 e	3.25 e	12	4.9	A-	4
BCE Inc	BCE	32	DC	19,827	3.25 ie	3.65 ei	9	6.0	B+	2
• Bell Atlantic Corp	BEL	50	DC	12,990	3.30 e	3.75 e	13	5.5	A-	5
• BellSouth Corp	BLS	54	DC	15,880	4.25 e	4.45 e	12	5.0	B+	3
§ Century Tel Enterp	CTL	30	DC	433	1.70 e	1.80 e	16	1.0	A	4
Cincinnati Bell	CSN	17	DC	1,090	1.15 e	1.25 e	14	4.7	B+	3
Empresas Telex-Chile ADS	TL	11	DC	83	0.50 e	0.60 e	18	1.5	NR	4
• GTE Corp	GTE	30	DC	19,748	2.45 e	2.50 e	12	6.1	B+	3
MFS Communications	MFST	33	DC	141	d2.10 e	d1.50 e	NM	Nil	NR	4
• NYNEX Corp	NYN	37	DC	13,408	2.15 e	3.15 e	12	6.4	B+	3
• Pacific Telesis Group	PAC	29	DC	9,244	2.60 e	2.75 e	10	7.6	B+	2
§ Rochester Telephone	RTC	21	DC	906	1.45 e	1.60 e	13	3.9	B+	3
§ Southern New Eng Telecom	SNG	32	DC	1,654	2.75 e	2.85 e	11	5.4	A-	3
• Southwestern Bell Corp	SBC	40	DC	10,690	2.80 e	3.05 e	13	3.9	A	4
Telecom Corp New Zealand ADS	NZT	51	MR	1,402	2.90 e	3.50 e	15	5.3	NR	4
Telefonica de Espana ADS	TEF	35	DC	9,063	2.45 e	2.60 e	14	2.9	NR	3
Telefonos de Mexico'L'ADS	TMX	41	DC	7,910	6.20 e	7.00 e	6	3.5	NR	4
§ Telephone & Data Sys	TDS	46	DC	591	0.95 e	1.20 e	38	0.7	B+	3
• U S West Inc	USW	36	DC	10,294	3.00 e	3.10 e	11	6.0	B+	4

Telecommunications (Long Distance)

• AT&T Corp	T	50	DC	67,156	3.00 e	3.55 e	14	2.6	A-	5

Peer Comparisons (*Continued*)

	Company	Symbol										
§	Comsat Corp	CQ	19	DC	640	1.85 e	2.00 e	9	4.1	B	4
§	LDDS Communications	LDDS	19	DC	1,145	1.05 e	1.30 e	15	Nil	B	4
•	MCI Communications	MCIC	18	DC	11,921	1.44 e	1.65 e	11	0.2	B	5
•	Sprint Corp	FON	28	DC	11,368	2.53 e	2.65 e	10	3.6	B	2

Textile/Apparel Manufacturers

	Company	Symbol										
§	Burlington Industries	BUR	10	SP	2,127 *	1.46 py	1.20 e	8	Nil	NR	3
	Collins & Aikman	CKC	9	JA	1,306	1.60 e	1.75 e	5	Nil	NR	4
	Fieldcrest Cannon	FLD	26	DC	1,000	2.85 e	3.00 e	9	Nil	B-	3
§	Fruit of The Loom'A'	FTL	27	DC	1,884	1.80 e	2.50 e	11	Nil	NR	4
	Guilford Mills	GFD	22	SP	704 *	1.82 p	2.30 e	10	2.6	B+	4
	Haggar Corp	HGGR	25	SP	491 *	2.95 p	3.20 e	8	0.7	NR	4
§	Hancock Fabrics	HKF	9	JA	368	0.40 e	0.55 e	16	3.6	NR	5
•	Hartmarx Corp	HMX	6	NV	732	0.30 e	0.55 e	11	Nil	C	4
	Kellwood Co	KWD	21	AP	1,203 *	1.71	1.85 e	11	2.8	A-	4
•	Liz Claiborne	LIZ	17	DC	2,204	1.50 e	1.75 e	10	2.6	A-	4
•	Oshkosh B'Gosh Cl'A'	GOSHA	14	DC	340	0.55 e	0.65 e	22	2.0	B	1
	Oxford Indus	OXM	22	MY	625 *	2.23	2.35 e	9	3.2	B+	5
§	Phillips-Van Heusen	PVH	15	JA	1,152	1.15 e	2.00 e	8	0.9	A	3
	Pillowtex Corp	PTX	10	DC	292	0.97 e	1.29 e	8	Nil	NR	2
•	Russell Corp	RML	31	DC	931	2.00 e	2.30 e	14	1.5	A-	4
•	Springs Industries'A'	SMI	37	DC	2,023	3.15 e	3.50 e	11	3.2	B+	4
	Thomaston Mills'A'	TMSTA	16	JE	279 *	1.63	1.00 e	16	1.7	B	2
•	V.F. Corp	VFC	49	DC	4,320	4.20 e	4.65 e	10	2.7	A-	4

Tobacco

	Company	Symbol										
•	Amer Brands	AMB	38	DC	13,701	3.20 e	3.45 e	11	5.3	A	4
§	Dibrell Bros	DBRL	20	JE	919 *	d0.69	0.80 e	25	3.9	B+	3
•	Philip Morris Cos	MO	58	DC	50,621	5.45 e	6.15 e	9	5.7	A+	3
	RJR Nabisco Holdings	RN	6	DC	15,104	0.45 e	0.55 e	10	Nil	NR	3
§	Univl Corp	UVV	20	JE	2,975 *	1.09 y	1.45 e	14	5.0	B+	1
•	UST Inc	UST	28	DC	1,110	1.85 e	2.15 e	13	4.6	A+	5

Toys

	Company	Symbol										
•	Hasbro Inc	HAS	29	DC	2,747	2.00 e	2.55 e	11	0.9	B+	5
•	Mattel, Inc	MAT	25	DC	2,704	1.45 e	1.90 e	13	0.9	B-	3
	Tyco Toys	TTI	6	DC	730	d0.60 e	0.75 e	8	Nil	NR	5

Transportation Miscellaneous

	Company	Symbol										
	Air Express Intl	AEIC	20	DC	726	1.13 e	1.27 e	16	0.8	B	3
§	Airborne Freight	ABF	21	DC	1,720	2.00 e	2.20 e	9	1.4	B	3
•	Federal Express	FDX	60	MY	8,479 *	3.65	5.00 e	12	Nil	B-	4
•	Pittston Services Group	PZS	26	DC	1,569	2.05 e	2.25 e	12	0.7	B	4
•	Ryder System	R	22	DC	4,217	1.95 e	2.25 e	10	2.7	B	4

Truckers

	Company	Symbol										
§	Arnold Indus	AIND	21	DC	273	1.20 e	1.40 e	15	2.1	A	3
	Carolina Freight Corp	CAO	10	DC	845	1.35 e	0.65 e	15	Nil	C	2
•	Consolidated Freightways	CNF	22	DC	4,192	1.10 e	2.10 e	11	1.7	B-	3
§	Hunt(JB)Transport	JBHT	15	DC	1,021	1.15 e	1.40 e	11	1.3	B+	3
•	Roadway Services	ROAD	57	DC	4,156	1.10 e	3.50 e	16	2.4	A-	2
	Rollins Truck Leasing	RLC	12	SP	451 *	0.86	1.00 e	12	1.3	A-	4
	Werner Enterprises	WERN	24	FB	433	1.55 e	1.73 e	14	0.4	A-	3
•	Yellow Corp	YELL	24	DC	2,857	d0.05 e	1.75 e	14	3.9	B-	3

5

The Outlook for the Economy

From a forecasting perspective, the economy in 1995 is beset with questions, as can be deduced from the following predictions by S&P's chief economist, David Blitzer. The most urgent questions concern how long the Fed will continue to tighten policy and what the economy's response to the current tightening will be.

The Fed is attempting a "soft landing." It would like to slow the economy just enough to nip any inflationary rebound, but not enough to bring on a recession. This has been tried before, and the results are not encouraging. The most recent effort was in 1989 and 1990; the result was the recession of 1990–1991. Since the end of World War II, there have been nine recessions and two soft landings that did not send the economy downhill. The success stories were in the mid-1960s and the mid-1980s. In effect, the odds therefore are 9–2 against the Fed in 1995.

Despite the long odds, we think the 1995 soft landing story is a good bet. First, we have psychology on our side this time. Consumers and businesses are upbeat and optimistic; they are willing to spend money, but are also aggressively resisting inflation. Second, we could get a boost from federal spending. Now that the deficit has been beaten down for the last three years, a president seeking re-election and a Congress looking for tax cuts could easily combine to boost fiscal stimulus in 1995–1996. Third, the rest of the industrial world is finally emerging from recession. Renewed economic activity overseas should give U.S. exports a boost next year and provide a little help.

But the key to seeing how 1995 will unfold is to examine where we are right now. With that information we can move on to the question of where we'll go.

Review and Outlook: 1994

If we had to use just one word to describe the economy, that word would be "strong." GDP growth for all of 1994 rose 4%. The growth was broad-based: there were no notably weak spots, but a number of strong ones. The growth was powered by the economy's own momentum. This is not a case of exports being driven by a recovery among trading partners, or easy money stimulating housing, or government spending pumping up some sensitive sectors. It is a case of an economic engine running on all cylinders.

- **Consumers.** Consumer spending has raised some questions from time to time, due to concerns that income is not keeping up and that people are drawing down savings or borrowing money. While consumers are dipping into savings and borrowing more, the underlying fundamentals look very good. We have something of a virtuous (as opposed to vicious) cycle: gains in jobs are adding to consumer income and supporting consumer sentiment. This in turn raises demand and spending and means good business. The good business echoes back to further gains in jobs. Although such cycles don't last forever, they are very nice while they do. The start of 1995 will qualify as just such a time. We expect to see 6% or better real annual growth rates for disposable personal income for all of 1995. That will be supported by further job gains, with increases in payroll employment averaging about 200,000 new jobs per month. This will mean more gains in consumer spending as well.

- **Autos.** It is now clear that the seemingly soft auto sales over the summer of 1994 were due to plant closings and spot shortages, not to any weakness in demand or rising financing costs. Even though spot shortages for some models occurred in 1994's fourth quarter, auto sales are advancing and are projected to climb a shade below 1% in 1995.

- **Business capital spending.** Business capital spending is also holding up. The Commerce Department's survey of spending plans for 1994 showed an 8.8% real increase. This number looked good for several reasons. First, it is above 1993's 7.3% pace. More important, however, the 8.8% is from a survey done in August and is an upward revision from an earlier survey done in May. Businesses don't increase spending if they are pessimistic about the economy and their own business. We project a 9.4% increase in aggregate capital spending (called nonresidential fixed investment by economists) for 1995.

In the category of producers' durable equipment (a component of aggregate capital spending), growth in investment slowed in the first half of 1994. The reason was less dramatic increases in computers and a slowdown in the volatile transportation sector. But construction surged in the fourth quarter of 1993, then paused in the first quarter of 1994, and rebounded in the second half of 1994. As a result, business capital spending will be part of overall economic growth for the next few quarters. A 9.1% advance is forecast for 1995.

■ **Housing.** Housing may not be a source of growth, but it won't be a source of weakness either. Housing starts opened 1994 on a strong note and topped 1.5 million (seasonally adjusted annual rate) in March, before pulling back to about 1.4 million in the latter months of 1994. This pullback is not so much a sign of damage from high interest rates as it was an acknowledgment that 1.5 million is unsustainable. In fact, the 1.4 million won't be sustained in the long run because the underlying demographic demand is for about 1.2 million to 1.3 million units annually. So, housing has leveled off. For the time being, however, we expect good income growth and strong consumer sentiment to keep housing from dropping sharply.

Rising interest rates will have some effect on housing, but not as great as many fear. Mortgage money may cost more than it did a year ago, but there is no shortage of it. In the old days, it was possible for tight money to shut down housing and for housing to threaten to shut down the economy because rising rates would force banks to limit cheap mortgages. (There was no such thing as an expensive mortgage in the controlled markets of the 1970s and before.) This time, rates are rising, but mortgages are readily available. Moreover, consumers have learned that they can often refinance a mortgage a year or two later at a better rate—most people did just that in 1993. Another factor is the availability of adjustable rate mortgages, which often have more liberal credit requirements. So rising interest rates price fewer people out of the mortgage market than used to be the case. Rising mortgage rates limit housing, but don't shut it down.

- **Imports and exports.**   Trade is one sector that did not help the economy in 1994. Exports grew, but they continued to be limited by weak economies among our industrial trading partners. Our strong domestic economy, however, caused imports to grow. Exports should pick up in the second half of 1995 and are projected to advance 7.1%, versus an 8.2% rise in imports, for the full year.

- **Government.**   The other mixed spot is government spending. On the federal level, defense reduction is still the order of the day. The result is reduced spending and stimulus. In the second half of 1994, federal purchases shrank, driven down by defense. State and local government spending didn't contract, but they weren't much of a growth engine either.

Add it all up, and we see a strong economy driven by consumers and helped by businesses and trade. Another plus is low inflation. Price inflation at the consumer level will hover around 3–3.5% through 1995.

The good inflation results combined with the strong economy seem to fly in the face of the conventional wisdom (and the Fed's theories) that the two cannot coexist. Nonetheless, we are currently enjoying an unusual combination of zealous objections to rising prices and optimism about the economy from most consumers and business people. With the memory of the difficult 1991–1993 recovery so fresh, everyone is aggressive about fighting price increases. People register their objection to high prices by shopping around, patronizing competitors, or doing without. That attitude is helping to keep inflation low. At the same time, however, people are upbeat and willing to buy—when the price is right. This buying is helping to spur the economy. So, we get good growth and little inflation.

The rare combination of sentiments suggests that if there is any time that policymakers could be less concerned about inflation, this is it. Maybe the Fed should not restrain things quite so much.

Looking Ahead

The 1995 economy will be one of leveling off, not dropping. Real GDP growth is expected to slow to about 1% in the second and third quarters. The slowing comes from a combination of restraint (from higher interest rates) and a gradual depletion of pent-up demand. Housing has already started leveling off; auto sales will follow. So will job growth, and with it consumer spending. Business investment growth will ease further, despite some gains in construction. But there's nothing in the outlook to suggest that a recession awaits us in 1995—if the Fed stops tightening in time.

Moreover, we expect the economy to beat the 9–2 odds we mentioned at the opening of this chapter and slip through a two-quarter soft landing before beginning to pick up speed in late 1995 and 1996. These are long odds, though, and the idea of beating them deserves some explanation.

First, we expect the Fed to ease up in time. While its recent record may not inspire a lot of confidence—it did miss in 1990, after all—the Fed has done reasonably well in looking after the economy and does not see much to gain by bringing on a recession and having to argue it out with Congress. If the Fed merely stops tightening by May or June, but doesn't reverse and ease, we may still escape recession.

Second, we expect some fiscal stimulus. It has been a long time since the government spent money or cut taxes to boost the economy. In fact, the Clinton Administration is now at the other extreme: it has reduced the deficit, both in dollars and as a proportion of GDP, for three consecutive years. But now that it has established its deficit-fighting credentials and is looking toward the 1996 elections, we think a new strategy will emerge. Moreover, if the current talk in Congress continues, there could be some effort to have Reagan-style tax cuts, with support on both sides of the aisle. The President could step in and let taxes be trimmed with his blessing. That would help boost the economy, giving us (and Bill Clinton) a better 1996.

Third, there may be a little help from the trade sector. In 1995, economies in Europe and Japan should finally begin emerging from their slump. Improvements in those economies will mean gains for U.S. exports. These exports, which are now growing slowly, will boost the economy and help avoid a recession. So, though the odds may seem long, there should be a way to avoid recession and see the third soft landing—not the tenth recession—since World War II.

Risks and What-Ifs

No forecast is ever exactly right. So, some consideration of how the numbers in the following table might be off is worthwhile. We talked about the odds of a soft landing being 9–2 against, with the apparently more likely outcome being recession. While we believe that we will escape with a soft landing, the other possibility is worth considering.

Since the final quarter of 1993, the economy has consistently been stronger than many expected. Growth numbers have been revised upward, and the pessimists have been disappointed. Yet this robust growth could be sowing the seeds of its own destruction: the old boom-and-bust cycle. Presume for a moment that the economy continues to outpace the forecasts and grows more rapidly than our numbers indicate. Two factors will point to this boom being followed by a bust.

First, the Fed is not likely to be scared off by some strong numbers. In fact, if the economy surges ahead instead of gently throttling back, the Fed will become more aggressive in raising interest rates and tightening. When the slowdown does eventually arrive, the Fed will have stomped on the brakes quite hard, making the chances of easing just enough to let things quiet down gently much slimmer than 9–2.

Second, the Fed's theory of inflation—that if you really run the economy too fast for too long, you get inflation—is true. While we may argue about the definition of "too fast" or "too long," there are indeed speed limits. If the economy truly goes into overdrive, the result will be inflation. Inflation is likely to bring forth a nasty response from the Fed. It is also likely to worry people and business, knock sentiment for a loss, and increase the general uncertainty. All of that will add to the economic turmoil.

But for those who play it right, there may be some positives to the boom-and-bust cycle. The boom, if we get it, would likely carry through most of 1995, giving us another year of strong growth and good profits.

If we manage to avoid a recession in 1995, that doesn't mean there won't be another. It will come—and most likely well before the end of this decade. But a soft landing in 1995 would mean a little extra life for the current expansion. After such a long slow recovery, maybe we deserve a second shot at the expansion before the inevitable slump.

The S&P Economic Outlook
(Seasonally Adjusted Annual Rates)

	1994 (%)	1995E (%)	1996E (%)
Gross Domestic Product			
Annual rate of increase	6.2	5.1	5.0
Annual rate of increase—real GDP	4.0	3.0	2.5
Annual rate of increase—GDP deflator	2.1	2.3	2.4
Components of Real GDP			
Personal Consumption Expenditures	3.5	3.0	2.3
Durable goods	8.5	5.4	2.8
Nondurable goods	2.9	2.2	1.7
Services	2.5	2.7	2.6
Nonresidential Fixed Investment	13.7	9.4	4.4
Producers' Durable Equipment	17.6	9.1	3.9
Residential Fixed Investment	8.3	(2.2)	3.7
Net change in business inventories	45.3	31.1	16.0
Gov't Purchase of Goods & Services	(−0.8)	1.2	1.5
Federal	(−5.4)	(3.4)	(1.2)
State & Local	2.1	3.9	2.9
Exports	8.7	7.1	7.4
Imports	13.7	8.2	4.8
Income & Profits			
Personal Income	6.1	5.9	5.3
Disposable personal income	5.8	5.9	5.3
Savings rate	4.1	4.0	4.0
Corporate profits before taxes	12.2	(0.2)	2.2
Corporate profits after taxes	10.2	(2.0)	2.7
Earnings per share (S&P 500 on trailing 4Q)	32.5	5.1	7.5
Prices & Interest Rates (Avg. for period)			
Consumer Price Index	2.6	3.0	3.3
Treasury bills	4.2	5.8	4.5
10 year notes	7.1	7.8	6.7
30 year bonds	7.4	7.9	6.9
New issue rate—corporate bonds	8.0	8.7	7.7
Other Key Indicators			
Industrial Production Index	5.3	3.2	2.5
Capacity utilization rate	83.4	83.6	82.7
Housing starts	11.9	(5.9)	2.3
Auto sales	5.9	0.7	(3.1)
Unemployment rate	6.1	5.5	5.6
U.S. dollar (Quarterly % chg. at quarterly rates)	(−1.5)	(1.9)	(1.7)

6

Sector Investing Through Mutual Funds

It frequently has been said that mutual funds maintain marital harmony, because it is easier to replace an underperforming mutual fund manager than it is to replace an underperforming spouse. So if you prefer mutual funds to individual stocks, but would like to practice sector investing, don't despair. There are plenty of sector funds available.

Sector funds are mutual funds that emphasize the purchase of stocks in a specific industry or overall sector. There are more than 100 such funds. When investors attempt to find these funds, however, they typically must start with the fund family and then see if that family offers a sector fund. In an attempt to reverse this process, and keep within the framework of this book, many of these funds have been assigned to one or more of the corresponding industries in the S&P 500. In situations where the fund invests in all industries of a particular sector, that fund has been assigned to one or more of the corresponding S&P 500 sectors. No fund has been assigned to both a particular industry and its overall sector. Funds are either industry-specific or sector-specific.

Along with the name of the fund and the corresponding sectors or industries, you will find the one-year and five-year total returns (share price appreciation plus dividends reinvested).

Please be aware that this list is by no means all-inclusive. In addition, these industry and sector funds are not likely to invest in only those companies found in the S&P 500. Shares of other domestic and international industry-related (as well as non-industry-related) companies may be bought and sold by the sector fund manager. Be sure to order the fund's prospectus and read it carefully. This will tell you about the full range of companies that the fund may own, as well as the fund's performance, expenses, minimum investment levels, limits to the number of switches per year, and other important information.

Sector Funds Listing

| S&P Sector | | | Total Returns (%) | |
S&P Industry	Distributor	Fund Name	1994	5-Yr.
Basic Materials	**Dean Witter Distributors**	**Natural Resources**	−0.9	3.8
	Fidelity Distributors	**Select Industrial Materials**	8.2	10.7
	Merrill Lynch Funds	**Natural Resources A**	1.2	3.6
	Putnam Mutual Funds	**Natural Resources A**	−2.8	3.7
	T. Rowe Price	**New Era**	5.2	5.3
Aluminum				
Chemicals	Fidelity Distributors	Select Chemical	14.8	13.4
Chemicals (Diversified)	Fidelity Distributors	Select Chemical	14.8	13.4
Chemicals (Specialty)	Fidelity Distributors	Select Chemical	14.8	13.4
Containers (Metal & Glass)	• • •	• • •		
Containers (Paper)	Fidelity Distributors	Select Paper & Forest Products	14.1	11.6
Gold Mining	Benham Distributors	Gold Equities Index	−16.7	−0.3
	Blanchard Group of Funds	Precious Metals	−15.0	0.9
	Bull & Bear	Gold Investors Ltd.	−13.8	0.6
	Dean Witter Distributors	Precious Metals	−11.5	NA
	Fidelity Distributors	Select American Gold	−15.5	2.6
	Fidelity Distributors	Select Precious Metals	−1.1	5.6
	Franklin Distributors	Gold	−4.7	2.4
	John Hancock	Freedom Gold & Government B	−15.5	2.6
	IDS Financial Services	Precious Metals	−9.6	1.8
	Invesco Funds Group	Strategic Portfolio - Gold	−27.9	−4.0
	Keystone Distributors	Precious Metals Holdings	−13.3	3.8
	Lexington Funds	Goldfund	−7.3	0.5
	Lexington Funds	Strategic Investments	11.3	−5.5
	Lexington Funds	Strategic Silver	−8.4	−3.7
	MFS Financial Services	Gold & Natural Resources B	−17.7	−1.7
	Oppenheimer Fund Mgmt.	Gold & Special Minerals	−6.0	0.1
	Scudder Investor Services	Gold	−7.5	0.8
	United Services Advisors	Gold Shares	−2.7	−9.9
	United Services Advisors	World Gold	−16.9	0.9
	USAA Investment Mgmt.	Gold	−9.4	−1.5
	Van Eck Securities	Gold/Resources	−15.6	0.3
	Van Eck Securities	International Investors Gold	−1.0	2.3
	Vanguard Group	Spec. Portfolio - Gold & Prec. Metals	−5.4	4.3
Metals (Miscellaneous)	• • •	• • •		
Paper & Forest Products	Fidelity Distributors	Select Paper & Forest Products	14.1	11.6
Steel	• • •	• • •		
Capital Goods	**Fidelity Distributors**	**Select Industrial Equipment**	**3.1**	**12.1**
Aerospace/Defense	Fidelity Distributors	Select Defense & Aerospace	1.8	9.7
	John Hancock	Freedom Nat'l Aviation & Tech.	−14.2	2.5
Electrical Equipment	Fidelity Distributors	Select Electronics	17.2	23.1
Engineering & Construction	Fidelity Distributors	Select Construction & Housing	−16.0	11.2
Heavy Duty Trucks & Parts	Fidelity Distributors	Select Automotive	−12.8	16.5
Machine Tools	• • •	• • •		
Machinery (Diversified)	• • •	• • •		
Manufacturing (Diversified)	Fidelity Distributors	Select Industrial Materials	8.2	10.7
Pollution Control	Fidelity Distributors	Select Environmental Services	−9.6	−1.4
	Invesco Funds Group	Strategic Portfolio - Environmental	−11.4	NA
Consumer Cyclical	**Fidelity Distributors**	**Select Consumer Products**	**−7.1**	**NA**
Auto Parts After Market	Fidelity Distributors	Select Automotive	−12.8	16.5
Automobiles	Fidelity Distributors	Select Automotive	−12.8	16.5
Broadcast Media	Fidelity Distributors	Select Leisure	−6.8	9.3
	Fidelity Distributors	Select Multimedia	4.0	12.1
	Invesco Funds Group	Strategic Portfolio - Leisure	−5.0	16.7
Building Materials	Fidelity Distributors	Select Construction & Housing	−16.0	11.2

Total Returns Courtesy of Lipper Analytical Services

Sector Funds Listing (*Continued*)

Entertainment	Fidelity Distributors	Select Leisure	−6.8	9.3
	Fidelity Distributors	Select Multimedia	4.0	12.1
	Invesco Funds Group	Strategic Portfolio - Leisure	−5.0	16.7
Hardware & Tools	Fidelity Distributors	Select Construction & Housing	−16.0	11.2
Homebuilding	Fidelity Distributors	Select Construction & Housing	−16.0	11.2
Hotel-Motel	Fidelity Distributors	Select Leisure	−6.8	9.3
	Invesco Funds Group	Strategic Portfolio - Leisure	−5.0	16.7
Household Furn. & Appliances	Fidelity Distributors	Select Construction & Housing	−16.0	11.2
Leisure Time	Fidelity Distributors	Select Leisure	−6.8	9.3
	Invesco Funds Group	Strategic Portfolio - Leisure	−5.0	16.7
Manufactured Housing	Fidelity Distributors	Select Construction & Housing	−16.0	11.2
Publishing	Fidelity Distributors	Select Leisure	−6.8	9.3
	Fidelity Distributors	Select Multimedia	4.0	12.1
	Invesco Funds Group	Strategic Portfolio - Leisure	−5.0	16.7
Publishing (Newspapers)	Fidelity Distributors	Select Leisure	−6.8	9.3
	Fidelity Distributors	Select Multimedia	4.0	12.1
	Invesco Funds Group	Strategic Portfolio - Leisure	−5.0	16.7
Restaurants	Fidelity Distributors	Select Food & Agriculture	6.1	12.4
	Fidelity Distributors	Select Leisure	−6.8	9.3
	Invesco Funds Group	Strategic Portfolio - Leisure	−5.0	16.7
Retail (Department Stores)	Fidelity Distributors	Select Retailing	−5.0	15.9
Retail (General Merchandise)	Fidelity Distributors	Select Retailing	−5.0	15.9
Retail (Specialty)	Fidelity Distributors	Select Retailing	−5.0	15.9
Retail (Specialty-Apparel)	Fidelity Distributors	Select Retailing	−5.0	15.9
Shoes	· · ·	· · ·		
Textiles	· · ·	· · ·		
Toys	Fidelity Distributors	Select Leisure	−6.8	9.3
	Invesco Funds Group	Strategic Portfolio - Leisure	−5.0	16.7
:onsumer Staples	**Fidelity Distributors**	**Select Consumer Products**	**−7.1**	**NA**
Beverages (Alcoholic)	Fidelity Distributors	Select Food & Agriculture	6.1	12.4
Beverages (Soft Drinks)	Fidelity Distributors	Select Food & Agriculture	6.1	12.4
Cosmetics				
Distributors (Consumer Prods)	Fidelity Distributors	Select Food & Agriculture	6.1	12.4
Foods	Fidelity Distributors	Select Food & Agriculture	6.1	12.4
Health Care (Diversified)	Dean Witter Distributors	Health Sciences Trust	−6.5	NA
	Fidelity Distributors	Select Health Care	21.4	18.5
	G.T. Global Financial Services	Global Health Care A	0.3	9.7
	Invesco Funds Group	Strategic Portfolio - Health Sciences	0.9	14.0
	Merrill Lynch Funds	Health Care A	−4.3	NA
	Putnam Mutual Funds	Health Sciences Trust A	15.2	12.1
	Vanguard Group	Spec. Portfolio - Health Care	9.5	15.6
Health Care (Drugs)	Dean Witter Distributors	Health Sciences Trust	−6.5	NA
	Fidelity Distributors	Select Health Care	21.4	18.5
	G.T. Global Financial Services	Global Health Care A	0.3	9.7
	Invesco Funds Group	Strategic Portfolio - Health Sciences	0.9	14.0
	Merrill Lynch Funds	Health Care A	−4.3	NA
	Putnam Mutual Funds	Health Sciences Trust A	15.2	12.1
	Vanguard Group	Spec. Portfolio - Health Care	9.5	15.6
Health Care (Miscellaneous)	Dean Witter Distributors	Health Sciences Trust	−6.5	NA
	Fidelity Distributors	Select Biotechnology	−18.2	16.3
	Fidelity Distributors	Select Health Care	21.4	18.5
	Fidelity Distributors	Select Medical Delivery	19.8	17.8
	G.T. Global Financial Services	Global Health Care A	0.3	9.7
	Invesco Funds Group	Strategic Portfolio - Health Sciences	0.9	14.0
	Merrill Lynch Funds	Health Care A	−4.3	NA
	Putnam Mutual Funds	Health Sciences Trust A	15.2	12.1
	Vanguard Group	Spec. Portfolio - Health Care	9.5	15.6
Hospital Management	Dean Witter Distributors	Health Sciences Trust	−6.5	NA
	Fidelity Distributors	Select Health Care	21.4	18.5
	Fidelity Distributors	Select Medical Delivery	19.8	17.8
	G.T. Global Financial Services	Global Health Care A	0.3	9.7
	Invesco Funds Group	Strategic Portfolio - Health Sciences	0.9	14.0
	Merrill Lynch Funds	Health Care A	−4.3	NA

Sector Funds Listing (*Continued*)

	Putnam Mutual Funds	Health Sciences Trust A	15.2	12.1
	Vanguard Group	Spec. Portfolio - Health Care	9.5	15.6
Household Products	Fidelity Distributors	Select Construction & Housing	−16.0	11.2
Housewares	Fidelity Distributors	Select Construction & Housing	−16.0	11.2
Medical Products & Supplies	Dean Witter Distributors	Health Sciences Trust	−6.5	NA
	Fidelity Distributors	Select Health Care	21.4	18.5
	G.T. Global Financial Services	Global Health Care A	0.3	9.7
	Invesco Funds Group	Strategic Portfolio - Health Sciences	0.9	14.0
	Merrill Lynch Funds	Health Care A	−4.3	NA
	Putnam Mutual Funds	Health Sciences Trust A	15.2	12.1
	Vanguard Group	Spec. Portfolio - Health Care	9.5	15.6
Retail (Drug Stores)	Fidelity Distributors	Select Retailing	−5.0	15.9
Retail (Food Chains)	Fidelity Distributors	Select Retailing	−5.0	15.9
Tobacco	Fidelity Distributors	Select Food & Agriculture	6.1	12.4
Energy	**Dean Witter Distributors**	**Natural Resources**	**−0.9**	**3.8**
	Fidelity Distributors	**Select Energy**	**0.4**	**2.2**
	Invesco Funds Group	**Strategic Portfolio - Energy**	**−7.3**	**−5.4**
	Merrill Lynch Funds	**Natural Resources A**	**1.2**	**3.6**
	PaineWebber	**Global Energy**	**−9.9**	**0.7**
	T. Rowe Price	**New Era**	**5.2**	**5.3**
	Putnam Mutual Funds	**Natural Resources A**	**−2.8**	**3.7**
	State Street Research	**Global Energy A**	**−4.4**	**NA**
	United Services Advisors	**Global Resources**	**−9.7**	**−1.7**
	Vanguard Group	**Spec. Portfolio - Energy**	**−1.6**	**5.5**
Oil & Gas Drilling	Fidelity Distributors	Select Energy Service	0.4	−0.4
	Fidelity Distributors	Select Natural Gas	−6.8	NA
Oil (Domestic Integrated)	• • •	• • •		
Oil (Exploration & Production)	Fidelity Distributors	Select Energy Service	0.4	−0.4
Oil (International Integrated)	• • •	• • •		
Oil Well Equip. & Serv.	Fidelity Distributors	Select Energy Service	0.4	−0.4
Financials	**Century Shares Trust**	**Century Shares**	**−3.9**	**8.1**
	Fidelity Distributors	**Select Financial Services**	**−3.7**	**14.6**
	John Hancock	**Freedom Regional Bank**	**−0.2**	**18.2**
	Invesco Funds Group	**Strategic Portfolio - Financial**	**−5.9**	**18.0**
	PaineWebber	**Regional Fin'l**	**−1.5**	**NA**
Insurance Brokers	Fidelity Distributors	Select Insurance	−0.3	10.2
Life Insurance	Fidelity Distributors	Select Insurance	−0.3	10.2
Major Regional Banks	Fidelity Distributors	Select Regional Banks	0.2	16.8
	Fidelity Distributors	Select Home Finance	2.6	23.6
	John Hancock	Freedom Regional Bank B	−0.2	18.2
	PaineWebber	Regional Financial	−1.5	NA
Money Center Banks	Fidelity Distributors	Select Regional Banks	0.2	16.8
	Fidelity Distributors	Select Home Finance	2.6	23.6
	John Hancock	Freedom Regional Bank B	−0.2	18.2
	PaineWebber	Regional Financial	−1.5	NA
Multi-Line Insurance	Fidelity Distributors	Select Insurance	−0.3	10.2
Personal Loans	Fidelity Distributors	Select Home Finance	2.6	23.6
Property-Casualty Insurance	Century Shares Trust	Century Shares	−3.9	8.1
	Fidelity Distributors	Select Insurance	−0.3	10.2
Savings & Loan Companies	Fidelity Distributors	Select Home Finance	2.6	23.6
	PaineWebber	Regional Financial	−1.5	NA
Financial (Miscellaneous)	Fidelity Distributors	Select Broker & Invest. Mgmt.	−17.3	14.7
Services				
Specialized Services	• • •	• • •		
Specialty Printing	• • •	• • •		
Technology	**Alliance Fund Distributors**	**Technology**	**28.5**	**22.0**
	Fidelity Distributors	**Select Technology**	**11.1**	**22.3**

Sector Funds Listing (*Continued*)

	Franklin Distributors	DynaTech	5.2	10.5
	John Hancock	Freedom Nat'l Aviation & Tech.	−14.2	2.5
	John Hancock	Freedom Global Technology	9.6	10.7
	Invesco Funds Group	Strategic Portfolio - Technology	5.3	22.5
	Kemper Financial Services	Technology	11.2	12.2
	Merrill Lynch Funds	Technology A	26.6	NA
	T. Rowe Price	Science & Technology	15.8	22.0
	Seligman Financial Svcs	Communications & Information A	35.3	24.6
Communication Equip./Mfrs.	Fidelity Distributors	Select Developing Communications	15.2	NA
	G.T. Global Financial Services	Global Telecommunications A	4.4	NA
	Montgomery Securities	Global Communications	−13.4	NA
Computer Software & Services	Fidelity Distributors	Select Software & Services	0.4	21.5
Computer Systems	Fidelity Distributors	Select Computers	20.5	24.0
Electronics (Defense)	Fidelity Distributors	Select Defense & Aerospace	1.8	9.7
Electronics (Instrumentation)	Fidelity Distributors	Select Electronics	17.2	23.1
Electronics (Semiconductors)	Fidelity Distributors	Select Electronics	17.2	23.1
Office Equipment & Supplies	Fidelity Distributors	Select Computers	20.5	24.0
Photography/Imaging	Fidelity Distributors	Select Leisure	−6.8	9.3
Telecom. (Long Dist.)	Fidelity Distributors	Select Telecommunications	4.3	11.3
	G.T. Global Financial Services	Global Telecommunications A	4.4	NA
	Montgomery Securities	Global Communications	−13.4	NA
Transportation	**Fidelity Distributors**	**Select Transportation**	**3.9**	**15.0**
Airlines	Fidelity Distributors	Select Air Transportation	−21.7	4.1
	John Hancock	Freedom Nat'l Aviation & Tech.	−14.2	2.5
Railroads	· · ·	· · ·		
Truckers	· · ·	· · ·		
Transportation (Miscellaneous)	· · ·	· · ·		
Utilities	**ABT Financial Services**	**Utility Income**	−12.2	3.2
	AIM Distributors	Utilities - A	−11.6	5.2
	American Capital	Utilitiy Income A	7.1	NA
	Benham Distributors	Utilities Income	−10.0	NA
	BT Investments	Utility	−11.7	NA
	Cappiello-Rushmore	Utility Income	−13.3	NA
	Colonial Investment Svcs.	Utilities	−11.0	NA
	Dean Witter Distributors	Utilities	−9.9	5.6
	Eaton Vance Distributors	Traditional Total Return Trust	−12.2	4.9
	Federated Securities	Fortress Utility	−7.9	8.0
	Federated Securities	Liberty Utility	−8.0	8.2
	Fidelity Distributors	Select Utilities	−7.4	7.0
	Fidelity Distributors	Utilities Income	−5.3	8.4
	Franklin Distributors	Utilities	−11.7	6.0
	IDS Financial Services	Utilities Income	−7.1	8.0
	Invesco Funds Group	Strategic Portfolio - Utilities	−9.9	6.8
	Liberty Financial	Utilities	−6.8	NA
	Merrill Lynch Funds	Global Utility	−10.0	NA
	Midwest	Utility	−2.0	7.4
	Prudential Mutual Funds	Global Utility	−7.8	10.6
	Prudential Mutual Funds	Utility	−8.5	5.1
	Putnam Mutual Funds	Utilities Growth & Income A	−7.0	NA
	Smith Barney Shearson	Utility B	−10.1	6.1
	Vanguard Group	Spec. Portfolio - Utilities Inc.	−8.6	NA
Electric Companies	Dreyfus Service Corp.	Edison Electric Index	−12.7	NA
Natural Gas	Fidelity Distributors	Select Natural Gas	−6.8	NA
	Rushmore	American Gas Index	−9.8	1.6
Telephone	Fidelity Distributors	Select Telecommunications	4.3	11.3
	G.T. Global Financial Services	Global Telecommunications A	4.4	NA
	Montgomery Securities	Global Communications	−13.4	NA
Other	Neuberger & Berman	Select Sectors	0.9	10.8
	MFS Financial Services	Managed Sectors A	−2.9	NA

Appendix A

The S&P 500 Composite Index
Sectors, Industries, and Companies and Their Percentage of the Overall Index as of 12/30/94

Sector / Industry		%OF 500
Basic Materials		**7.10**
Aluminum		0.49
AL	Alcan Aluminium Ltd.	0.17
AA	Aluminum Co. of America.	0.23
RLM	Reynolds Metals.	0.09
Chemicals		2.71
APD	Air Products & Chemicals	0.15
DOW	Dow Chemical	0.56
DD	Du Pont (E.I.)	1.14
EMN	Eastman Chemical	0.12
GR	Goodrich (B.F.).	0.03
HPC	Hercules, Inc.	0.14
MTC	Monsanto Company	0.24
PX	Praxair, Inc	0.08
ROH	Rohm & Haas.	0.12
UK	Union Carbide.	0.13
Chemicals (Diversified)		0.44
AVY	Avery Dennison Corp.	0.06
EC	Engelhard Corp	0.06
FMC	FMC Corp	0.06
FRM	First Mississippi Corp	0.02
PPG	PPG Industries	0.24
Chemicals (Specialty)		0.48
GRA	Grace (W.R.) & Co.	0.11
GLK	Great Lakes Chemical	0.12
MII	Morton International	0.13
NLC	Nalco Chemical	0.07
SIAL	Sigma-Aldrich.	0.05
Containers (Metal & Glass)		0.13
BLL	Ball Corp.	0.03
CCK	Crown Cork & Seal.	0.10
Containers (Paper)		0.17
BMS	Bemis Company.	0.04
STO	Stone Container.	0.05
TIN	Temple-Inland.	0.08
Gold Mining		0.63
ABX	American Barrick Res	0.23
ECO	Echo Bay Mines Ltd	0.04
HM	Homestake Mining	0.07
NEM	Newmont Mining	0.09
PDG	Placer Dome Inc.	0.15
GLD	Santa Fe Pacific Gold Corp	0.05
Metals (Miscellaneous)		0.34
AR	ASARCO Inc	0.04
CYM	Cyprus Amax Minerals Co.	0.07
N	Inco, Ltd.	0.10
PD	Phelps Dodge	0.13
Paper & Forest Products		1.31
BCC	Boise Cascade.	0.03
CHA	Champion International	0.10
FBO	Federal Paper Board.	0.04
GP	Georgia-Pacific.	0.19
IP	International Paper.	0.28
JR	James River.	0.05
LPX	Louisiana Pacific.	0.09
MEA	Mead Corp.	0.09
PCH	Potlatch Corp.	0.03
UCC	Union Camp.	0.10
W	Westvaco Corp.	0.08
WY	Weyerhaeuser Corp.	0.23

Sector / Industry		%OF 500
Steel		0.40
AS	Armco Inc.	0.02
BS	Bethlehem Steel.	0.06
IAD	Inland Steel Ind. Inc.	0.05
NUE	Nucor Corp	0.14
X	USX-U.S. Steel Group	0.08
WTHG	Worthington Ind.	0.05
Capital Goods		**9.06**
Aerospace/Defense		1.77
BA	Boeing Company	0.48
GD	General Dynamics	0.08
LK	Lockheed Corp.	0.14
ML	Martin Marietta.	0.13
MD	McDonnell Douglas.	0.17
NOC	Northrop Grumman Corp.	0.06
RTN	Raytheon Co.	0.25
ROK	Rockwell International	0.23
UTX	United Technologies.	0.23
Conglomerates		0.66
ITT	ITT Corp	0.28
TDY	Teledyne Inc	0.03
TGT	Tenneco Inc.	0.22
TXT	Textron Inc.	0.13
Electrical Equipment		3.73
AMP	AMP Inc.	0.23
EMR	Emerson Electric	0.42
GE	General Electric	2.61
GSX	General Signal	0.04
GWW	Grainger (W.W.) Inc.	0.09
HON	Honeywell.	0.12
RYC	Raychem Corp	0.05
TNB	Thomas & Betts	0.04
WX	Westinghouse Electric.	0.13
Engineering & Construction		0.16
FLR	Fluor Corp	0.11
FWC	Foster Wheeler	0.03
MRN	Morrison Knudsen	0.01
ZRN	Zurn Industries.	0.01
Heavy Duty Trucks & Parts		0.32
CUM	Cummins Engine Co., Inc.	0.06
DCN	Dana Corp.	0.07
ETN	Eaton Corp	0.11
NAV	Navistar International Corp.	0.03
PCAR	PACCAR Inc	0.05
Machine Tools		0.04
CMZ	Cincinnati Milacron.	0.02
GIDL	Giddings & Lewis	0.02
Machinery (Diversified)		0.91
BGG	Briggs & Stratton.	0.03
CAT	Caterpillar Inc.	0.33
CKL	Clark Equipment.	0.03
CBE	Cooper Industries.	0.12
DE	Deere & Co	0.17
HPH	Harnischfeger Indus.	0.04
IR	Ingersoll-Rand	0.10
NC	NACCO Ind. Cl. A	0.01
TKR	Timken Co.	0.03
VAT	Varity Corp.	0.05

Sector Industry		%OF 500
Capital Goods (continued)		
Manufacturing (Div. Ind.)		**0.91**
ALD	AlliedSignal	0.29
CR	Crane Company.	0.02
DOV	Dover Corp	0.09
ITW	Illinois Tool Works.	0.15
JCI	Johnson Controls	0.06
MIL	Millipore Corp	0.04
PLL	Pall Corp.	0.06
PH	Parker-Hannifin.	0.07
TNV	Trinova Corp	0.03
TYC	Tyco International	0.10
Pollution Control		**0.56**
BFI	Browning-Ferris Ind.	0.17
REN	Rollins Environmental.	0.01
WMX	WMX Technologies Inc	0.38
Consumer Cyclical		**13.80**
Auto Parts After Market		**0.40**
CTB	Cooper Tire & Rubber	0.06
ECH	Echlin Inc	0.05
GPC	Genuine Parts.	0.13
GT	Goodyear Tire & Rubber	0.15
SPW	SPX Corp	0.01
Automobiles		**2.32**
C	Chrysler Corp.	0.52
F	Ford Motor	0.85
GM	General Motors	0.95
Broadcast Media		**0.97**
CBS	CBS Inc.	0.10
CCB	Capital Cities/ABC	0.39
CMCSK	Comcast Class A Special.	0.11
TCOMA	Tele-Communications.	0.37
Building Materials		**0.23**
MAS	Masco Corp	0.11
OCF	Owens-Corning Fiberglas.	0.04
SHW	Sherwin-Williams	0.08
Entertainment		**1.61**
KWP	King World Productions	0.04
TWX	Time Warner Inc.	0.40
VIA.B	Viacom Inc	0.43
DIS	Walt Disney Co	0.74
Hardware & Tools		**0.15**
BDK	Black & Decker Corp.	0.06
SNA	Snap-On Inc.	0.04
SWK	Stanley Works.	0.05
Homebuilding		**0.05**
CTX	Centex Corp.	0.02
KBH	Kaufman & Broad Home Corp.	0.01
PHM	Pulte Corp	0.02
Hotel-Motel		**0.29**
HLT	Hilton Hotels.	0.10
MAR	Marriott Int'l	0.10
PRI	Promus Inc	0.09
Household Furn. & Appliances		**0.23**
ACK	Armstrong World.	0.04
BSET	Bassett Furniture.	0.01
MYG	Maytag Corp.	0.05
WHR	Whirlpool Corp	0.11
ZE	Zenith Electronics	0.02

Sector Industry		%OF 500
Leisure Time		**0.08**
BLY	Bally Entertainment Corp	0.01
BC	Brunswick Corp	0.05
HDL	Handleman Co	0.01
OM	Outboard Marine.	0.01
Manufactured Housing		**0.04**
FLE	Fleetwood Enterprises.	0.03
SKY	Skyline Corp	0.01
Publishing		**0.40**
DNB	Dun & Bradstreet	0.28
MHP	McGraw-Hill.	0.10
MDP	Meredith Corp.	0.02
Publishing (Newspapers)		**0.69**
DJ	Dow Jones & Co	0.09
GCI	Gannett Co	0.22
KRI	Knight-Ridder Inc.	0.08
NYT.A	New York Times Cl. A	0.07
TMC	Times Mirror	0.12
TRB	Tribune Co	0.11
Restaurants		**0.70**
LUB	Luby's Cafeterias.	0.02
MCD	McDonald's Corp.	0.61
RYAN	Ryan's Family Steak Hse.	0.01
SHN	Shoney's Inc	0.02
WEN	Wendy's International.	0.04
Retail (Department Stores)		**0.79**
DDS	Dillard Department Stores.	0.09
MA	May Dept. Stores	0.25
MST	Mercantile Stores.	0.04
NOBE	Nordstrom.	0.10
JCP	Penney (J.C.).	0.31
Retail (General Merchandise)		**2.27**
DH	Dayton Hudson.	0.15
KM	K mart	0.18
S	Sears, Roebuck & Co.	0.48
WMT	Wal-Mart Stores.	1.46
Retail (Specialty)		**1.49**
CC	Circuit City Stores.	0.06
HD	Home Depot	0.62
LOW	Lowe's Cos	0.17
MES	Melville Corp.	0.10
PBY	Pep Boys	0.06
PCCW	Price/Costco Inc	0.07
TAN	Tandy Corp	0.09
TOY	Toys R Us.	0.26
Z	Woolworth Corp	0.06
Retail (Specialty-Apparel)		**0.37**
CHRS	Charming Shoppes	0.02
GPS	Gap (The).	0.13
LTD	Limited, The	0.19
TJX	TJX Companies Inc.	0.03
Shoes		**0.30**
BG	Brown Group.	0.02
NKE	NIKE Inc	0.16
RBK	Reebok International	0.10
SRR	Stride Rite.	0.02

Sector Industry		%OF 500	Sector Industry		%OF 500
Consumer Cyclical (continued)			**Health Care (Miscellaneous)**		**0.79**
Textiles		**0.21**	AZA	ALZA Corp. Cl. A	0.04
HMX	Hartmarx Corp.	0.01	AMGN	Amgen.	0.23
LIZ	Liz Claiborne, Inc	0.04	BEV	Beverly Enterprises.	0.04
GOSHA	Oshkosh B'Gosh	0.01	MNR	Manor Care	0.05
RML	Russell Corp	0.04	USHC	U.S. Healthcare Inc.	0.20
SMI	Springs Industries Inc	0.02	UNH	United HealthCare Corp	0.23
VFC	V.F. Corp.	0.09			
			Hospital Management		**0.47**
Toys		**0.21**	COL	Columbia/HCA Healthcare Corp	0.39
HAS	Hasbro Inc	0.08	CMY	Community Psych Centers.	0.01
MAT	Mattel, Inc.	0.13	NME	National Medical Enterprise.	0.07
			Household Products		**2.59**
Consumer Staples		**22.36**	CLX	Clorox Co.	0.09
Beverages (Alcoholic)		**0.80**	CL	Colgate-Palmolive.	0.27
BUD	Anheuser-Busch	0.39	KMB	Kimberly-Clark	0.24
BF.B	Brown-Forman Corp.	0.06	PG	Procter & Gamble	1.27
ACCOB	Coors (Adolph)	0.02	SPP	Scott Paper.	0.16
VO	Seagram Co. Ltd.	0.33	UN	Unilever N.V	0.56
Beverages (Soft Drinks)		**2.84**	**Housewares**		**0.33**
KO	Coca Cola Co	1.98	NWL	Newell Co.	0.10
PEP	PepsiCo Inc.	0.86	PMI	Premark International.	0.09
			RBD	Rubbermaid Inc	0.14
Cosmetics		**0.78**			
ACV	Alberto-Culver	0.02	**Medical Products & Supplies**		**0.77**
AVP	Avon Products.	0.12	BCR	Bard (C.R.) Inc.	0.04
G	Gillette Co.	0.49	BOL	Bausch & Lomb.	0.06
IFF	International Flav/Frag.	0.15	BAX	Baxter International Inc	0.24
			BDX	Becton, Dickinson.	0.10
Distributors (Consumer Products)		**0.22**	BMET	Biomet, Inc.	0.05
FLM	Fleming Cos. Inc	0.03	MDT	Medtronic Inc.	0.19
SVU	Supervalu Inc.	0.05	STJM	St. Jude Medical	0.06
SYY	Sysco Corp	0.14	USS	U.S. Surgical.	0.03
Foods		**3.02**	**Retail (Drug Stores)**		**0.24**
ADM	Archer-Daniels-Midland	0.32	LDG	Longs Drug Stores.	0.02
CPC	CPC International.	0.24	RAD	Rite Aid	0.06
CPB	Campbell Soup.	0.33	WAG	Walgreen Co.	0.16
CAG	ConAgra Inc.	0.23			
GIS	General Mills.	0.27	**Retail (Food Chains)**		**0.60**
HNZ	Heinz (H.J.)	0.27	ABS	Albertson's.	0.22
HSY	Hershey Foods.	0.13	ASC	American Stores.	0.11
K	Kellogg Co	0.39	BRNO	Bruno's Inc.	0.02
PT	Pet Inc.	0.06	GFS.A	Giant Food Cl. A	0.04
OAT	Quaker Oats.	0.12	GAP	Great A & P.	0.02
RAL	Ralston-Ralston Purina Gp.	0.13	KR	Kroger Co.	0.08
SLE	Sara Lee Corp.	0.36	WIN	Winn-Dixie	0.11
WWY	Wrigley (Wm) Jr.	0.17			
			Tobacco		**1.88**
Health Care (Diversified)		**3.72**	AMB	American Brands Inc.	0.23
ABT	Abbott Labs.	0.79	MO	Philip Morris.	1.48
AGN	Allergan, Inc.	0.05	UST	UST Inc.	0.17
AHP	American Home Products	0.57			
BMY	Bristol-Myers Squibb	0.88	**Energy**		**9.90**
JNJ	Johnson & Johnson.	1.05	**Oil & Gas Drilling**		**0.04**
MKG	Mallinckrodt Group Inc	0.07	HP	Helmerich & Payne.	0.02
WLA	Warner-Lambert	0.31	RDC	Rowan Cos.	0.02
Health Care (Drugs)		**3.31**	**Oil (Exploration & Production)**		**0.20**
LLY	Lilly (Eli) & Co	0.57	BR	Burlington Resources	0.13
MRK	Merck & Co	1.43	MXS	Maxus Energy	0.01
PFE	Pfizer, Inc.	0.73	ORX	Oryx Energy Co	0.04
SGP	Schering-Plough.	0.42	SFR	Santa Fe Energy Resources.	0.02
UPJ	Upjohn Co.	0.16			

The S&P 500 Composite Index (*Continued*)
Sectors, Industries, and Companies and Their Percentage of the Overall Index as of 12/30/94

Sector Industry		%OF 500	Sector Industry		%OF 500
Energy (continued)			**Money Center Banks**		**1.96**
	Oil (Domestic Integrated)	**1.72**	BAC	BankAmerica Corp	0.44
AHC	Amerada Hess	0.13	BT	Bankers Trust N.Y.	0.13
ASH	Ashland Oil.	0.06	CMB	Chase Manhattan.	0.19
ARC	Atlantic Richfield	0.49	CHL	Chemical Banking Corp.	0.26
KMG	Kerr-McGee	0.07	CCI	Citicorp	0.49
LLX	Louisiana Land & Exploration	0.04	FNB	First Chicago Corp	0.13
OXY	Occidental Petroleum	0.18	JPM	Morgan (J.P.) & Co	0.32
PZL	Pennzoil Co.	0.06			
P	Phillips Petroleum	0.26	**Multi-Line Insurance**		**1.23**
SUN	Sun Co., Inc	0.09	AET	Aetna Life & Casualty.	0.16
MRO	USX-Marathon Group	0.14	AIG	American Int'l. Group.	0.93
UCL	Unocal Corp.	0.20	CI	CIGNA Corp	0.14
	Oil (International Integrated)	**7.18**	**Personal Loans**		**0.17**
AN	Amoco.	0.88	BNL	Beneficial Corp.	0.06
CHV	Chevron Corp	0.87	HI	Household International.	0.11
XON	Exxon Corp	2.25			
MOB	Mobil Corp	1.00	**Property-Casualty Insurance**		**0.78**
RD	Royal Dutch Petroleum.	1.72	CB	Chubb Corp	0.20
TX	Texaco Inc	0.46	CIC	Continental Corp	0.03
			GRN	General Re Corp.	0.30
	Oil Well Equip. & Serv.	**0.76**	SAFC	SAFECO Corp.	0.10
BHI	Baker Hughes	0.08	SPC	St. Paul Cos	0.11
DI	Dresser Industries	0.10	FG	USF&G Corp	0.04
HAL	Halliburton Co	0.11			
MDR	McDermott International.	0.04	**Savings & Loan Companies**		**0.18**
SLB	Schlumberger Ltd	0.37	AHM	Ahmanson (H.F.) & Co	0.06
WAI	Western Atlas.	0.06	GDW	Golden West Financial.	0.06
			GWF	Great Western Financial.	0.06
Financials		**10.73**			
	Insurance Brokers	**0.19**	**Financial (Miscellaneous)**		**2.49**
AAL	Alexander & Alexander.	0.02	AXP	American Express	0.45
MMC	Marsh & McLennan	0.17	AGC	American General	0.17
			DWD	Dean Witter, Discover & Co	0.17
	Life Insurance	**0.44**	FRE	Federal Home Loan Mtg.	0.27
JP	Jefferson-Pilot.	0.08	FNM	Federal Natl. Mtge	0.60
LNC	Lincoln National	0.10	KRB	MBNA Corp.	0.10
PVN	Providian Corp	0.09	MER	Merrill Lynch.	0.20
TMK	Torchmark Corp	0.07	SB	Salomon Inc.	0.12
UNM	UNUM Corp.	0.08	TA	Transamerica Corp.	0.10
USH	USLIFE Corp.	0.02	TRV	Travelers Inc.	0.31
	Major Regional Banks	**3.29**	**Services**		**0.64**
ONE	Banc One Corp.	0.31	**Specialized Services**		**0.41**
BKB	Bank of Boston	0.08	HRB	Block H&R.	0.12
BBI	Barnett Banks Inc.	0.11	ECL	Ecolab Inc	0.04
BOAT	Boatmen's Bancshares	0.08	IPG	Interpublic Group.	0.07
CFL	CoreStates Financial	0.11	NEC	National Education	0.00
FFB	First Fidelity Bancorp	0.11	NSI	National Service Ind	0.04
I	First Interstate Bancorp	0.15	OG	Ogden Corp	0.03
FTU	First Union Corp	0.22	SK	Safety-Kleen	0.03
FLT	Fleet Financial Group.	0.13	SRV	Service Corp. International.	0.08
KEY	KeyCorp.	0.18			
MEL	Mellon Bank Corp	0.13	**Specialty Printing**		**0.23**
NBD	NBD Bancorp Inc.	0.13	DLX	Deluxe Corp.	0.07
NCC	National City Corp	0.12	DNY	Donnelley (R.R.) & Sons.	0.14
NB	NationsBank.	0.37	JH	Harland (J.H.)	0.02
NOB	Norwest Corp	0.22			
PNC	PNC Bank Corp.	0.15	**Technology**		**12.83**
SNC	Shawmut National	0.06	**Communication Equip./Mfrs.**		**0.74**
STI	SunTrust Banks	0.17	ANDW	Andrew Corp.	0.04
USBC	U.S. Bancorp	0.07	CSCO	cisco Systems.	0.27
WB	Wachovia Corp.	0.16	DIGI	DSC Communications	0.12
WFC	Wells Fargo & Co	0.23	MAI	M/A-Com, Inc	0.01
			NT	Northern Telecom	0.25
			SFA	Scientific-Atlanta	0.05

The S&P 500 Composite Index (*Continued*)
Sectors, Industries, and Companies and Their Percentage of the Overall Index as of 12/30/94

Sector / Industry		%OF 500
Technology (continued)		
Computer Software & Services		**2.53**
ACAD	Autodesk, Inc.	0.06
AUD	Automatic Data Processing Inc.	0.25
CEN	Ceridian Corp.	0.04
CA	Computer Associates Intl	0.23
CSC	Computer Sciences Corp	0.08
FDC	First Data	0.16
LOTS	Lotus Development.	0.06
MSFT	Microsoft Corp	1.06
NOVL	Novell Inc	0.19
ORCL	Oracle Systems	0.38
SMED	Shared Medical Systems	0.02
Computer Systems		**2.15**
AMH	Amdahl Corp.	0.04
AAPL	Apple Computer	0.14
CPQ	COMPAQ Computer.	0.31
CYR	Cray Research.	0.01
DGN	Data General	0.01
DEC	Digital Equipment.	0.14
INGR	Intergraph Corp.	0.01
IBM	International Bus. Machines.	1.29
SUNW	Sun Microsystems	0.10
TDM	Tandem Computers Inc	0.06
UIS	Unisys Corp.	0.04
Electronics (Defense)		**0.16**
EGG	E G & G Inc.	0.02
ESY	E-Systems.	0.04
LOR	Loral Corp	0.10
Electronics (Instrumentation)		**0.82**
HWP	Hewlett-Packard.	0.76
PKN	Perkin-Elmer	0.03
TEK	Tektronix Inc.	0.03
Electronics (Semiconductors)		**2.28**
AMD	Advanced Micro Devices	0.07
INTC	Intel Corp	0.79
MU	Micron Technology.	0.13
MOT	Motorola Inc	1.01
NSM	National Semiconductor	0.07
TXN	Texas Instruments.	0.21
Office Equipment & Supplies		**0.62**
ASN	Alco Standard.	0.10
MCL	Moore Corp. Ltd.	0.06
PBI	Pitney-Bowes	0.15
XRX	Xerox Corp	0.31
Photography/Imaging		**0.52**
EK	Eastman Kodak.	0.48
PRD	Polaroid Corp.	0.04
Telecommunications (Long Distance)		**3.01**
T	AT&T Corp.	2.35
MCIC	MCI Communications	0.37
FON	Sprint Corp.	0.29
Transportation		**1.66**
Airlines		**0.28**
AMR	AMR Corp	0.12
DAL	Delta Air Lines.	0.08
LUV	Southwest Airlines	0.07
U	USAir Group.	0.01

Sector / Industry		%OF 500
Railroads		**1.09**
BNI	Burlington Northern.	0.13
CSX	CSX Corp	0.22
CRR	Conrail Inc.	0.12
NSC	Norfolk Southern Corp.	0.24
SFX	Santa Fe Pacific Corp.	0.10
UNP	Union Pacific.	0.28
Truckers		**0.11**
CNF	Consolidated Freightways	0.02
ROAD	Roadway Services	0.07
YELL	Yellow Corp.	0.02
Transportation (Miscellaneous)		**0.18**
FDX	Federal Express.	0.10
PZS	Pittston Services Group.	0.03
R	Ryder System	0.05
Utilities		**10.02**
Electric Companies		**3.94**
AEP	American Electric Power.	0.18
BGE	Baltimore Gas & Electric	0.10
CIN	CINergy Corp	0.10
CPL	Carolina Power & Light	0.13
CSR	Central & South West	0.13
ED	Consolidated Edison.	0.18
DTE	Detroit Edison	0.11
D	Dominion Resources	0.18
DUK	Duke Power	0.23
ETR	Entergy Corp	0.15
FPL	FPL Group.	0.20
HOU	Houston Industries	0.14
NMK	Niagara Mohawk Power	0.06
NSP	Northern States Power.	0.09
OEC	Ohio Edison.	0.08
PE	PECO Energy Co	0.16
PPW	PacifiCorp	0.15
PCG	Pacific Gas & Electric	0.31
PEG	Public Serv. Enterprise Inc.	0.19
SCE	SCEcorp.	0.20
SO	Southern Co.	0.39
TXU	Texas Utilities.	0.22
UCM	Unicom Corp.	0.15
UEP	Union Electric Co.	0.11
Natural Gas		**0.90**
CGP	Coastal Corp	0.08
CG	Columbia Gas System.	0.04
CNG	Consolidated Natural Gas	0.10
EFU	Eastern Enterprises.	0.02
ENE	Enron Corp	0.23
ENS	ENSERCH Corp	0.03
GAS	NICOR Inc.	0.04
NAE	NorAm Energy Corp.	0.02
OKE	ONEOK Inc.	0.01
PET	Pacific Enterprises.	0.05
PEL	Panhandle Eastern.	0.09
PGL	Peoples Energy	0.03
SNT	Sonat Inc.	0.07
E	Transco Energy	0.02
WMB	Williams Cos	0.07

The S&P 500 Composite Index (*Continued*)
Sectors, Industries, and Companies and Their Percentage of the Overall
Index as of 12/30/94

Sector Industry		%OF 500	Sector Industry		%OF 500
Utilities (continued)			*Other*		**1.85**
Telephone		**5.18**	**Miscellaneous**		**1.85**
AT	ALLTEL Corp.	0.17	ATI	AirTouch Communications.	0.43
AIT	Ameritech.	0.66	AGREA	American Greetings Cl A.	0.06
BEL	Bell Atlantic.	0.65	GLW	Corning Inc.	0.20
BLS	BellSouth.	0.80	DL	Dial Corp.	0.06
GTE	GTE Corp	0.87	H	Harcourt General Inc	0.08
NYN	Nynex.	0.46	HRS	Harris Corp.	0.05
PAC	Pacific Telesis.	0.36	JOS	Jostens Inc.	0.03
SBC	SBC Communications Inc	0.72	MMM	Minn. Mining & Mfg	0.67
USW	US West Inc.	0.49	PHYB	Pioneer Hi-Bred International.	0.09
			TRW	TRW Inc.	0.13
			WH	Whitman Corp	0.05

Appendix $\mathbf{B}$

Sector and Industry Returns by Phase of the Economic Cycle

| | Average Index % Change During the Previous: | | | | |
| | 4 Economic Expansions | | | 5 Contractions | |
Sector Industry	Early	Middle	Late	Early	Late
Basic Materials	**15.46**	**22.43**	**21.59**	**-13.33**	**15.86**
Aluminum	10.03	19.37	27.14	-16.07	8.41
Chemicals	16.10	25.24	5.66	-10.23	11.09
Chemicals (Diversified)	33.07	31.38	20.62	-19.10	21.18
Chemicals (Specialty)	NA	32.82	38.33	-19.19	26.99
Containers (Metal & Glass)	31.43	27.77	9.01	-14.25	12.35
Containers (Paper)	20.79	37.18	9.66	-16.87	18.13
Gold Mining	-9.74	22.76	48.37	8.21	23.42
Metals (Miscellaneous)	4.73	4.17	49.47	-19.33	19.12
Paper & Forest Products	23.84	18.23	8.69	-15.22	10.94
Steel	8.93	5.42	-1.02	-11.30	6.91
Capital Goods	**27.99**	**23.03**	**33.96**	**-22.55**	**21.65**
Aerospace/Defense	43.40	18.20	18.70	-19.64	16.17
Electrical Equipment	16.88	18.07	10.96	-17.86	18.21
Engineering & Construction	NA	-19.42	155.79	-20.05	36.79
Heavy Duty Trucks & Parts	32.26	0.71	-1.07	-22.73	9.38
Machine Tools	19.39	17.07	20.63	-29.42	17.15
Machinery (Diversified)	19.92	17.14	13.50	-16.30	12.09
Manufacturing (Div. Inds.)	NA	78.88	32.59	-23.83	30.51
Pollution Control	36.09	53.58	20.61	-30.57	32.89
Consumer Cyclical	**29.94**	**16.55**	**17.99**	**-20.28**	**33.19**
Auto Parts After Market	20.73	19.57	-6.07	-17.77	20.48
Automobiles	28.96	9.88	-6.27	-17.36	14.67
Broadcast Media	55.68	35.20	11.61	-16.75	22.21
Building Materials	18.10	16.23	6.36	-19.50	23.25
Entertainment	9.52	46.92	26.08	-12.66	30.60
Hardware & Tools	11.57	13.69	3.34	-20.73	24.01
Homebuilding	8.26	4.95	13.23	-34.57	53.61
Hotel-Motel	24.46	33.25	-7.67	-31.76	34.11
Household Furn. & Appliances	19.12	10.21	-4.69	-16.49	25.45
Leisure Time	62.02	10.04	-9.10	-23.93	34.80
Manufactured Housing	19.15	3.94	-7.84	-21.23	55.04
Publishing	34.43	23.85	-0.70	-18.88	26.04
Publishing (Newspapers)	36.52	24.37	0.02	-14.88	26.67
Restaurants	47.69	34.87	11.16	-15.81	21.51
Retail (Department Stores)	19.87	11.10	28.40	-12.65	26.01
Retail (General Merchandise)	15.77	11.05	9.34	-10.66	22.36
Retail (Specialty)	88.08	6.70	125.05	-28.75	62.74
Retail (Specialty-Apparel)	NA	11.92	121.05	-30.00	70.22
Shoes	26.46	13.05	35.40	-16.58	37.62
Textiles	29.50	18.30	12.73	-25.13	32.37
Toys	22.87	-11.64	16.34	-19.84	33.18
Consumer Staples	**15.87**	**30.51**	**33.90**	**-8.65**	**23.86**
Beverages (Alcoholic)	9.84	45.34	6.70	-6.61	8.48
Beverages (Soft Drinks)	21.86	32.90	26.99	-10.69	13.52
Cosmetics	5.69	32.18	9.44	-20.08	16.06
Distributors (Consumer Products)	25.09	5.03	98.57	-12.12	40.86
Foods	21.76	28.14	16.42	-7.71	16.90
Health Care (Diversified)	NA	51.27	69.17	-3.53	21.73
Health Care (Drugs)	10.84	28.71	24.07	-10.56	14.70
Health Care (Miscellaneous)	NA	11.90	-18.18	14.95	37.03
Hospital Management	18.33	-12.81	78.43	-10.09	45.20

Sector and Industry Returns by Phase of the Economic Cycle (Continued)

Sector Industry	Average Index % Change During the Previous:				
	4 Economic Expansions			5 Contractions	
	Early	Middle	Late	Early	Late
Consumer Staples (Cont'd)					
Household Products	6.32	34.18	15.01	-4.91	14.21
Housewares	NA	95.21	99.19	-19.05	29.17
Medical Products & Supplies	8.23	31.29	5.16	-9.40	14.54
Retail (Drug Stores)	34.49	30.99	6.64	-20.28	38.25
Retail (Food Chains)	8.63	15.58	32.20	-8.14	25.52
Tobacco	19.29	27.78	38.63	-1.62	21.70
Energy	**31.34**	**8.58**	**37.36**	**-13.66**	**5.64**
Oil & Gas Drilling	27.47	4.46	42.23	-21.47	10.66
Oil (Domestic Integrated)	38.34	-0.17	39.56	-13.79	9.20
Oil (Exploration & Production)	NA	NA	NA	-6.45	-11.94
Oil (International Integrated)	27.59	11.54	17.08	-7.62	10.30
Oil Well Equip. & Serv.	31.97	18.47	50.56	-18.99	10.00
Financials	**20.78**	**12.36**	**10.99**	**-18.66**	**24.19**
Financial (Miscellaneous)	NA	NA	NA	-27.42	37.03
Insurance Brokers	NA	19.73	49.97	-2.80	11.19
Life Insurance	30.34	14.14	7.88	-20.27	23.25
Major Regional Banks	5.17	10.35	4.70	-20.22	16.49
Money Center Banks	5.96	7.50	9.41	-14.02	14.78
Multi-Line Insurance	31.54	14.19	11.89	-12.99	8.79
Personal Loans	23.74	5.27	-0.92	-25.50	33.36
Property-Casualty Insurance	31.93	9.43	9.43	-14.94	16.15
Savings & Loan Companies	16.81	18.24	-4.46	-29.77	56.69
Services	**50.45**	**66.36**	**6.50**	**-19.94**	**27.92**
Specialized Services	50.45	66.36	6.50	-19.94	27.92
Specialty Printing	NA	NA	NA	NA	NA
Technology	**23.93**	**17.48**	**25.80**	**-16.93**	**23.03**
Communication Equip./Mfrs.	22.47	-4.89	49.07	-14.72	24.91
Computer Software & Services	41.06	36.15	19.52	-18.97	33.66
Computer Systems	18.12	8.65	-4.30	-18.20	16.25
Electronics (Defense)	NA	6.39	39.27	-4.46	26.67
Electronics (Instrumentation)	19.93	27.08	14.51	-17.99	29.97
Electronics (Semiconductors)	24.93	18.87	21.47	-19.24	19.19
Office Equipment & Supplies	17.09	30.67	4.23	-24.40	31.21
Photography/Imaging	NA	NA	NA	NA	NA
Telecommunications (Long Dist.)	NA	16.92	62.60	-17.47	2.42
Transportation	**34.19**	**12.76**	**3.39**	**-19.67**	**22.18**
Airlines	32.57	12.50	1.45	-21.11	18.48
Railroads	33.43	5.83	17.35	-14.87	16.17
Transportation (Miscellaneous)	NA	NA	NA	-31.60	23.63
Truckers	36.58	19.95	-8.64	-11.10	30.44
Utilities	**20.22**	**18.79**	**18.87**	**-4.66**	**6.82**
Electric Companies	12.01	4.45	-3.05	-5.95	8.18
Natural Gas	28.44	7.22	15.54	-10.69	11.97
Telephone	NA	44.71	44.13	2.67	0.31
Other	**38.71**	**17.99**	**25.37**	**-16.49**	**13.86**
Conglomerates	38.71	13.08	3.46	-22.58	13.49
Miscellaneous	NA	22.90	47.27	-10.40	14.23
S&P 500	**19.70**	**12.09**	**12.28**	**-13.92**	**14.34**

About The Author

Sam Stovall is editor of *S&P's Industry Reports* and a
member of S&P's Investment Policy Committee. He is a
frequent guest on CNBC's "Buy, Hold or Sell" program,
as well as CNN's "Moneyline." Mr. Stovall is a board
member of the New York Chapter of the American
Association of Individual Investors and is an adjunct
professor of finance at Marymount Manhattan College in
NYC.

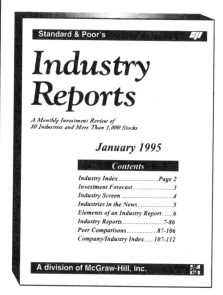

Standard & Poor's

Industry Reports

A Monthly Investment Review of 80 Industries and More Than 1,000 Stocks

January 1995

Contents

A division of McGraw-Hill, Inc.

Let **S&P INDUSTRY REPORTS** help you track which sectors are leading the market

Monthly "snapshots" of 80 key industries and their investment prospects give you a comprehensive, easy-to-use investment tool

S&P INDUSTRY REPORTS provides you with investment-oriented research covering key industries and leading stocks in each sector.

Each issue brings you monthly quick-reference "snapshots" of 80 industries and provides evaluations of each industry's near- and long-term investment outlook, including:

■ **PRICE PERFORMANCE** — Quick-reference chart displaying the monthly price performance for the S&P 500 industry group over 5 years plus the 7-month moving average.

■ **STATISTICAL SNAPSHOT** — Lets you see at a glance how the industry has performed over the past quarter, year and three years in numerical terms, and includes S&P's Industry group STARS ranking.

■ **STOCK RANKINGS** — Alphabetical list of up to 10 of the highest-ranked stocks. This list is based on S&P's exclusive STARS ranking system for evaluating price-appreciation potential.

■ **INDUSTRY OVERVIEW** — Gives you the current investment outlook for each industry.

■ **GROUP RATIOS** — Year-end results for 10 of the most commonly used valuation and profitability measurements, plus a seven-year average to help you keep current valuations in perspective.

■ **Plus** — A wealth of timely and topical economic, market and industry news, screens and analysis. Also features peer comparisons reviewing statistics and ratios for 1,000 companies in all 80 industries.

SAM STOVALL, *M.B.A., CFP, is Editor of S&P* INDUSTRY REPORTS. *He is also a frequent guest on CNBC's* Buy, Sell or Hold *program.*

ISA-035

 STANDARD & POOR'S A division of McGraw–Hill, Inc. 25 Broadway, New York, NY 10004